PRINCIPLES OF CATERING DESIGN

PRINCIPLES OF CATERING DESIGN

by Fred Lawson

Architectural Press

725·71

42216

ISBN 0 85139 533 3
© Fred Lawson 1973
First published 1973 by Architectural Press Ltd.
Filmset and printed in Great Britain by
BAS Printers Limited, Wallop, Hampshire

PREFACE

The need for a comprehensive source of reference on the physical facilities used in catering is widely recognized. On the one hand, the architect or engineer often requires advice on the practical interpretation of design requirements whilst, on the other, proprietors and managers of catering establishments increasingly find it necessary to obtain guidance on the technical aspects of their equipment and buildings. With increasing sophistication of catering technology and the introduction of metrication in design, the need for technical information will become more acute in the near future.

In addition, a knowledge of catering design is required by many whose work is associated with the industry; for example, the manufacturers of catering equipment, food technologists, public health inspectors and others concerned in the administration of legal requirements and, not least, those involved in the teaching of hotel and catering management subjects on whose shoulders lies the responsibility of disseminating knowledge.

Catering facilities design is concerned with food storage, preparation and cooking and the distribution and service of meals. A companion book, *Restaurant Planning and Design*, is devoted, more specifically to the design of dining rooms and their associated areas, that is to say, those areas used by the customer.

With a wide topic of this nature, it is necessary to draw boundaries of limitation but, where necessary, reference has been made to related subjects to show the interlinkage of information. Further, to familiarize the catering manager with metric units and their relative sizes, dual units have been quoted throughout and a summary of metrication changes has been included for reference.

The text contains mainly factual information which is supported by illustrations to show practical examples of recent catering schemes. The latter have been compiled from contributions by most of the leading authorities in this field in Britain and, whilst it is difficult to select but a few out of the many names involved, I am greatly indebted to the following companies for their co-operation: Trust Houses Forte Ltd., Berni Inns Ltd., Concorde Catering Equipment Ltd. Glynwed Foundaries Ltd., Oliver Toms (Catering Equipment) Ltd., James Stott and Co (Engineers) Ltd., G. F. E. Bartlett and Son Ltd., Staines Kitchen Equipment Co. Ltd., the Plessey Co. Ltd., the King's Fund Catering Advisory Service.

The drawings were adapted for printing by Tielman and Roselyne Nicolopoulos.

Professor Medlik kindly gave advice on catering statistics and information has been provided by many of my colleagues. Most of all, I am grateful to my wife for her tolerance and fortitude.

F. R. Lawson

CONTENTS

SYMBOLS USED ON PLANS

Number	Symbol	Equipment

A STORAGE AREAS

1 Shelving

2 Vegetable racks

3 Vegetable bins

4 Storage bins

5 Weighing machine

6 Mobile racks

7 Trolleys

B PREPARATION AREAS

8 Work table or bench

9 Work bench with cupboards/drawers

10 Work bench with waste bin

11 Worktop with shelves

12 Single sink with drainer

13 Double sink unit

14 Mobile sink

15 Wash-hand basin

16 Marble-topped bench

17 Vegetable rack

18 Salad preparation unit

19 Pot rack

20 Trolley

21 Mobile tray racks

22 Refrigerator

23 Mobile refrigerator/refrigerated trolley

24 Deep freezer

25 Potato peeler

26 Chipping machine

27 Mixing machine

28 Slicing machine

29 Chopping block

30 Cutting board

COOKING AREA

31 Proving oven

32 General purpose oven

33 Pastry oven or pizza oven

34 Forced-air convection oven

35 Steaming oven

36 Microwave oven

37 Boiling top—general

38	Boiling top with open top burners	66	Tray stand
39	Boiling top with solid top	67	Ice cream conservator
40	Bratt pan	68	Cutlery stand
41	Oven range with boiling top	69	Tray rail
42	Griller or salamander	70	Cashier's desk
43	Deep fat fryer		
44	Boiling pan—rectangular type		
45	Boiling pan—circular		

WASH-UP AREA

46	Open well bain-marie	71	Receiving table for soiled dishes
47	Extraction hood over equipment	72	Stacking table for clean dishes
48	Griddle plate	73	Dishwashing machine—semi-automatic
49	Toaster	74	Dishwashing machine—'flight' type

SERVING AREA

50	Plate lowerator or dispenser	75	Clearing trolley
51	Hot cupboard unit	76	Waste-disposal unit or scraping point
52	Hot cupboard with bain-marie top	77	Water boiler
53	Bench type bain-marie unit	78	Water softening equipment
54	Pass-through unit—heated	79	Refuse bins
55	Pass-through unit—cold		
56	Refrigerated under-cupboard		
57	Refrigerated cupboard with doleplate		

BAR AREA

58	Refrigerated display cabinet	80	Wine refrigerator
59	Milk dispenser	81	Ice-making machine
60	Beverage unit	82	Bottle storage racking
61	Coffee unit	83	Glass storage racking
62	Counter unit—unheated	84	Beer engine or dispense points
63	Counter unit—with infra red lamps above	85	Glass-washing machine
64	Counter display cabinet	89	Chilled water dispenser

DINING AREAS

65	Compressor or boiler under counter	90	Beverage vending unit
		91	Food vending unit
		92	Waiter/waitress serving station

INTRODUCTION

1 CATERING AS AN INDUSTRY

1.01 As an industry, catering is a heterogeneous grouping of many different types of establishment, ranging from hotel restaurants and banqueting rooms to snack bars and canteens, which have one purpose in common—to provide meals and refreshments away from home for consumption on the premises.

The size of the catering industry today reflects the expansion which has taken place over the last 30 years or so and which stems, to a great extent, from wartime developments—food rationing and communal feeding on a large scale:

(1) Food rationing for the public was introduced at an early date in the war and provided much inducement to eating out in catering establishments, particularly as food supplies were rationed to caterers, but not to their customers.

(2) With a view to ensuring that the best use was made of the limited food supplies available, and that all civilians could have at least one hot meal a day, hundreds of British restaurants and other catering establishments were opened during the war for the public in all parts of the country.

(3) Factory Canteen and other Orders requiring the provision of canteen facilities for employees, issued between 1940 and 1943, gradually extended the scope of employee feeding to most companies and organizations employing more than 250 people. Before the war started there were about 1,000 canteens in Britain; when the war ended their number was 25,000.

(4) Section 49 of the Education Act, 1944, imposed a duty on Local Education Authorities to provide meals for pupils in the schools maintained by them and made grants available for this purpose.

Size of Industry

1.02 In 1964 the Board of Trade (now Department of Trade and Industry) identified some 172,000 catering outlets in Britain providing meals and refreshments and, within this total, there were 9,000 licensed hotels and holiday camps, 33,000 commercial restaurants, 17,000 fish and chip shops, 69,000 public houses, 23,000 licensed and registered clubs and 21,000 canteens. The Inquiry did not cover unlicensed hotels, guest and boarding houses, hospital catering, school meals, nor a number of other forms of catering. If these establishments are added, the catering industry consists of well over 200,000 establishments in which meals and refreshments are provided; there is,

therefore, one catering outlet for about 250 people in Britain.

Employees

1.03 Well over a million people are engaged in the hotel and catering industry, of whom some 600,000 are in the commercial sectors and about the same number in various catering services provided as an ancillary function to some other main purpose of an organization—in industry, education, hospitals and other institutions. Employees engaged directly in various catering occupations, such as cooks and waiters, represent one-third of the manpower in the commercial sectors and well over one-half in the whole industry.

From the National Census of Population, 1961, it would appear that over 80 per cent of the occupations classified as waiters, restaurateurs, counterhands and kitchen-hands are filled by women. In the more specialist roles of cooks, butchers and bakers, about one-half of those employed in commercial restaurants are women although, in other sectors—school meals, employee catering and similar services—women occupy over four-fifths of these positions.

Turnover

1.04 In 1964 the total turnover in the sectors covered by the Board of Trade Inquiry was £2,239 million, of which sales of meals and refreshments accounted for £664 million. By 1970 the total turnover had risen to over £3,000 million, of which some £900 million was represented by meals and refreshments, and the remainder on accommodation, alcoholic drink or other services.

Changes in catering

1.05 Over the last few years the main impact of change in catering has not been reflected so much in real growth as in substitution. In facing the difficulties created by shortages of skilled labour and rising costs of rent and operation, the catering industry is undergoing a process of rationalization. Following the same trend which has lead to the corner shop being largely replaced by the supermarket, the whole concept of catering is changing from the traditional domestic approach to that of a highly organized and competitive industry.

This involves not only increased efficiency in management and operational techniques but also a more sophisticated approach to the design of catering premises, greater deliberation in the selection of equipment and increasing reference to work study, safety, hygiene and other functional considerations when planning the catering facilities. Specific technical information on these aspects is often lacking in the literature on catering and such details as are available tend to be limited to promoting particular products or services. It is with the objective of providing a general technological background to the subject of catering facilities design that this book has been written.

1 INFLUENCES ON DESIGN

1 ORGANIZATION

1.01 Whilst there are normally wide variations in function, size and style between different establishments, the catering industry is concerned with two main areas of activity:

(a) *Commercial catering*—which includes restaurants, cafés, coffee shops, snack bars and other facilities operated as a separate business or forming part of an hotel or retail premises. The primary motivation is profit and the catering activity is directed at the general public.

(b) *Catering servicing or contracting* to an organization whose main interests lie in some other field and for which catering is operated as a service to staff or participants. Examples of catering services include industrial canteens, school meal services, hospital catering and welfare catering.

This distinction between areas of catering is tending to become less significant as more catering services are operated, under contract, by commercial caterers rather than by the employing organizations themselves. In other cases, although the catering is provided as a direct service, it may be operated on a financially independent basis comparable to a commercial enterprise.

2 COMMERCIAL CATERING

Market Surveys

2.01 As a preliminary to planning a restaurant, snack bar or other kind of catering investment, it is essential that an assessment is made of the likely demand for both this and alternative facilities. Such information is obtained by carrying out a survey of the market for potential customers taking into account such factors as:

(a) the size and features of the area which is likely to be served;

(b) the numbers of possible customers and their social characteristics;

(c) the types of meals which most probably will be required and the frequency of this demand;

(d) the extent and likely effects of competition including the possibility of acquiring custom by displacement.

From an analysis of this information, it should be possible to determine not only the best location for a catering venture but also the type and size of establishment which is likely to be most successful and the level of investment in the premises which can attract the highest percentage return.

Specific information from market surveys and feasibility studies is often lacking when an architect is briefed on a scheme and, as a result, the design of the premises and decisions on the selection of equipment tend to be pursued in isolation. Through this lack of direction, it is not uncommon to find that the catering facilities provided are inappropriate for the situation and type of meals required.

One way of reducing the element of risk involved with new premises is to adopt a formula of style and size which has been proved to be commercially successful elsewhere; and the competition engendered by copying is often, in itself, a spur to further innovation and development.

Location

2.02 Many factors affect the suitability of a site as an investment for commercial catering but the fundamental considerations are the number and types of people who are likely to use the facility, ie. the density and structure of the market. This will, initially, influence the choice of location and size of investment, secondly, the level of sophistication of the service and, ultimately, the commercial viability of the enterprise.

It is, therefore, understandable that most catering establishments are conveniently located in city centres, in business areas, in seaside resorts and recreational areas, along main highways: wherever there is a sufficiently dense concentration of potential users. In other instances, where the prestige of an establishment is so well recognized that it attracts customers from a very wide catchment area, the exact location of the premises may be of less significance.

Although frequently assumed to be a secondary factor, the location of the premises is also important in terms of access. Safe means of access and adequate car parking facilities are often vital requirements for obtaining planning approval to a scheme. In addition, suitable provision must be made for deliveries of food and for the removal of refuse without congestion or nuisance.

Size

2.03 On average, the size of commercial restaurants is small. The Attwood survey of 1965, covering some 28,400 premises and subsequent investigations, indicate that over 50 per cent of the catering premises in Great Britain have seating capacities of 40 or less; approximately 20 per cent can each accommodate between 40 and 60 customers; whilst fewer than 4 per cent have seating for 150 or more customers.

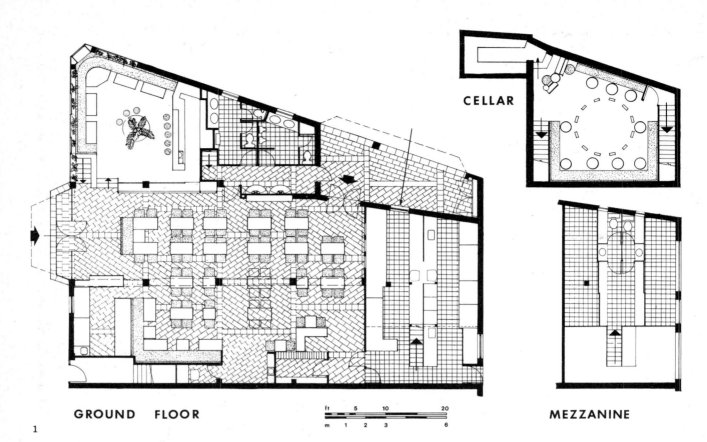

GROUND FLOOR

| ft | 5 | 10 | 20 |
| m | 1 | 2 | 3 | 6 |

CELLAR

MEZZANINE

1

The Chipper, Kings Road, Chelsea. Architect—Lucas Mellinger, associated with Peter Young.
As an example of the increasing sophistication in fish restaurant design, these premises, constructed 1971, are fully licensed and include provision for a small orchestra and dancing in the 'cellar' area of the restaurant in addition to a high quality *take-away service. The character of the interior is based on that of a market place with various activities forming local focal points of interest—the bar, viewing windows into the kitchen, the coffee counter, etc. Wall surfacings include marble chippings and textured mirror mosaics whilst the specially designed furniture has copper plated frames and edgings.*

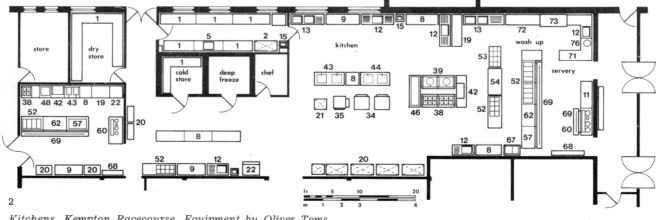

| ft | 5 | 10 | 20 |
| m | 1 | 2 | 3 | 6 |

2

Kitchens, Kempton Racecourse. Equipment by Oliver Toms Ltd.
The layout of the kitchen has been adapted to suit the area available and serves two restaurants in addition to a number of mobile catering units.

Allied to reductions in the size of dining areas, the tendency is for kitchens to be made smaller thereby achieving a greater proportion of revenue-earning space. Economies in both space and equipment are mainly obtained by reducing the amount of food preparation which needs to be carried out in the premises and this has been made possible by the development of 'convenience' foods, supplied ready prepared in a blanched, chilled or frozen state.

Ownership

2.04 The majority of catering outlets are independently owned and operated although, of the total 33,000 restaurants, cafés, snack bars, etc recorded in the Board of Trade Survey in 1964, some 2,300 were operated by multiple organizations. In addition, most hotels are in group ownership.

Franchising is also used in catering—although to a limited extent in the United Kingdom—with individual operators

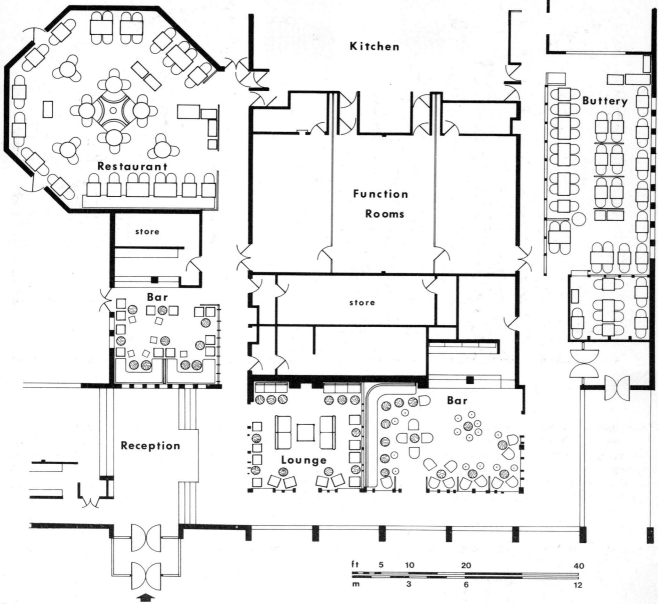

Kitchen

Function Rooms

Restaurant

store

Buttery

Bar

store

Bar

Reception

Lounge

| ft | 5 | 10 | 20 | 40 |
| m | | 3 | 6 | 12 |

3

Post House, Ipswich. Trust Houses Forte Ltd.
Plan showing the layout of the restaurants in the Ipswich Post
House, constructed 1971/2.

investing in premises to supply a range of branded food
products which have been developed and promoted by the
franchisors. As an example, many of the Wimpey Bars
are run under a franchise arrangement.

Premises operated by group organizations tend to be
standardized in design and the equipment is generally
specified in detail in order to ensure uniformity in the
quality of the catering products. Most of the leading
hotel and catering companies employ full-time specialists
for the planning and development of their facilities and
much of the innovation in catering design has been derived
from this expertise.

Trends

2.05 Commercial catering is subject to many customer
influences and the design of catering facilities must take
account of changes in eating habits, fashion and technology.

(a) *Types of meals*

The trend in eating habits, brought about mainly by
pressures on time, is towards shorter meals, quicker
service and greater flexibility in meal times. In most
situations, customers choose self service or bar service
rather than being waited on at the table and an *à la carte*
menu is preferred to a set meal. A typical size of restaurant meal in the UK today is more likely to be two
courses than three whilst in the USA single course meals
are most common.

To meet the demand for less formal meals, selected and
prepared to order, catering equipment is increasingly
chosen for speed and convenience in use and is often based
on grilling, frying and microwave processes of accelerated
cooking. Such equipment may be mounted as back-bar
units within or immediately adjacent to the dining area
in order to save space and time in service. In some cases
the end-cooking processes may be carried out in view of

the customers and the equipment is often purposely designed for this use in order to provide a visually attractive feature of interest.

(b) Cycles of design

As a reflection of the affluence of the consumer public and higher standards of living and leisure, fashion cycles in restaurant design are becoming very short, necessitating replacement of the décor, furniture and fittings after a limited market life. The average operating cycle of a restaurant is probably in the order of 5 to 7 years but this may be as little as 3 to 5 years where the modernity of design and service are important features of attraction. In contrast, an expensive restaurant serving food of the highest quality would possibly adopt a more traditional décor, less subject to the influence of fashion, which will be determined mainly by considerations of maintenance. In this case, an operating period of 7 to 10 years would be a reasonable estimate.

Whilst the operational life of the restaurant design concept may be relatively short, the preparation, cooking and serving equipment used in catering is generally capable of practical use over a considerably longer time. For most items of heavy equipment, 10 years would normally be regarded as an economic period of service, although obsolescence and the cost of maintaining the more highly sophisticated or specialized equipment may warrant sooner replacement. Taking this into account, it is often an advantage to plan the kitchen—with its reception and storage areas—as an efficient unit independent of the design of the restaurant.

(c) Flexibility of use

To counteract the greatly reduced use of dining room facilities by residents at lunch and dinner, many city centre hotels are finding it is increasingly necessary to attract outside custom. To some extent this is achieved by introducing speciality restaurants, buttery bars, coffee shops and small dining areas to cater for popular trends in lieu of the traditional hotel dining rooms and in many new hotels this division of function is emphasized by separating the public areas from the construction of the bedroom block. The need for a large restaurant may also be obviated by providing room service with continental breakfast and this is now a common feature in modern hotels with various arrangements for self-service and self catering being introduced where appropriate.

These changes in type and size of restaurant also affect the function of the kitchen. Often a large single kitchen, planned on traditional lines, is insufficiently flexible and uneconomic to allow part use. The equipment is frequently too large and unwieldy and the layout too extensive for efficient operation. In some cases, it may be possible to adapt such a kitchen to serve as a central production unit in which the food for several outlets is prepared and initially cooked but the trend is to provide separate service kitchens associated with each restaurant.

Flexibility is also an important feature in the design of conference and banqueting facilities. In most cases, the large areas provided for this purpose must be capable of sub-division and rearrangement to suit different groups of users and the catering service and equipment must be equally adaptable to meet these varying requirements of use.

(d) Innovations in equipment

Changes in basic cooking equipment are a relatively recent development and derive mainly from the use of frozen 'convenience' foods and the need to accelerate the cooking and service of meals. Processes now widely employed in catering include the use of forced air convection, air-cooled radiant heat, microwaves and steam and fat at high pressures. Much of this equipment is highly sophisticated, designed to be self-regulating and, to a large extent, automatic in operation.

In addition, the increasing proportionate cost of labour and the scarcity of skilled staff warrant the use of labour-saving devices for all types of routine work both in preparing meals and in cleaning.

Not least in importance, is a growing awareness of the advantages of mobility in meal preparation facilities as represented by the use of mobile sinks and preparation equipment, transporters for food, mobile holding cabinets which may be heated or refrigerated, mechanized conveying systems, movable benches, storage racks and counters and various designs of trolleys. The mobility of plant and adaptability in the arrangement of work areas are important factors in achieving higher efficiencies of work with less effort.

(e) Centralization of production

By concentrating food preparation into large central production units it is possible to achieve economies in the bulk purchasing of raw materials, in more efficient and continuous use of workers and machinery and better control over the cost and quality of the products. Centralized production has been made possible on a large scale by the development of rapid freezing techniques which reduce the temperature of the prepared food to temperatures at which bacteriological and chemical deterioration is virtually arrested, ensuring a greatly extended storage life.

The use of 'deep frozen' and other convenience foods enables a wide range of choice of meal to be offered with the minimum of preparation and cooking and this facility has widespread applications in all sectors of the catering industry. In particular, the reduction in kitchen space and catering equipment can achieve considerable savings in capital outlay and in rental charges where the restaurant occupies an expensive town centre site. Further, this saving in space will often allow a corresponding increase in the size of the dining area thereby extending the revenue-earning capacity of the enterprise.

3 CATERING SERVICES AND CONTRACTS

3.01 A wide variety of catering activities are involved in providing meals and refreshments as ancillary services to other organizations. As a broad classification these include the following:

Type of catering	Application
1 Employee catering	Employees and management in all types of industrial and commercial organizations.
2 School catering	Children and students in schools, nurseries and other educational establishments.
3 University catering	Students, staff and visitors in colleges and universities.
4 Hospital catering	Patients and special dietary requirements in hospitals and convalescent homes.
5 Institutional catering	Residents in public and private institutions and centres.
6 Welfare catering	Residents and non-residents

4

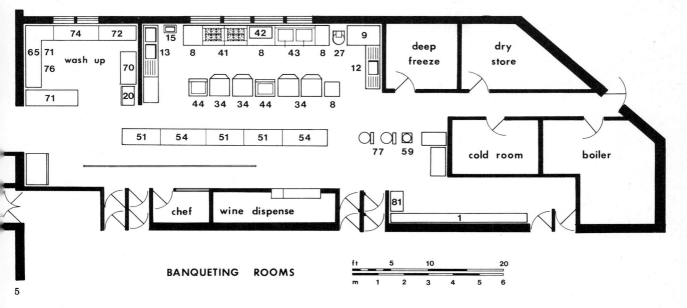

BANQUETING ROOMS

```
ft        5      10           20
m    1    2   3    4   5   6
```

5

The Kitchens, Portsmouth Centre Hotel. Centre Hotels Ltd.
Equipment by Oliver Toms Ltd.
Based on convection ovens, the kitchen is designed to serve
over 500 at one banquet sitting.

6

7

Evolution of kitchen equipment. Module 36 Equipment by Stotts of Oldham.
Examples showing restaurant kitchen equipment installed 12 years ago with a seemingly unplanned array of cooking equipment.

8

9

More recent kitchen equipment in a well planned kitchen but with appliances still largely unrelated and each supplied with individual services.

A modern kitchen using interchangeable Module 36 equipment in a matching suite. All gas, electricity and water pipes and cables are contained in a central service chamber.

	served by Local Authority schemes including 'meals on wheels'.
7 Transport catering	Passengers in transit by road, rail or air services.
8 Services catering	Armed forces and other service personnel.

Organizations

3.02 The majority of organizations provide and operate the catering and related services themselves, recruiting catering staff as direct employees. An increasing proportion of canteens are provided by the main organization but operated, under contract, for them by one of a number of commercial companies specializing in this field. Most contracts are based on the operating costs plus a servicing fee but some are let on the basis of an inclusive charge. The Report on Industrial Catering produced by the Commission on Industrial Relations, 1971, indicated that, of the total of 24,560 industrial canteens, about 3,880 (18·4 per cent) were operated by contractors and 20,880 operated directly.

From the designer's point of view, both the type of operation required and its eventual management are important considerations which must be decided at the outset. Where it is proposed to let a catering concession or to employ a catering contractor, the kitchen must be designed to suit the particular system of catering which will be used and, in many cases, the catering company will specify in some detail their precise requirements for space and facilities.

Trends in catering services

3.03 Recent changes in the operation of catering services, parallel to those in the commercial sector, are having an appreciable influence on the design of new facilities. In addition, the production, distribution and service of meals on a large scale—which is more common in catering services—are affected by more specific developments directed towards increasing speed and efficiency.

(a) *Types of meals*

Catering services frequently involve a responsibility for the welfare of the users and dietary considerations play an important part in the selection and preparation of food. There is, nonetheless, a trend towards more varied lighter meals as influenced by consumer preferences. The Industrial Society surveys, which are carried out

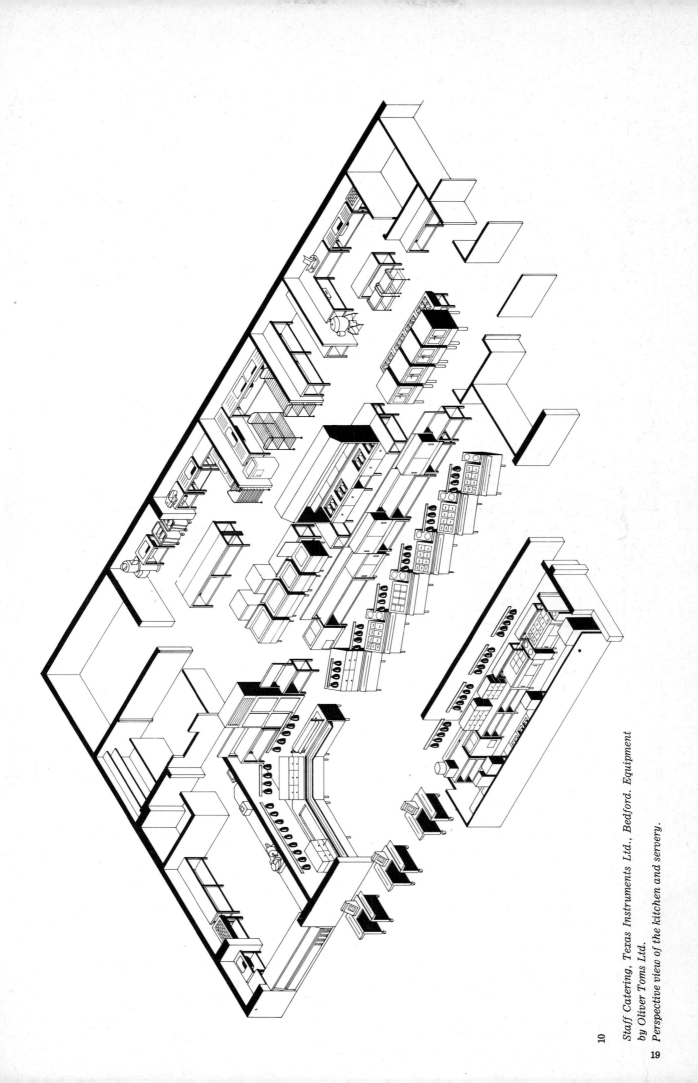

Staff Catering, Texas Instruments Ltd., Bedford. Equipment by Oliver Toms Ltd.
Perspective view of the kitchen and servery.

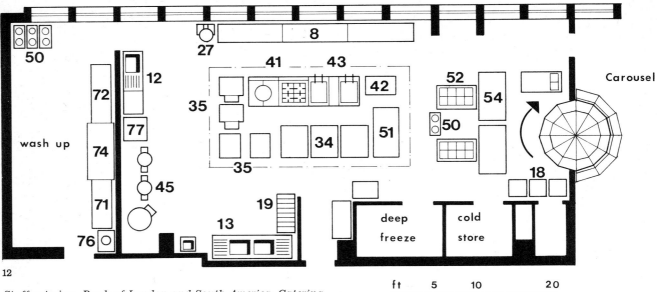

12

Staff catering, Bank of London and South America. Catering by Gardner Merchant.
An example of kitchen layout based on the use of pre-prepared frozen food. Approximately one sixth of the total kitchen space is taken up by cold storage. Fast service is made possible by the use of a continuously rotating counter or carousel.

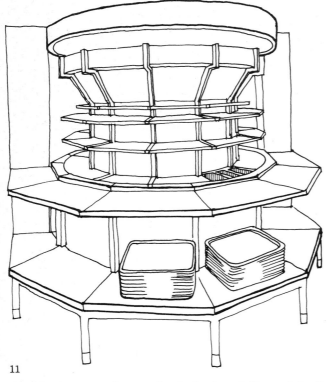

11

Sketch of a carousel or mechanised rotary table used for the service of food. Similar equipment may be used to receive dirty tableware enabling this to be conveyed direct to a wash-up area screened from view.

13

LASMEC equipment by Stotts of Oldham.
The Local Authorities School Meals Equipment Consortium was set up in 1961 to develop a range of equipment which would combine simplicity and economy of installation operation and maintenance with attractive appearance and that would be of more suitable design for the restricted space normally available in school kitchens. Since the introduction of the LASMEC modular range by Stotts in 1965, over 1400 new and existing kitchens have been equipped with these appliances and the space saving potential of the modular equipment has found many applications in other catering installations.
Prototype of the LASMEC kitchen 1965.

annually, indicated that an increase in the take-up of meals by employees from an average of 35 per cent in 1969 to 38 per cent in 1970 could be attributed to the growing popularity of breakfast type meals and cooked light meals. Such changes in demand have a significant effect on the selection of equipment for preparing and cooking food.

(b) *Service of meals*
For employee catering the key factor in food service is speed and a number of developments—such as the free-flow food hall, carousel service and automatic vending—have been introduced to accelerate service and minimize the need to queue.
In industrial catering, vending machines are now used

15

16

Employee catering facilities, Department of the Environment.
Equipment by Glynwed Foundries Ltd.
View of the interior of the canteen showing the serving area screened by a mural covered partition. (16) The canteen facilities are housed in an octagonal shaped building at ground and first floor levels. (17)

14

LASMEC Mark 2 equipment installed 1971.

17

Staff catering facilities, The Plessey Co. Ltd., Ilford.
Equipment by Oliver Toms Ltd.
The main canteen showing the central area of wood block flooring cleared for social functions.

extensively for beverages (62 per cent of industrial premises), for snacks (31 per cent) and to provide a 24-hour service of hot meals for shift workers (23 per cent).

Speed is also a necessity in other areas of catering in which extended lines of distribution are liable to affect the temperature and quality of the prepared meals. New techniques in hospital catering and other areas of food service include the use of individual hotplates and conveyor systems.

(c) *Innovation and centralization*

The limitations of a defined market facilitate forward planning and the development of specific systems of catering to meet particular requirements. In the immediate post-war era, the formation of the Local Authorities School Meals Equipment Consortium (LASMEC) lead to specialization in equipment and, within the last 2 to 3 years, the Leeds University experiments have pioneered the development of 'cook-freeze' systems in school meals and hospital catering. Centralization of

food preparation into food production units, central kitchens and commissaries are also being developed in industry and—on a vast scale—for airport catering.

(d) *Dining areas*

An appreciation of the importance of 'atmosphere' in the design of dining rooms has done much to remove the utilitarian appearance of canteens whilst ensuring that the needs of maintenance and other operational features have not been neglected. There is a growing tendency in modern technological industries for executives and other employees to share common dining facilities although separate provision is generally preferred at directorship level.

In many instances it may be necessary to temper the cost of providing a large dining area by designing this space for multi-purpose use—such as social, assembly, exhibition and recreational purposes.

Where a large number of women are employed it may be advantageous to extend the catering services to include

21

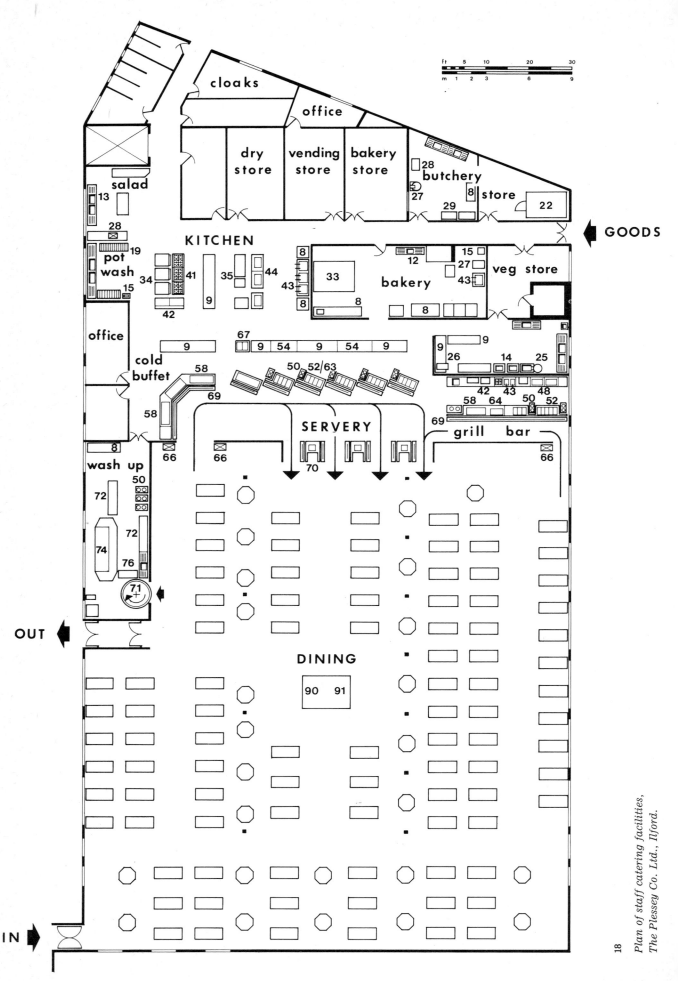

GOODS

KITCHEN

cloaks

office

dry store

vending store

bakery store

butchery

store

22

salad

13

28

19

pot wash

34 41 42 35 44 9 43 8 33 8 8 8

15

office

cold buffet

58

58 69

9 67 9 54 9 54 9

50 52/63

bakery

12 15 27 43

veg store

9 9 26 14 25

42 43 50 48

58 64 50 52

69 grill bar

SERVERY

66 66 70 66

DINING

90 91

wash up

72 72 74 76

50

71

OUT

IN

Plan of staff catering facilities,
The Plessey Co. Ltd., Ilford.

18

19

Staff catering facilities, The Plessey Co. Ltd., Ilford. Equipment by Oliver Toms Ltd.
An impressive modern kitchen designed to cater for 1500–2000 employees with midday meals served in two sittings over a

period of 1½ hours. The equipment includes 3 convection ovens with separate boiling tables, 3 steam ovens and 3 double deep fryers. A practical and decorative effect has been achieved by the patterning of floor tiles.

a food shop counter where domestic purchases of meat and other food commodities can be obtained during the meal breaks.

4 CHARACTERISTICS OF CATERING FACILITIES
Design features
4.01 To identify design requirements for particular catering needs it is useful to adopt some method of classifying restaurants and similar facilities into groups which have certain features in common. A classification based on those aspects of catering operation which have a marked influence on planning and design could include considerations of size, occasions of use, types of meals and their method of service, level of sophistication and extent of specialization.

Such a classification has been adopted in the book *Restaurant Planning and Design*, taking into account the features most commonly associated with specific types of establishment and identifying the following categories of service and specialization:
Service
· Snack bar
· Café
· Self-service cafeteria
· Counter
· Coffee shop
· Buttery bar
· Banquet
· Remote service—including automatic vending
Specialization
· Speciality
· Traditional
· Entertainment

The range of different catering outlets and the variety in individual restaurant designs are so extensive that these groupings cannot be regarded as exclusive nor precise in definition. However, for the purpose of determining basic catering requirements, it is important to establish from the beginning, the type of operation which is envisaged and, for this, some form of grouping is useful.

Application
4.02 Whilst these descriptions can be applied to catering establishments generally, the main value in identifying different types of restaurant is in the commercial sector. A restaurant, café, snack bar or other kind of catering premises needs to be identified with the market demand for that facility and be easily recognized as providing the type of meals, service, 'atmosphere', price, and other features which the potential customer expects.
In contrast, where the catering provision forms a secondary service for a market which is usually semi-captive, other factors assume greater importance. Although the dining area may be recognized as being a restaurant, self-service cafeteria or coffee shop, etc., it is considerations of efficiency, speed of service, scheduling, distribution, dietary requirements, cleaning, maintenance and other operational conditions which generally determine the planning and design of the catering services.

Operational features in catering services
4.03 Typical requirements for catering services can be summarized under the main areas of application using the classification in paragraph 3.01 of this chapter as a guide.

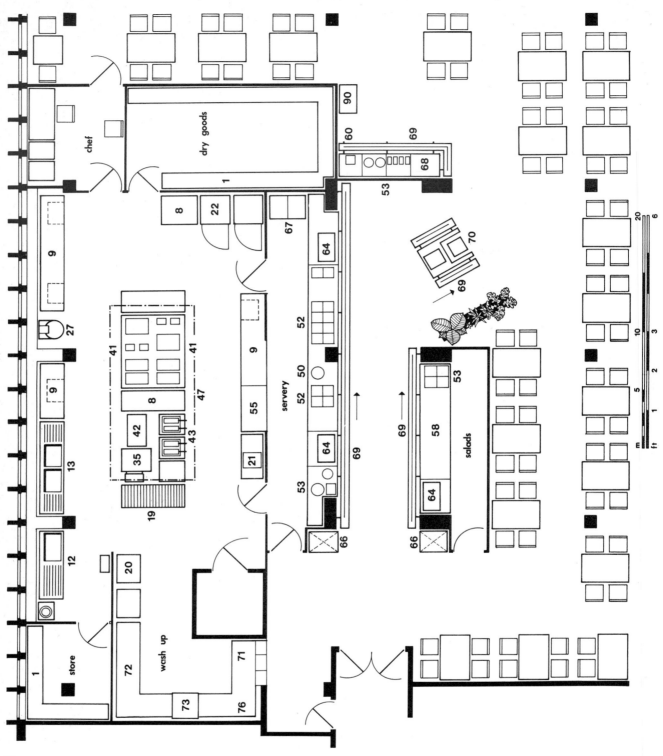

British Relay Ltd., Crawley. Concorde Catering Equipment
Co. Ltd.

The plan illustrates a self-service restaurant designed to serve
350 dinners over a 1½ hour period. An island salad bar has been
provided to divide the flow and increase the speed of service,
in addition to allowing a better presentation.

21

22

Mercedes Benz (Agam), Utrecht, Holland. Concorde Catering Equipment Ltd.
First floor restaurant used for senior staff and visitors which operates on self-service and waiter systems.[21] The modular counters have been arranged in echelon for greater interest

and the illuminated frieze above shows typical dishes obtainable. The restaurant occupies a balcony position over-looking the main car showroom on the floor below, thus combining business interests.[22]

23

24

Mercedes Benz (Agam), Utrecht, Holland. Concorde Catering Equipment Ltd., for the Sutcliffe Catering Co. Ltd.
Illustrations of the kitchens used for the staff catering showing cooking equipment arranged in islands[23] with peripheral sinks and food preparation facilities.[24]

(a) Employee catering

This service usually involves the provision of cooked mid-day meals with, often, limited use for light meals and refreshments at other times of the day. Although the size of installation will vary considerably, preparation of food on a large scale is frequently required and the servery must be designed to meet the peak demand for meals with minimum waiting and congestion. Various self-service arrangements—cafeteria, free-flow systems, etc— are used to meet this requirement and simplified payment facilities may also be adopted. Removal of used tableware may be by means of trolley collection or self-clearance and this must be facilitated in the layout and design.

Vending machines are frequently used to supply beverages and to supplement the main meal service, installed either within the main dining room or in separate areas. The dining area may need to be flexible to allow multi-purpose use—such as for social meetings—but the interior surfaces,

furniture and fittings must be designed on functional lines to withstand heavy usage with the minimum of cleaning and maintenance.

Depending on policy and size, separate dining facilities may be required for directors, executive and/or administrative staff. These may be linked to the main kitchen or have independent cooking areas and may include facilities for self service or for waitress service to the tables.

(b) School catering

The preparation and cooking of mid-day meals for large numbers of children and staff is usually provided in individual school kitchens although meals may be supplied from a central commissary or production kitchen ready prepared for use and delivered in a frozen, chilled or hot state. Emphasis is given to inexpensive but appealing meals which must be nutritionally balanced whilst choice may need to be limited to one or two alternative dishes.

25

A large school kitchen incorporating 3 Module 36 suites.

The school kitchen is designed to facilitate rapid service over a short peak period, normally with several sittings in close succession. Small group seating in the dining room is generally preferred to allow staff-student contact and informal supervision. To allow multi-purpose use, the dining room may need to be easily adaptable in layout with means of isolating the servery and kitchen. Furniture is normally of a simple standard design capable of being easily stacked or linked together.

Special conditions apply to nursery and primary schools where dietary requirements and social benefits may assume important aspects of the meal service and the sizes of units of furniture and fittings must be reduced to suit different age groups.

(c) University catering

The catering facilities for colleges and universities are essentially similar to those required in employee catering but must provide greater flexibility for extending or limiting the service at different meal and break times and for various periods of the year. Separate provisions are usually made for a snack bar service in addition to licensed bars and lounges although these may be supplied with food initially prepared in the main kitchen. For a large university there may also be cost advantages in operating a central commissary kitchen together with bulk storage facilities rather than a number of independent units.

(d) Hospital catering

Special features of hospital catering include the preparation of appetizing balanced meals, often on a large scale with separate dietary kitchens or sections to cater for special needs; facilities for plating meals for remote service where required; carefully planned arrangements for conveying food from the main kitchen to the wards and dining rooms with the minimum of delay and for the return of crockery, containers, etc.; provisions for accurate scheduling of meal production and for keeping the food hot during transit or reheating chilled or frozen meals in service kitchens.

In addition to serving patients, the hospital catering facilities will normally be required to provide meals for residential and non-residential employees, including night staff, and may supply light meals and refreshments for visitors.

(e) Institutional catering

As a rule, catering facilities in institutions must provide all meals throughout the day for staff and residents who may be handicapped by age or infirmity or under confinement. Security measures may be required and a simple method of food service is usually adopted with table or self-service arrangements as appropriate. In some cases, particularly in institutional buildings provided by Local Authorities, meals may be supplied through a delivery

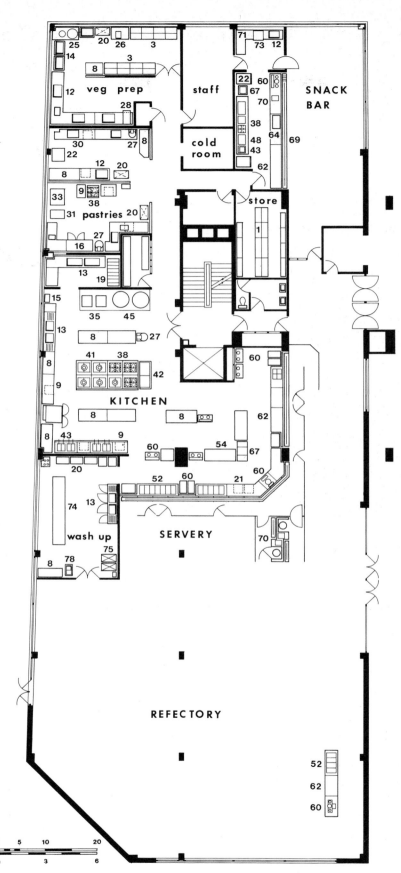

Student refectory, Brighton Technical College. Equipment by Glynwed Foundries Ltd.
This new refectory has a seating capacity of 500 and caters for 1000 for mid-day meals and morning and afternoon breaks. During the short, busy break periods, double beverage and light refreshment points (4 in all) are brought into use. A microphone unit having two-way communication with the kitchen, larder and pastry areas, is situated on the service counter.

Included in the facilities is a modern call order unit snack bar which can cater for 70 separately from the main area and is used, particularly, for the evening meals.
The whole area has been designed for use in conjunction with the Hotel and Catering Department of the College, which has, in addition, extensive teaching kitchens and demonstration facilities.

27

28

Brighton College of Technology. Equipment by Glynwed Foundries Ltd.
Views of the serving counter[27] *and refectory as seen from the reverse side.*[28]

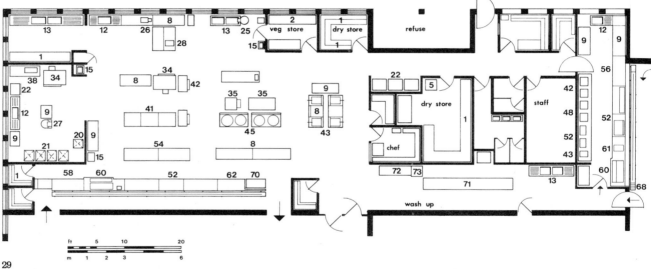

29

30

31

Kitchen layout, Cornwall House Social Centre, University of Exeter. Equipment by G. F. E. Bartlett & Son Ltd.
View of kitchen showing a range of boiling pans, tables and hot cupboards and the near side of the serving counter.

Much of the equipment used for food preparation has been made mobile, including the vegetable sinks and mixing machine. In the foreground is a modern convection oven.

32

Kitchen layout, Cornwall House Social Centre, University of Exeter. Equipment by G. F. E. Bartlett and Son Ltd.
View of the serving counter which is open to the kitchen but separated from the restaurant by a brick partition wall. The kitchen serves snack meals for up to 140 people at a time twice daily.

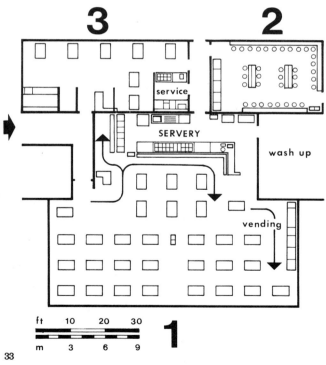

33

King's Fund Catering Advisory Service.
A Plan incorporating proposals for hospital staff catering for a peak of 500 staff meals at mid-day and smaller numbers at other times. The scheme provides for three areas to meet different needs, namely:
(1) A main dining area for some 350 people.
(2) A snack bar area for 60–100 people.
(3) A more expensive area, for about 40–60, operated with waitress service.
Vending units—giving a 24 hour service—are included in the snack bar and main restaurant.

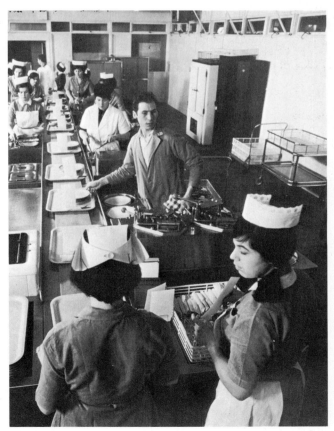

34

Hospital catering. Equipment by Glynwed Foundries Ltd.
A typical example of the 'Ganymede' system using a conveyor belt arrangement for assembling trays with food from mobile units. The heated pellet/dish machine is shown in the foreground.

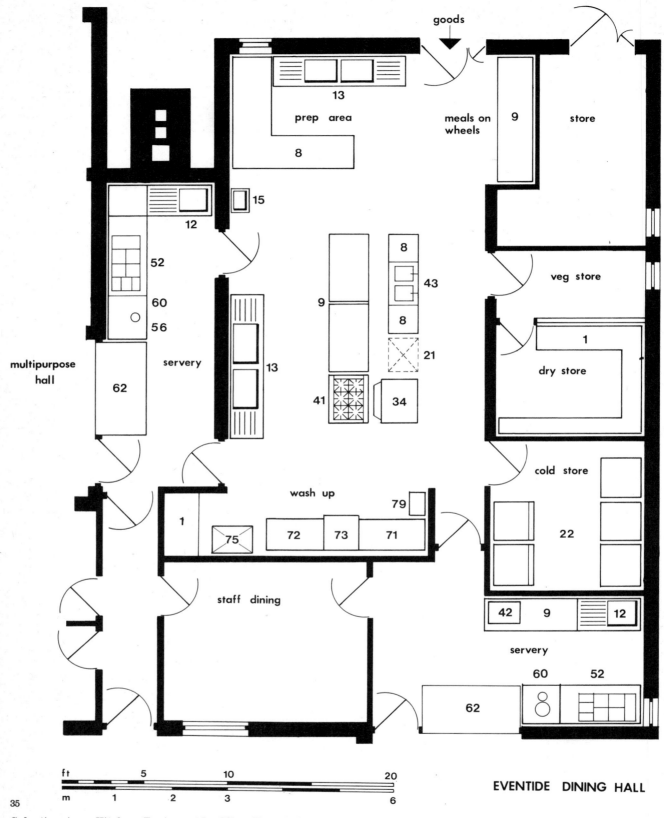

goods

prep area
13
8

meals on wheels

store
9

15

12

52

60

56

multipurpose hall
62

servery

13

8
43
9
8

21

41
34

veg store

1
dry store

cold store
22

42 9 12

servery
60 52

wash up
79
1 75 72 73 71

staff dining
62

ft		5		10				20
m		1	2	3				6

35

EVENTIDE DINING HALL

Salvation Army Kitchen. Equipment by Oliver Toms Ltd.
Plan showing kitchen designed to serve dining rooms and
'meals on wheels' service.

service operating from a central commissary and, in others, the food commodities may be purchased in bulk through a central agency.

The dining room is often used as a focal point for social gatherings and where possible should be attractively designed for this purpose with means of closing off the servery when this is not in use. Special design considera-

tions may apply, for instance where the residents are physically handicapped or issues of security are involved.

(f) *Welfare catering*

Preparation facilities for meals supplied through welfare centres usually include provisions for remote distribution of hot meals to other areas and to individual homes. Space

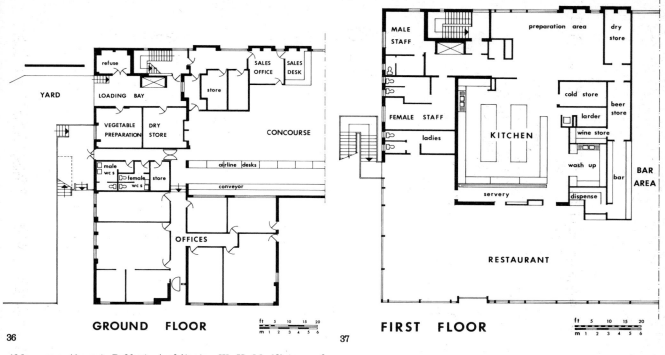

GROUND FLOOR ft 5 10 15 20 / m 1 2 3 4 5 6

36

FIRST FLOOR ft 5 10 15 20 / m 1 2 3 4 5 6

37

Aldergrove Airport, Belfast. Architects—W. H. McAlister and Partners.
Plans of the ground floor servicing area[36] from which food and other goods are transported by lift to the first floor kitchen which is located adjacent to the restaurant.[37]

and washing equipment must be available for the utensils, trolleys and containers used for this purpose and adequate arrangements made for car and van parking.

The dining areas are invariably designed for multi-purpose use and should include provision for serving beverages and refreshments outside the main meal periods.

(g) *Transport catering*

Due to restrictions on space and time, on short journeys meals are normally fully or mainly prepared in advance and often prepacked ready for immediate service. Transport catering is a highly specialized field, requiring considerable preplanning and scheduling of meals to take account of travelling conditions and timetables. The kitchens on aircraft, trains and in many ships are small and must be ergonomically designed to allow efficient use without congestion. The fittings are specifically designed and accelerated cooking equipment—such as convection and microwave ovens—is normally installed. Operational problems may arise when prepared food has to be stored over delayed or prolonged journeys and from the effects of reduced air pressure (in aircraft), repeated handling, spillage and vibration.

(h) *Services catering*

Catering facilities provided for the armed forces and other service personnel are generally complex, involving large-scale production of a wide range of meals in permanent installations and provision for emergency feeding using mobile units. The planning of such facilities is normally carried out by internal design staff and much of the portable equipment is specifically developed for the purpose.

5 TECHNICAL INFORMATION

5.01 Separation of catering services into various groupings is particularly relevant when considering standards, cost-limitations and other design guidelines. Most sectors of the catering industry are individually regulated by specific requirements determined by the Government Department or other authority responsible for the expenditure involved whilst, in other cases much valuable information is provided by organizations, operating in an advisory capacity. As a summary of some of the main sources of information, reference should be made to the following:

(a) Educational establishments

School catering services are regulated by the Department of Education and Science and the maximum allowances, in terms of costs per school place, are laid down for various types of educational establishments. As a guide to design standards Building Bulletin No 11, *Design of School Kitchens* (1955), originally published by the Ministry of Education, provided a foundation of technical details. In addition, most Local Education Authorities employ catering advisers to co-ordinate the organization of school meals services.

(b) Universities

Expenditure on university buildings—including dining facilities—is determined by the University Grants Committee. The limits of such expenditure can be calculated from the *Non-Recurrent Grants—Notes on Procedure*, from which the following figures are derived for illustration purposes. Both the policy towards capital expenditure on university accommodation and the cost limits allowed are under review.

Capital grants and expenditure limits for kitchen and dining areas are assessed on the following Planning Norms:

1 *The maximum meal demand* (usually at weekday lunch)
This rarely exceeds the total student numbers and may be considerably less. A typical provision is 75% of the equivalent full-time student population.

2 *The pattern of demand*
The demand for different types of meals will also vary but are normally in the proportions:

type	examples	% of meals served
Main meals	meat and two vegetables	40
Snacks	egg and chips; beans on toast	35
Hand snacks	coffee and sandwich; pie and pint	25

3 *Dining areas*
Depending on the types or meals provided, dining rooms should be based in the following areas:

Type of dining room	Area per dining place, -usable	-gross*	Times used each meal-time	Gross area per meal served
	m²	m²		m²
Cafeteria	1·1	1·65	2·5	0·67
Snacks	1·1	1·65	2·5	0·67
Waitress Service	1·1	1·65	1·5	1·10
Formal dining	1·1	1·65	2·0†	0·85

* including a balancing allowance of 50% on the usable area
† with coffee service in separate lounges or common rooms

4 *Kitchen areas*
Calculations of kitchen areas are also based on the types of meals provided;

Type of meals provided	Kitchen area per meal -usable	-gross*
	m²	m²
3 main meals including breakfast	0·45	0·68
1 main meal per day	0·40	0·60
Cooked snack meals	0·30	0·45
Coffee sandwich service	0·10	0·15

* Including a balancing allowance of 50% on the usable area.

5 *Rate per square metre*
The standard rate in 1971–2 for calculating expenditure limits was £66.20 per square metre of the gross floor area. This rate allows for building accommodation—including floor finishes—and the normal engineering services but excludes furniture and equipment.

6 *Unit allowances for furniture and fittings*
Expenditure limits are set for heavy kitchen equipment, additional light kitchen equipment, dining room equipment and furniture and for crockery and cutlery.

(a) Heavy kitchen equipment

Number of meals per day	Conventional menus full meal service basic	per meal	1 main meal and and up to 30% of second meal basic	per meal	2 light meals basic	per meal
Up to 200		£47·00		£37·60		£23·50
200 to 600	£4600 +	£24·00	£3680 +	£19·20	£2300+	£12·00
600 to 1500	£11500 +	£12·50	£9200 +	£10·00	£5750+	£6·20
Over 1500	£14500 +	£10·50	£11600 +	£8·40	£7250+	£5·20

(b) Light kitchen equipment

Number of meals per day	Cost allowance
Up to 200	£3·60 per meal
200 to 800	£420 + £1·50 per meal
Over 800	£1140 + £0·60 per meal

(c) Isolated Coffee service

Customer demand at any one period	Cost allowance
For 250 to 500	£875 + £1 per additional customer over 250
For over 500	£1750 + £1 per additional customer over 500

(d) Dining room equipment, furniture furnishings and fittings

For main and light meals, irrespective of numbers	£10·75 per place

(e) Crockery and cutlery

	Main meals	Light meals
Single sittings	£5·00 per place	£2·50 per place
Two or more sittings	£10·00 per place	£5·00 per place

Reference University Grants Committee, Capital Grants, Notes on Procedure, 1971, and Planning Norms for University Buildings, 1972.

(c) Hospital buildings
Guidance on the standards of provision and costs for hospital catering facilities are contained in Building Notes issued by the Department of Health and Social Security.

Hospital Building Notes	Standards of accommodation and engineering
No 10—Kitchens	services
No 11—Dining rooms	

Hospital Equipment Notes	Requirements for equipment utensils,
No 10—Kitchens	furniture and tableware
No 11—Dining rooms	

Procedure Notes	Departmental cost and area guide
No 6—Cost Control	

An indication of these recommendations is shown in the following summary. The figures quoted (1970) are subject to review, and the appropriate Department should be consulted prior to planning a catering scheme.

Functional unit	Basic Accommodation (To nearest 5 m²) (m²)	Departmental area* (m²)	Cost guide to nearest £1000 † (£)	Optional additions Bulk food stores (a) including dairy (b) including dairy and butchers shop
Central Kitchens (Building Note 10)				(£) (a) (£) (b)
300 meals	270	345	36 000	2000 4000
400 ,,	315	390	41 000	3000 5000
500 ,,	380	475	46 000	4000 6000
750 ,,	475	595	58 000	5000 9000
1000 ,,	565	705	70 000	7000 13 000
1250 ,,	650	820	81 000	9000 16 000
1500 ,,	695	875	92 000	11 000 19 000
Staff Dining Rooms (Building Note 11)				
125 meals	140	160	11 000	
250 ,,	230	260	18 000	Costs for temporary
500 ,,	425	485	32 000	guidance
750 ,,	625	715	46 000	

* Includes an allowance to cover possible additional accommodation.
† Up to June 1972.

(*Reference:* Appendix 7, Hospital Procedure Note No 6, Department of Health and Social Security, HMSO).

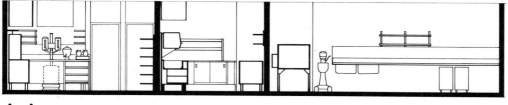

A – A

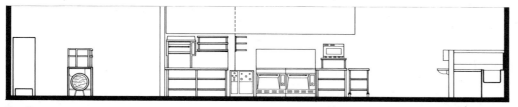

B – B

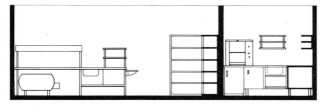

C – C

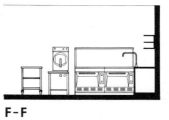

D – D

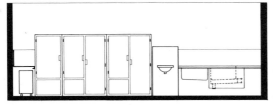

E – E

F – F

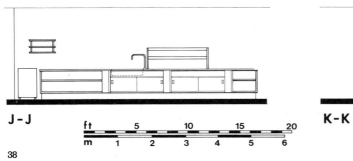

G-G

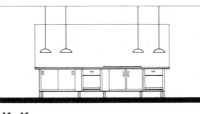

H – H

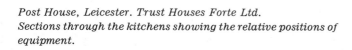

J – J

K – K

ft	5	10	15	20
m	1	2	3	4	5	6

38

Post House, Leicester. Trust Houses Forte Ltd.
Sections through the kitchens showing the relative positions of
equipment.

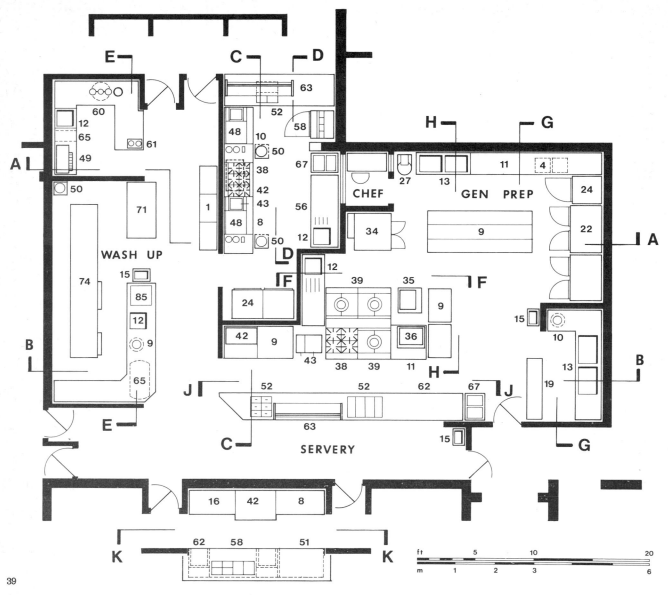

39

Post House, Leicester. Trust Houses Forte Ltd.
Plans showing the layout of the main kitchen for all the hotel
catering except that provided for staff. A separate kitchen
caters exclusively for staff meals.

(d) Institutional and welfare catering

Guidance on cost limitations for Local Authority buildings provided for institutional training centres, and
residential accommodation for elderly people and for the
mentally disordered is given in the Department of Education and Science, Local Authority Building Note 1,
Appendix F: Cost Allowances (1972). From the allowance
for basic accommodation—which includes food preparation facilities—the following deductions may be made if a
meals delivery service is used.

Meals delivery service for		Deduction
		£
50–99	meals provided	1880
100–150	„ „	2475

(e) Industrial canteens

Annual surveys of canteen prices costs and subsidies are
conducted by the Industrial Society (48 Bryanston Square,

London W1) and the survey reports contain a wealth of
information relating to employee catering facilities.

(f) Inter-unit comparison surveys

The Centre for Hotel and Catering Comparisons (Scottish
Hotel School, University of Strathclyde, Glasgow) con-
ducts annual surveys of participating hotels, motels and
restaurants from which comparative financial statistics
are summarized and published in annual reports.

(g) National Economic Development Office

Arising from studies organized through its Economic
Development Committees, the NEDO has published a
number of reports and guides of direct relevance to catering investment. In this context, the following are most
valuable as sources of reference.
i *Hotel and Catering EDC: Investment in hotels and catering,
1968*—Results of an investment study; *Economic assessment
to 1972*—Growth, projections for the hotel and catering
industry up to 1972; *Your market, 1971*—Sources of market

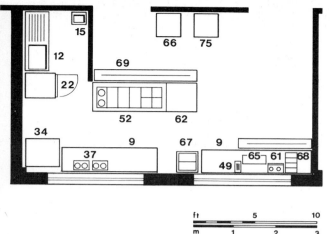

40

Staff catering facilities, Post House, Leicester. Trust Houses Forte Ltd.
Designed for frozen precooked meals, the staff kitchen has the minimum of cooking equipment, namely, a two deck convection oven and two twin boiling units. The serving counter comprises a bain-marie hot cupboard—with an infra-red shelf above— and a cold counter unit.

information; *Marketing in a small business, 1970*—Practical aspects of marketing.
ii *Food Manufacturers EDC: Food Statistics, 1971*—A guide to official and unofficial UK sources.

(h) Other sources
A list of further sources of information relative to catering practice is given in Chapter 8.

Technical standards
5.02 Reference is made, particularly in relation to catering equipment, to the standards of quality, safety and performance recommended in British Standard Specifications published by the
  British Standards Institute,
  Park Lane, London W1A 2BS.
Such standards are intended for British practice although the basic functional requirements are generally relevant on an international scale.
Reference may also be made to the standards recommended by other national agencies and, in particular, the following are widely recognized:
  American National Standards Institute (ANSI)
  1430 Broadway,
  New York, NY 10018, USA.
  American Society for Testing Materials (ASTM)
  1916 Race St,
  Philadelphia 3, PA, USA.
  Association Française de Normalization (AFNOR)
  Tour Europe,
  92 Courbevoie, Paris.
  Deutscher Normenausschuss (DNA)
  1000 Berlin 30,
  Burgrafenstrasse 4–7.

2 FOOD STORAGE

1 GENERAL REQUIREMENTS

Catering policy

1.01 The amount of space allocated for storage of food and other commodities varies considerably from one catering establishment to another, being mainly related to the size and type of catering involved but also, to a large extent, influenced by considerations of management policy.

1.02 In practice, the areas allocated for stores in existing catering premises are rarely found to be excessive and are often inadequate both in space and facilities. This is possibly because, like staff accommodation, stores tend to be regarded as non-revenue producing areas and, consequently, are reduced to the minimum. However, the congestion which frequently results from inadequate or unsuitable storage creates problems in maintaining proper food cost control, rotation of stocks, records and other aspects of supervision. In turn this can lead to substantial losses from deterioration of food, abuses in food use and pilfering. Considered from a commercial point of view, efficient storage can have a significant bearing on the profitability of the business.

1.03 The main factor to be taken into account in assessing storage requirements is the size of the catering operation and its turnover in terms of the number of meals produced each day. Other aspects such as the type of catering, the range of choice offered on the menu and the price of the meals will also affect the quantities of food used.

1.04 Whilst a preliminary indication of storage areas can be assumed from average figures for catering operations of similar size, the requirements for any particular establishment will depend on the operating conditions and other circumstances.

If space is restricted and/or the site expensive it may be more practicable for the caterer to arrange such frequent deliveries of all, or most, of the food supplies so that the stores can be kept to a minimum. In other cases, larger than normal reserves of food will be required where the premises are isolated or deliveries unreliable.

Details of the requirements for storage space and the conditions of storage for different food commodities are described under their respective headings.

2 PURCHASING

2.01 Storage requirements are also closely linked with the management's approach towards food purchasing and this should be considered at the same time.

Food supplies may be bought wholesale, retail or through contract arrangements, in bulk or otherwise, and obtained direct or through a central agency.

Wholesale

2.02 Food commodities obtained in the wholesale market show savings of up to 25 per cent or more compared with retail prices. There are other advantages in that it is often easier to obtain particular foods which are scarce or in limited demand and wholesale packs and containers, being in larger sizes, are usually more convenient for catering use.

Bulk purchases

2.03 If the catering organization, whether in one premises or as a group, is sufficiently large there may be even greater financial savings by buying food materials in bulk—either wholesale or direct from the supplier. Such economies are often obtained through central agencies buying for several catering establishments as in Local Authority school meals services, hospitals, hotel groups and large industrial companies.

Centralized systems

2.04 Central buying provides other advantages in that the bulk storage facilities may be sited in almost any convenient place and this does not necessarily have to form part of the catering premises. Considerations, such as the value of the land and other development costs, convenience of access and location for distribution purposes, can be taken into account in selecting the site and the building can be purposely designed for storage purposes. With this arrangement it is often feasible to carry out some initial preparation, eg washing and peeling vegetables; jointing, boning and portioning meat, before the food is dispatched, thus saving space, labour and equipment at the catering outlets.

The efficient operation of a centralized system does, however, require well organized distribution facilities and the costs of both premises and transport need to be taken into account in assessing the potential viability of such a scheme.

Centralized facilities are being used increasingly in the production of catering products such as butchery, bakery and confectionery items which require expensive specialized equipment and skilled staff. This could apply, for example, to an hotel company which has a number of hotels and restaurants operating within the same area

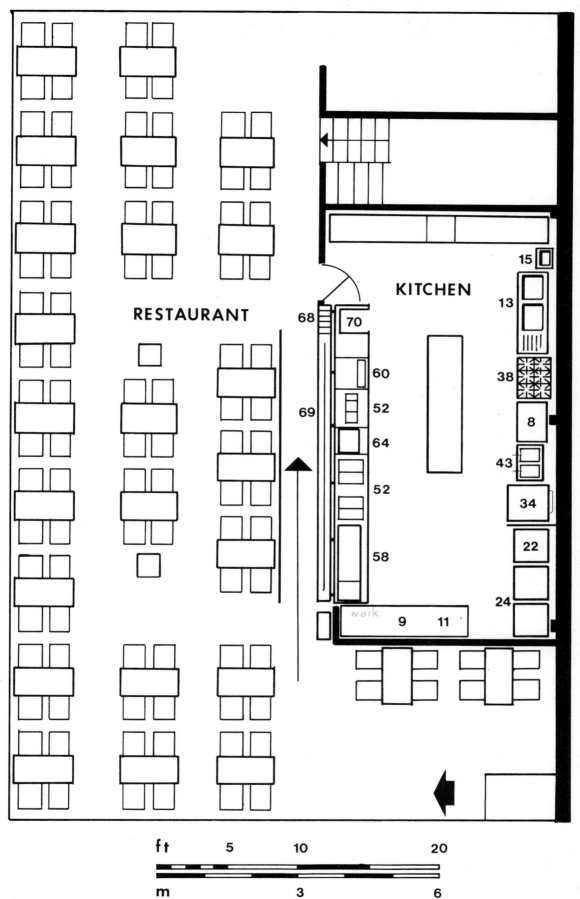

KITCHEN

RESTAURANT

15
13
38
8
43
34
22
24

68
70
60
52
64
52
58
69

work   9   11

ft   5   10   20

m   3   6

1

*Employee Catering Facilities, Change Ware Ltd. Equipment by
Oliver Toms Ltd.
Based on the use of frozen foods, the kitchen has the minimum
of preparation facilities.*

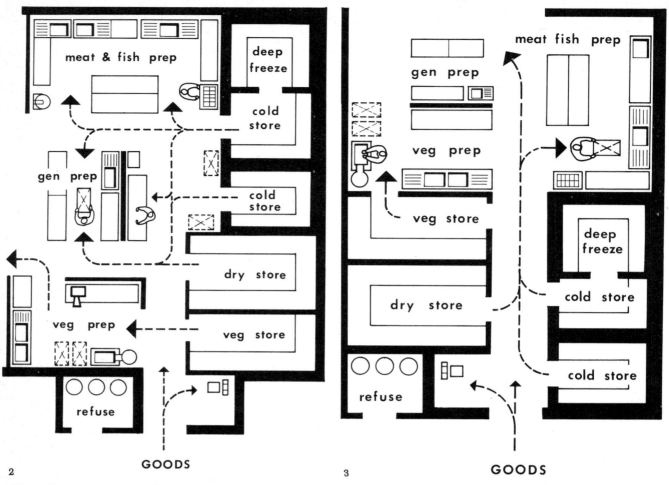

2

3

GOODS   GOODS

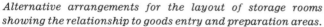

Alternative arrangements for the layout of storage rooms showing the relationship to goods entry and preparation areas.

and where it is possible to adapt one or more of the kitchens to supply others within the same group.

Similarly, in some seaside resorts, the advantages of collective buying are being obtained through the formation of hotel and restaurant voluntary co-operatives and this trend is evolving towards the collective use of centralized processing and freezing facilities. 'Cook-freeze' and similar central production arrangements have been adapted to hospital and school meals catering and this subject is covered in detail in Chapter 7.

Contract buying

2.05 Many Local Authorities and other public bodies buy food and other commodities through a system of contracts. A contract is let, under tender, for the supply of specified goods and provisions over a fixed period of time which may be as long as 12 months, although shorter periods—up to 3 months—are generally recommended for food provisions. With contract arrangements the caterer is restricted in choice of supplier and by the conditions laid down in the contract.

Retail arrangements

2.06 For a small catering establishment, food supplies are frequently most conveniently obtained from local retailers under negotiated terms which usually allow discounts and provide for frequent deliveries.

Convenience foods

2.07 Many catering premises necessarily occupy expensive town centre sites and are very restricted in accommoda-

tion. Under these conditions it is important that as much of the space as possible is incorporated into the revenue-producing restaurant area. Savings in space, kitchen equipment and labour can be achieved by the use of food which has been partly or fully prepared before delivery to the premises.

Prepared foods as supplied to caterers range from washed, peeled vegetables to fully prepared, pre-cooked frozen foods—the so-called 'convenience foods'—which require only to be reheated (or regenerated) to form the basis of a meal.

The changes in production methods taking place in the catering industry are having a considerable effect on storage requirements. With the use of frozen convenience foods there is no need for a conventional vegetable store. On the other hand, the volume of refrigerated storage must be considerably increased and must provide for the lower ranges of temperature which are involved.

3 SPACE REQUIREMENTS

3.01 Whilst storage requirements are generally quoted in terms of floor areas, the amount of storage space obtained from any particular area, and its convenience in use, will depend on several variables, such as the way food commodities are stacked, the height of shelves, the shape and dimensions of the room and space required for access including passages and doorways. Illustrations of layouts are shown in *8* and *11*.

Associated with storage, it is often necessary to provide some work space in the area, eg for sorting and weighing commodities in the dry goods store and for washing and

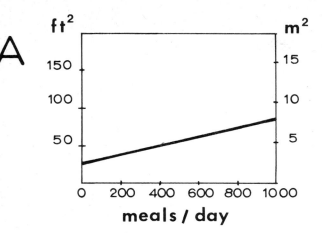

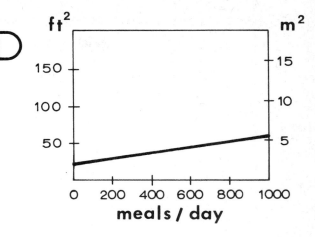

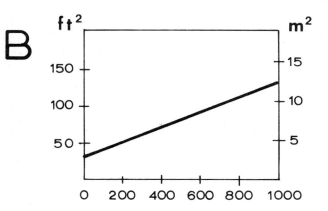

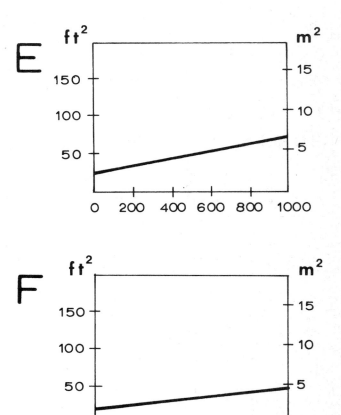

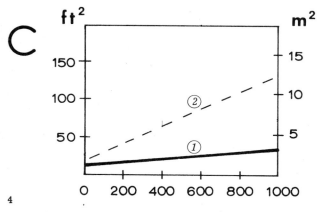

4

Space requirements for food storage in:
A—Vegetables store—with 3 deliveries/week.
B—Dry goods store—for 3 days supply.
C—Low temperature refrigeration—7 days supply.
① Conventional use ② Frozen precooked meals.
D—Cold room—daily delivery of perishable food.
E—Goods entry area including weighing and checking.
F—Refuse storage where bins are used.

These areas are based on the number of meals produced per day in a modern conventional kitchen using a proportion of frozen food items. Where the kitchen uses mainly precooked frozen meals, a separate vegetable storage area may not be required and the low-temperature refrigeration ('deep freeze') will be increased as indicated.

peeling operations in the vegetable store.

3.02 In contrast to other storage areas, cold stores and refrigerators are quoted in terms of cubic capacity. This is to facilitate calculation of refrigeration and insulation requirements since the whole volume of the store is involved. Unless the actual dimensions of a cold store are stated the nominal internal height is taken to be 2100 mm (7′ 0″).

The design capacity of a refrigerator is critical and must not be overloaded.

3.03 Typical storage requirements, based on the floor areas of stores in relation to the number of main meals served per day, are given in 4 and 5.

Small kitchens

3.04 Proportionately, the percentage of space required for storage as compared with the total area of the kitchen increases as the size of the catering operation decreases because, to allow space for access and movement, a store-

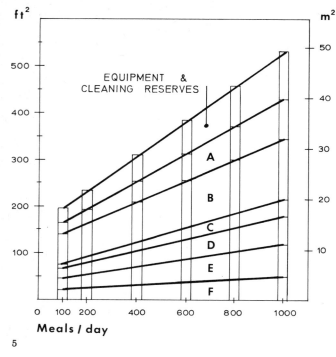

5

Total storage requirements for conventional kitchens based on the number of meals prepared per day.

room cannot be used so efficiently when the area becomes very small. When the number of meals produced per day is 50 or less it is usual to combine the dry stores and larder together and vegetables may be stored in racks which are grouped with other facilities rather than in a separate area. This would also apply in a larger premises where food is supplied at frequent intervals ready prepared for use and conventional storage requirements can be reduced to a minimum.

4 FOOD PACKAGING

4.01 In detailing the layout of food stores it is necessary to have regard to the methods of packaging used in wholesale food distribution. The sizes and weights of the containers will affect the arrangements for receiving, handling and storing food commodities and will determine features such as the design of racks and shelving, corridor widths and floor loadings.

Food containers are designed to provide protection, ventilation or insulation, so as to reduce damage and deterioration of food during transport and transitory storage. To a certain extent the sizes, shapes and materials used for traditional containers derive from historical associations but also have a practical foundation such as the need to facilitate easy transport and handling.

At the present time the distribution and methods of packaging are undergoing considerable change. This is

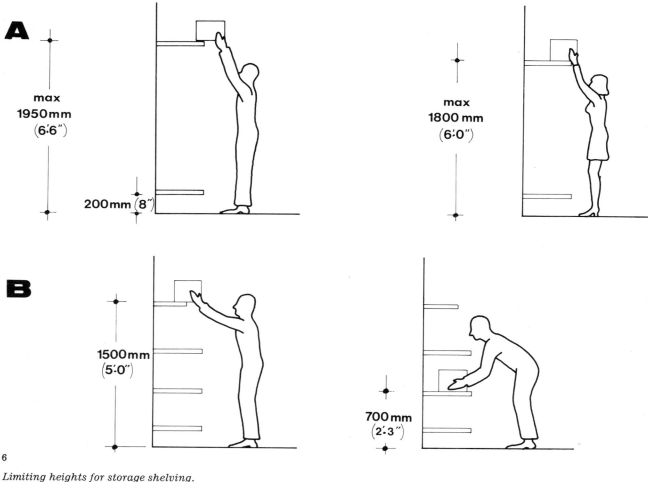

6

Limiting heights for storage shelving.
A—Maximum reach.
B—Within convenient reach for heavy and frequently used items.

being brought about partly by increased mechanization in agriculture and the washing, trimming and prepacking of farm produce at the source, and partly by the substitution of plastic and cardboard for more expensive traditional materials.

Further changes in food packaging will arise with the introduction of metric sizes. The proposals for metrication currently under consideration by the British Standards Institute, the Food Trades Metrication Committee and others are taking account of Continental sizes with the view to achieving standardization.

Storage of containers
4.02 Shelves and storage units should be of a height and width appropriate for the sizes of food containers and be sufficiently strong to carry the weights involved. An interspace of about 40 to 50 mm should be allowed between packages for easy positioning and removal.

The average vertical reach for men is about 2100 mm and the height of the top shelf should be limited to about 1950 mm (6′ 6″) to enable easy lifting without the use of ladders. This top shelf should only be used for light weight items.

At the other extreme, shelves and open bins must be kept at least 200 mm (8″) above the floor to leave a clear space underneath for access and cleaning, and to deter rodents. Shelves for frequently used items or heavy containers are best positioned between 700 and 1500 mm high (2′ 3″ to 5′ 0″).

Food commodities in bags and sacks are normally transferred to bins or racks for protection and convenient access.

Expensive containers such as casks, churns and—in some cases—tins may have to be returned to the supplier for reuse and, in addition to providing storage for food, there is a need for space, preferably separate, for empty containers awaiting collection. Such storage areas must be constructed to facilitate cleaning and provide protection against contamination.

5 GOODS ACCESS
5.01 Vehicle access is required to catering premises both for delivering food and other goods and for the removal of refuse and food waste. Typical delivery arrangements—although these will depend very much on the situation and size of the establishment—are as follows:

Dry goods — weekly or fortnightly
Vegetables — once or twice weekly
Perishable foods — daily
Refuse and
waste removal — usually once or twice weekly

5.02 Minimum dimensions of access roads for occasional use by goods lorries and refuse vehicles:

Single-lane carriageway		minimum
on the straight, minimum width	—	3200 m (10′ 6″)
on sharp turns, width increased up to	—	4400 m (14′ 6″)
swept turning area, minimum radius	—	11 000 m (36′ 6″)

Dimensions of typical refuse vehicle*
of 27/38 m³ capacity
Length 7400 m (24′ 4″), Width 2390 m (7′ 10″), Height 3280 m (10′ 9″)

* *Note:* Access requirements for refuse, etc vehicles must be verified by the Local Authority.

To allow delivery vans and lorries to pull right up to the door of the building, it is usually most convenient for the goods entrance to open on to a yard. The yard must have an impervious even surface such as concrete or tarmacadam, and be properly drained.

Refuse storage
5.03 If refuse and swill bins are accommodated in the yard these should be kept in a suitable enclosure raised off the ground and covered to give protection against the sun and rain. A water standpipe and hose are essential for washing down the area.

In most cases, conventional refuse and waste bins are used for storage but bulk containers (0.57 m³ or 0.85 m³ (20–30 cu ft) capacity) may be used instead of bins. Such containers must have close-fitting and, preferably, hinged lids. When bulk containers are used for refuse, extra space is required for loading and unloading the vehicle.

With a view to reducing decomposition of food waste intended for pig food and to eliminate odour and fly nuisance, waste bins may be sited in a refrigerated enclosure kept at a temperature of 2.0 to 5.0°C. There is also an increasing tendency to use waste disposal units for discharge of food waste direct to the drainage system. This facility greatly improves hygiene but may be subject to some abuse and the discharge of large quantities of solid waste to public sewers is restricted by some Local Authorities.

Fuel storage and other access requirements
5.04 Access may be required for solid or liquid fuel supplies stored in the vicinity of the building. Fuels and similar contaminating materials must be kept separate from any food area or utensil store and problems of dust, odour and possible seepage must be considered in siting the fuel store.

Risk of fire must also be taken into account including the use of this area as a potential fire escape route and as a means of entry to the premises for fire-fighting vehicles and equipment. Aspects of safety and fire precautions in restaurants are covered in detail in the book *Restaurant Planning and Design*.

6 GOODS ENTRANCE
6.01 Off-loading and carrying goods into the premises is generally done by the delivery men but the goods must be checked on receipt against invoices and weighed prior to being taken into store.

The arrangements for receiving, weighing and checking deliveries depend on the size of the premises and the relative positions of the storage areas. For a small catering establishment it may be sufficient to provide a table and weighing scales sited just inside the entrance or within the area of the stores, whichever is more convenient. A purposely designed goods receiving area should be provided in larger premises and, for efficient control, this must be sited immediately adjacent to the goods entrance and conveniently accessible to the food stores.

Where the latter is not possible due to the location of the stores, the goods receiving area may serve as a transit store for deliveries awaiting transport elsewhere in the building. Such arrangements may apply where food is conveyed—by lift or otherwise—to other floors or dispatched to substores serving different kitchens within the same catering organization. However, as a general rule it is undesirable to delay food from being taken direct to the stores. Double handling is wasteful of time and labour, is liable to lead to congestion and confusion, increases space requirements and construction costs and, in any event, must be avoided where the food is perishable

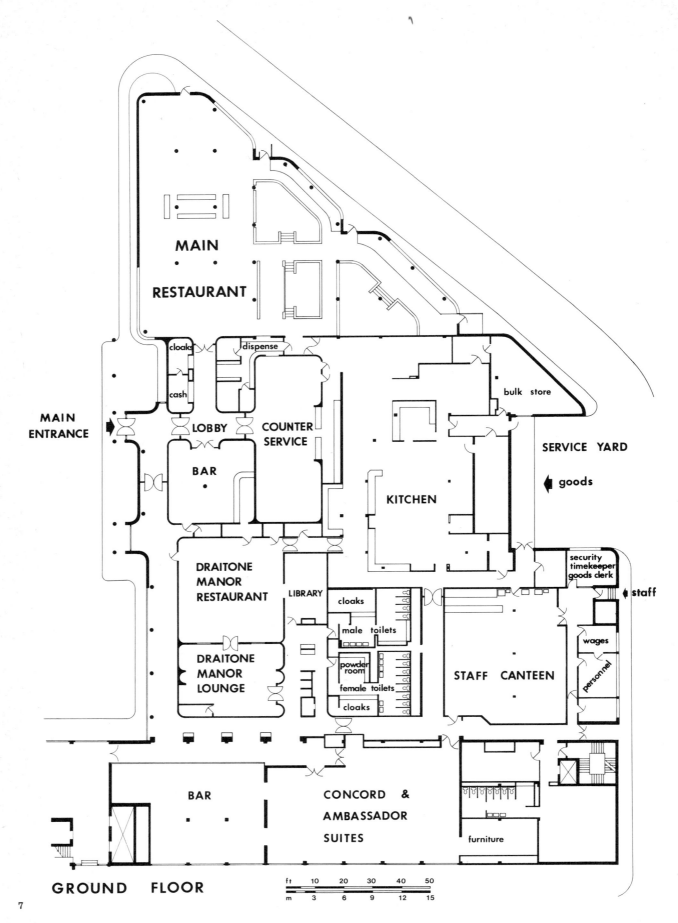

MAIN

RESTAURANT

cloaks

dispense

MAIN
ENTRANCE

cash

LOBBY

COUNTER
SERVICE

bulk store

SERVICE YARD

goods

BAR

KITCHEN

security
timekeeper
goods clerk

staff

DRAITONE
MANOR
RESTAURANT

LIBRARY

cloaks

male toilets

wages

personnel

DRAITONE
MANOR
LOUNGE

powder
room

female toilets

cloaks

STAFF CANTEEN

BAR

CONCORD &
AMBASSADOR
SUITES

furniture

GROUND FLOOR

ft   10   20   30   40   50

m   3   6   9   12   15

7

Excelsior Hotel, London Airport. Trust Houses Forte Ltd.
Ground floor plan showing layout and inter-relationship of
restaurants, kitchens, stores and other catering facilities for
the Excelsior Hotel.

or liable to contamination.

Construction

6.02 Where substantial quantities of food are involved it is an advantage to provide a raised platform or unloading bay at tailboard height for convenient off-loading from vehicles. To reduce damage the front edge of the bay should be protected with steel angle (say 150 mm × 150 mm).

6.03 Loading Bays

Bay widths for loading and unloading of vehicles are shown in the following table:

No of vehicles at one time	Recommended width of bay		Minimum width of bay		Minimum depth of bay (within building)	
	(m)	(ft)	(m)	(ft)	(m)	(ft)
Side loading						
1	11	36	10	33		
2	18	60	16	53	18 to 19	59 to 63
3	24	80	22	72		
End loading						
Per vehicle	4	13	3·75	12' 6"	14	46

(*Source: A J Metric Handbook,* Architectural Press.)

The area of the bay must allow for possible stacking of goods during unloading, for trolleys and other equipment, for weighing and checking facilities—which may include a small office—and for adequate work space in handling large containers. Special facilities may be required, such as overhead rail lines for carcase meat, etc and trolleys for exposed food which—to avoid possible contamination —must not be placed within 450 mm (1' 6") from the ground. The floors of the goods receiving area and corridors leading to the stores must be of durable, impervious material having a cleansable but non-slip surface. Granolithic concrete finished with a carborundum surface or quarry tiles are suitable materials for this purpose. Walls must be smooth, non-absorbent, easily cleansable and resistant to impact and scraping damage. Glazed tiles or glazed bricks are ideal but expensive and difficult to replace. Cement rendered walls, preferably painted, also meet these requirements. All junctions should be coved for easy cleaning and the whole area must be efficiently drained to allow hosing down.

Doors to the goods entrance and stores must be sufficiently wide, well hung and strong to withstand the damage likely to be received. Stout two-way swing doors, 1050 mm (3' 6") (single) or 1500 mm (5' 0") (double) wide, faced with sheet metal edging and kicking plates are probably most suitable for external use but a swing door of this type must have a wired glass or perspex viewing window to avoid accidents. All external doors must be fitted with substantial bolts and locks.

There must be no steps between the goods entrance and stores nor between the stores and preparation areas. Changes in level may be accommodated by ramps which should not, normally, have an incline greater than 10°. Food commodities may also be transported vertically by lifts and conveyors.

7 CONDITIONS AFFECTING STORAGE

7.01 Optimum conditions for storage depend on the type of food and range from a moderately cool dry atmosphere —which is suitable for dried goods—to one which is very cold and humid, as appropriate for most perishable foods. In general terms it is possible to distinguish the following categories of foods each of which requires specific storage conditions:

Category of food	Storage conditions
Frozen food	'Deep freeze' to —20°C (0°F) depending on length of storage required.
Chilled perishable and prepared foods	Cooled to between 0°C and 4°C (32°F and 40°F) but maintained above freezing point.
Dehydrated or dried food	Moderately cool (10–15°C (50–59°F)) and essentially dry.
Fresh vegetables and fruit	Cool (5–10°C) (41–50°F) well ventilated but protected from frost and high humidities.
Canned or bottled foods	No specific requirements but affected by extremes of temperature, humidity (rust) and rough handling (perforation).
Wines, Beers	Temperature very critical for the type of wine, beer, etc within range 10–16°C (50–60°F).

7.02 To provide for these variations, food storage is usually divided into separate areas namely:

(a) *Vegetable store*—for vegetables and fruit but excluding frozen items.

(b) *Dried goods store*—for dehydrated, dried, packaged, canned, bottled and miscellaneous food commodities. Sometimes referred to as 'general stores'. Day-to-day requirements are usually kept in small 'kitchen stores' situated in, or near to, the preparation areas.

(c) *Cold stores*—these include refrigerated cabinets and purpose built cold rooms which are mechanically cooled and larders used in small kitchens.

8 VEGETABLE STORES

Situation

8.01 The vegetable store must be sited near to the goods entrance so that deliveries can be taken directly into the store without having to pass through other areas. There must also be direct access from the store to the vegetable preparation area of the kitchen. Separate vegetable stores are seldom warranted in kitchens catering for less than 50 meals per day. In this case, storage racks are provided near the vegetable preparation equipment in the kitchen.

Design considerations

8.02 Vegetables are best stored away from daylight— although artificial lighting must be available—and must be protected from frost. The ideal temperature range for a vegetable store is between 5–10°C (41–50°F) (except bananas—stored above 13·5°C (56°F)). Higher temperatures accelerate ripening and drying out and green vegetables rapidly wilt and turn yellow when the ambient temperature is above 20°C (68°F).

Humidity is also an important factor in preserving the fresh, crisp texture of fruit and vegetables. In most cases, a relative humidity up to 95 per cent is desirable but this must be accompanied by good ventilation. Ventilation is essential to reduce mould growth which becomes rapidly established on dead and decaying material—such as bruised surfaces—and spreads, through the formation of spores, to other moist food surfaces particularly where the air is stagnant. Air circulation enables the correct conditions of temperature and humidity to be maintained throughout the whole area and helps to disperse and dilute odours. The minimum rate of ventilation for stores is 2 air changes per hour.

Light fittings must be positioned over the corridors to give an even light distribution around the shelves without

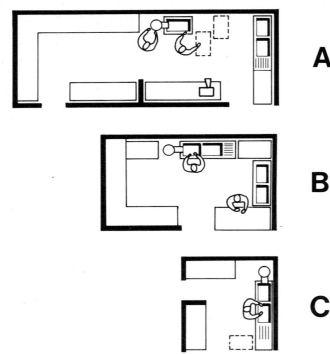

A

B

C

8

Vegetable preparation arrangements for A—large, B—medium and C—small size kitchens.

strong shadows. The design level of illumination for food stores is 200 lux (18·6 lumens/ft²) with a limiting Glare Index of 25 but a higher intensity should be provided— 400 lux (37·2 lumens/ft²)—over work areas such as the vegetable sink.

Construction

8.03 Constructional features in vegetable stores are similar to those in other storage rooms but more frequent washing down is usually necessary and the operations of washing, paring and preparing vegetables are liable to cause splashing of the adjacent walls and floor. Walls in the vicinity of any work area should, preferably, be of glazed tiles up to 1800 mm (6′ 0″). In other areas the walls are usually cement rendered and preferably painted with washable paint (oil bound distemper, gloss or plastic emulsion paint). Floors must also be impervious and laid to slight falls for drainage to a grating covered channel inside the room which discharges to a trapped silt gulley preferably sited outside the building. The ceiling should be plastered to a smooth even surface.

Fittings

8.04 Shelves, supported by racks, are used to increase storage capacity by allowing vertical stacking. At the same time stored vegetables and fruit should be easy to locate and handle without bruising. To allow air circulation, slatted shelves are used for packaged items and wire

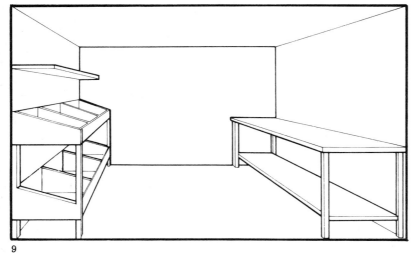

9

Perspective view of vegetable store with purposely designed storage bins and trolley for mobile storage.

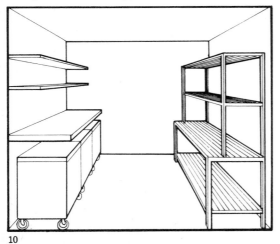

10

Diagram of dry goods store showing shelving arrangement and use of mobile rack units.

mesh racks or metal bins for loose vegetables and fruit. Racks are usually designed with a slight slope towards the front and may be fitted with a dust tray underneath. For green vegetables the shelves are kept shallow to avoid having to pile the vegetables on top of each other—which leads to rapid deterioration.

To facilitate ventilation and cleaning and to reduce rat and mice harbourage, bins and shelves should be supported 200 mm (8″) clear of the floor. It is not good practice to leave root crops such as potatoes in their original sacks on the floor nor on duckboards, and sufficient separated rack space must be provided to enable proper storage of all vegetables without having to tip new supplies on top of old stock.

Fresh fruit, including citrus fruits, are liable to cause tainting and are kept in a separate part of the vegetable store with shallow racks to minimize bruising. Salad items are also kept in a separate area within the store to minimize contamination. Details of vegetable storage arrangements are shown in 8 and 9.

9 DRY GOODS STORE

9.01 Storage of commodities such as flour, sugar, cereals, dried fruit and canned and bottled foods is grouped together in the dry goods (or general) stores. In large catering establishments this is usually divided into two stages, viz:

(a) Bulk or issue store

Sited near the goods receiving area this serves as the main store for bulk purchases and reserve stocks of dry goods. Quantities of various food commodities required for day-to-day use are weighed and measured in the store prior to issue. Central bulk stores are essential where there are several kitchens operating within the same establishment.

(b) Kitchen stores

Food ingredients for immediate use are normally kept in a small store or cupboard sited in or adjacent to the preparation area. The use of two stores may not be feasible in a small kitchen but some system of control over food usage and costs is always essential.

Construction

9.02 The siting and construction of a dry goods store must ensure that food does not come into contact with damp surroundings nor is exposed to excessive humidity, eg. from the kitchen. All dehydrated and dried commodities are susceptible to damage by moisture and deliquescent substances such as salt are rapidly affected. The floor, walls and roof of the store must be fully damp-proofed. Thermal insulation ('U' value below $1.70 \, \text{W/m}^2 \, °\text{C}$ or $0.3 \, \text{Btu/ft}^2 \, \text{h} \, °\text{F}$) is important to minimize fluctuations in temperature and risk of condensation in winter.

The positioning of doors and ventilators must not allow steam to enter from other areas. A supply of water—with standpipe and hose—should be available nearby for cleaning, but not sited in the store.

Natural lighting is not necessary but if windows are provided they must be carefully positioned to avoid direct entry of sunlight—and overheating—during the day, and condensation damage at night. Artificial lighting must be provided to give good illumination (200 lux; limiting Glare Index 25) without obscuration over the shelves and work areas.

Dry goods are not normally affected by moderate changes in temperature but insect pests in cereals, etc grow most rapidly at 28–35°C (83–95°F) and some foods, eg dried eggs and dried fruit, deteriorate under hot conditions (above 16°C (61°F)). A fairly constant temperature of between 10–15°C (50–59°F) is the optimum for storage. The store must be well ventilated giving at least 2 air changes an hour with the ventilators being positioned and protected to avoid entry of dust, smoke, odours, insects and vermin. Constructional requirements for a dry goods store are similar to those for other areas in which food is stored. The floors and walls, etc must be non-absorbent and readily cleansable. It is not necessary to provide drainage channels but the floor should have gradual slope towards the door to facilitate floor washing and drying. As in other areas all junctions should be coved and there should be no unnecessary ledges and ornamentation.

Storage fittings

9.03 To avoid dampness and contamination food must not be stored on the floor. Most packaged items are accommodated on shelves but dry goods in large quantities such as flour, sugar, cereals and dried fruit, are better kept in stainless or vitreous enamelled steel, anodised aluminium or plastic bins, which are fitted with wheel bases or castors to enable them to be moved easily in or out for use and cleaning. The bins must have rounded corners and close-fitting hinged lids and are usually housed under the shelving. Scoops must be provided.

Fittings and shelving must be designed for easy cleaning and should be easily demountable to allow redecorating of the store. Shelves should be designed to take a load density of $800 \, \text{kg/m}^3$ ($50 \, \text{lb/ft}^3$) and are usually formed from wood slats ($50 \, \text{mm} \times 12.5 \, \text{mm}$) ($2″ \times \frac{1}{2}″$) spaced 50 mm (2″) apart although purposely designed metal shelving is preferable.

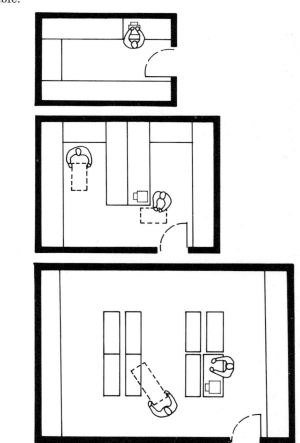

11
Arrangements for shelving in dry goods stores including the use of mobile rack units to facilitate transport and cleaning.

The back edge is fitted with a lip and kept 50 mm (2″) clear of the wall for cleaning. The main shelving is between 700 and 1500 mm (2′ 3″ and 5′ 0″) height and shelves above this, up to 2000 mm (6′ 6″) high, are limited to lightweight items and empty containers. Where bins are stored, a shelf clearance of about 1000 mm (3′ 3″) is required. To allow for different sizes of containers, shelves may be of different widths and spacing and adjustable shelving facilitates changes in the arrangement. Flexibility in layout is also provided by the use of mobile racks of shelving which permit easy removal for cleaning or transport.

The layout of the shelving racks will depend on the size and dimensions of the room but maximum access and use of the area will usually be obtained using double sided racks extending into the room at right angles to a wall. Gangways between shelves must be at least 1200 mm (4′ 0″) wide. Details of dry goods stores are shown in 10 and 11.

Shelf Loadings

| Spacing between shelves | | Loading per foot length of shelf of width— (a) | | | Loading per metre length of shelf of width— (a) | | |
| | | 16 in | 20 in | 24 in | 400 mm | 500 mm | 600 mm |
in	mm	lbf/ft	lbf/ft	lbf/ft	kN/m	kN/m	kN/m
12	300	50	70	80	0·8	1·0	1·2
16	400	70	90	110	1·0	1·3	1·5
20	500	90	110	130	1·3	1·6	1·9
24	600	110	130	160	1·5	1·9	2·3

Rack Loadings

| Overall height of storage on rack (b) | | Loading per foot length of rack of mean width— (a) | | | Loading per metre length of rack of mean width— (a) | | |
| | | 16 in | 20 in | 24 in | 400 mm | 500 mm | 600 mm |
in	mm	lbf/ft	lbf/ft	lbf/ft	kN/m	kN/m	kN/m
72	1800	280	360	430	4·1	5·2	6·2
84	2100	340	420	510	4·9	6·2	7·4

Notes
(a) Based on a load factor of 800 kg/m³ (50 lb/cu ft) and 80% utilisation of the storage space to allow for clearance and access.
(b) For storage on racks it is assumed that the shelves are spaced to obtain maximum capacity and that the lowest shelf has a clearance of 200 mm (8 in) from the floor.
(c) Loadings are rounded off to the nearest 10 lbf/ft and 0·1 kN/m.

Equipment

9.04 Within, or immediately adjacent to, the dry goods store there should be a workbench or table and weighing scales so that large packages of food can be sorted, divided and weighed ready for use. Both table and larger floor-mounted weighing scales are needed but the latter may be sited near the goods entrance. A tool rack with wire cutters and a lever and hammer, etc. is also required for opening containers.

The table and other surfaces which come into contact with 'open' food must be impervious, non-tainting and easily cleaned. For this purpose, stainless steel is most satisfactory but hard laminated plastic surfaces are also used and a marble slab is preferred for pastry work.

10 STORAGE OF PERISHABLE FOODS

10.01 The storage life of any food commodity will depend on its nature and composition, on the extent of contamination and on the temperature and storage conditions.

Foods described as perishable provide suitable media for the growth of putrefying organisms and are liable to undergo rapid decomposition. Spoilage of such foods can be reduced by limiting the number of organisms introduced through contamination and by restricting their growth and multiplication.

Contamination

10.02 Contamination is reduced by enforcing cleanliness and hygiene in the handling of food and the requirements of the Food Hygiene (General) Regulations, 1970, lay down legal standards which must be taken into account when the premises are initially designed. Congestion, neglect and lack of cleanliness frequently arise through inadequate consideration and provision of facilities. Apart from risk of spoilage and loss of quality, food may be contaminated by pathogenic organisms responsible for food-borne disease and bacterial food poisoning.

Temperature control

10.03 The growth and multiplication of food contaminating organisms, whether pathogenic or otherwise, is generally most rapid in warm conditions, particularly in the temperature range between 10°C and 62·7°C (50–145°F). Food spoilage and risk of food poisoning can, therefore, be reduced by maintaining the temperature of the food above or below this 'growth' zone. Higher temperatures are practicable in cooking and holding food immediately prior to service but in storage it is more appropriate to keep perishable food at temperatures below 10°C.

10.04 In chilled stores the refrigerating equipment is set to operate just above freezing point (0 to 4°C) (32–39°F) to avoid ice forming in the food and possibly altering its 'fresh' appearance. The storage life of most perishable foods is limited to about 1 to 4 days, although bacterial decomposition is retarded, since chemical changes resulting from enzymes naturally present in the food cause loss of condition and flavour. Both enzyme and bacterial activity slow down further as the temperature reduces below freezing point and practically cease at temperatures below −18°C (0°F). Hence, for long term storage over 6 months or more without deterioration of the food, it is necessary to use 'deep freeze' methods capable of maintaining these very low temperatures.

10.05 Refrigerated Storage Temperatures

It is important to appreciate that neither chilling nor freezing destroys the organisms in food and these will begin to multiply rapidly again if the temperature rises above 10°C. When frozen food is thawed out, its keeping qualities are no better than those of freshly prepared food kept under similar conditions.

Chilling and, to some extent, freezing do not greatly retard mould growth and moulds and their spores are frequently present in cold stores. In practice, control over moulds is most effectively provided by cleanliness— such as the frequent washing down of the interiors and fittings of refrigerators with disinfectants or purposely designed fungicides. As indicated earlier, air circulation is also valuable in reducing isolated pockets of fungal growth.

Preservation of food

10.06 Other techniques employed in preservation of food, which may affect the storage requirements of different food commodities, are summarized as follows:
1 Storage in *artificial gas* (eg carbon dioxide) to retard respiration and ripening of fruit.

Type of food	Normal temperature range °C	Comments
Deep frozen foods		
long period storage	−22 to −18	In sealed wrappings
short period storage	−15 to −10	Storage life depends on
1 to 2 days	3 to 5	temperature
Ice cream		
brick ice cream	−20 to −18	
bulk ice cream	−15 to −12	In containers
soft ice cream	−10 to −5	For machine or scoop
Fresh meat, bacon, ham	0 to 3	Carcase meat is hung to allow air circulation and avoid wetting
Poultry	0 to 3	Eviscerated and cleaned before storing
Offal	0 to 2	Stored in shallow trays
Fish	0 to 2	Kept separate in special wet fish trays stored in loose ice
Eggs	2 to 5	High humidity necessary but protected from condensation and wetting
Cheese		
hard cheese, blue cheese,	2 to 4	Wrapped. Storage
cream cheese, cottage cheese,	4 to 6	temperature depends on
soft cheese, Stilton	10 to 12	type of cheese, length of storage and ripeness
Milk, cream	2 to 6	Storage life depends
Butter, margarine	2 to 6	on temperature
General provisions and cooked foods	3 to 5	Refrigerator temperature for general use
Green salads (lettuce, chicory, endive, watercress)	1 to 6	Improved by sprinkling with ice
Tomatoes, melons	10 to 14	Damaged below 4°C
Oranges, grapefruit	5 to 10	Damaged below 0°C
Soft fruits (strawberries, blackcurrants, raspberries, etc)	5 to 10	Damaged by condensation and mould
(Note : certain fruits, eg bananas, are damaged by refrigeration)		
Beer	13 to 14	
Red wines	14 to 16	
White wines, sparkling wines	10 to 12	
Iced water dispensers	10 to 12	
Bottle cooling display	9 to 14	
Semi-open display	10 to 12	For counter use
Enclosed display	4 to 7	

2 Addition of *natural preservatives* (eg salt, vinegar, sugar) to inhibit the growth of food spoilage organisms.

3 Addition of *artificial preservatives* (eg sulphur dioxide, benzoic acid). This is strictly controlled by law.

4 *Dehydration*. Removal of moisture to prevent growth of bacteria and mould.

5 *Heat treatment*. Heat destroys organisms in food and is used in two processes—

(a) *Sterilization*—Complete destruction of all the organisms by a high temperature sustained for a fairly long period which invariably also alters the character of the food.

(b) *Pasteurization*—A modified process whereby food is heated to a lower temperature and/or shorter period sufficient only to destroy pathogenic (disease producing) organisms.

Pasteurized foods, of which milk is a common example, do not have a greatly extended storage life since spoilage organisms can survive the treatment. The character of the fresh food is, however, retained.

Sterilized food will keep indefinitely in a suitable sealed airtight container (eg canning).

6 *Packing* in a protective cover reduces contamination and damage. Some packing materials—such as polythene films and aluminium foil—also prevent loss of water vapour and dehydration during storage. Surface oxidation of food is reduced. Bright metallic foils assist in maintaining a more equal inner temperature by reflecting

12

Skyline Hotel, London Airport. Equipment by Foster Refrigeration UK Ltd.

A bank of 'walk in'-type refrigeration rooms built to modular design. In the foreground is a quick-freezer room and behind are rooms used, individually, for meat, dairy, vegetables and general products and for deep freeze storage.

radiant heat. Similarly, expanded plastic and corrugated paper, used in cartons, provide thermal insulation in addition to protection against damage.

Vacuum packing excludes air and thereby reduces surface oxidation, mould and bacterial spoilage.

11 COLD STORAGE

11.01 Refrigerated stores may be classified into two main groups:

(a) *Chilled Stores*—Cold rooms and refrigerators operating at temperatures just above freezing point to preserve appearance and extend storage life of perishable foods. Chilling is also used for cooling prepared foods and drink prior to service and in vending machines.

(b) *Deep Freeze Stores*—Subzero temperatures (at about −18°C) for prolonged storage of frozen foods. Deep freeze stores may be purposely built rooms or cabinets (conservators) used specifically for frozen foods or ice cream.

Situation

11.02 For a very small kitchen one refrigerator may be adequate for all purposes including the storage of meat and dairy produce, etc and the chilling of prepared foods awaiting service. In larger establishments, it is usually practical and convenient to provide refrigeration facilities in several areas for different uses.

Type of storage, etc	Situation
(1) Bulk cold stores with separate deep freeze storage	Near goods receiving area
(2) Kitchen stores—refrigerated cabinets and cold rooms	In or adjacent to the preparation area
(3) Refrigerated pass-through units, display cabinets and counters	In or adjacent to the servery
(4) Ice-making machines	In or adjacent to the bar
(5) Vending machines for drinks and meals	Near the servery or in an independent area
(6) Beer cellars and wine stores	Accessible from goods entrance and to bar and restaurant counters
(7) Cold stores for food waste	Near collecting area accessible from kitchen

Bulk cold stores

11.03 Large cold stores are frequently divided into separate storage areas for different food commodities in order to provide the specific equipment and conditions required.

(a) *Meat*—Hanging rails and special racks provided. Direct access to the butchery section of the preparation room.

Optimum condition for fresh meat, 0.5 to 3.0°C (33–38°F); 85 per cent relative humidity.

(b) *Fish*—Special cabinets with deep metal drawers for wet fish bedded in ice. Provision for drainage of melting water. Temperature 0 to 2.0°C (32–36°F). Kept in saturated condition.

Salted and smoked fish are kept in a separate sealed section.

(c) *Other perishable foods*—Dairy produce, eggs, fats, etc liable to be tainted by strongly odoriforous food (fruits, spices, vegetables). Usually stored at 2.0 to 5.0°C (36–41°F) with a relative humidity about 85 per cent but there is an optimum temperature and condition for each type of food.

(d) *Frozen foods*—Heavily insulated deep freeze cabinets and cold rooms. To minimize refrigerator loading and temperature fluctuation the deep freeze section is usually entered through a cold store operated at higher chilling temperature. This serves as an airlock, for precooling food prior to freezing and for thawing out food prior to use.

Cold storage in the preparation areas

11.04 Refrigerators and cold rooms are sited in or adjacent to the preparation areas for daily requirements of perishable foods and for chilling prepared foods prior to serving. The usual temperature setting is 3 to 5°C (37 to 41°F).

Frozen food and ice cream conservators may also be located in this area and are normally of the 'well' type which causes minimum disturbance to cold air in the interior when the lid is opened. Ice cream conservators should be mobile for use in the servery. The operating temperature is in the range −22 to −18°C (−7 to 0°F).

Larders

11.05 A larder is not refrigerated but relies on its location to maintain a suitably cool interior temperature. Larders are frequently used in small kitchens for a variety of purposes.

(a) To cool cooked foods before they are placed in the refrigerator.

(b) For prepared food waiting to be served cold but not chilled.

(c) For food returned unused from the servery until needed.

The larder must be sited away from cooking equipment and hot surroundings and should, preferably, be located on the north or north-east side of the building. Refrigerating cabinets—which give our heat externally—must not be enclosed in the room but may open into the larder with the advantage of providing some cooling when the door is opened. Larders are also used as annexes to cold rooms with the same objective.

In other situations it is often difficult maintaining the temperature of the larder below 10°C (50°F) as required by the Food Hygiene Regulations and, for larger premises, it is generally more suitable to provide a refrigerated cold room to replace the function of the larder.

Types of refrigerated storage

11.06 There are three main types of refrigerated stores:

(a) *Individual refrigerators*—Composed of an insulated cabinet with refrigeration equipment incorporated as a complete 'package'. General purpose refrigerators fall into two main types depending on size:

(1) 'Reach in' service cabinets which have capacities from about 1.4 to 2.8 m³ (50 to 100 cu ft) and are supplied fully assembled.

(2) 'Walk in' cabinets of 2.8 m³ (100 cu ft) and larger sizes are assembled on site from performed sections. In this case the compressor and condenser unit can be sited above or away from the cabinet and is often fixed outside the building for more efficient operation.

(b) *Cold rooms*—Larger capacities are provided by constructing a room in site to meet the design requirements. Costs/m² are higher than separate refrigerators but the equipment occupies less space and is easier to site. The compressor-condenser can be put in any convenient space or remote from the room (up to 6 m distance) (20').

(c) *Miscellaneous refrigerating equipment*—Purpose-built equipment designed for special uses include ice cream and deep freeze conservators, ice making machines, bottle coolers and display counters and cases.

Size requirements

11.07 For normal use, cold storage requirements are generally based on 0.015 m³/main meal/day (0.5 cu ft) but this provision will depend greatly on the extent to which prepared frozen foods are used and the frequency of deliveries.

Location of cold rooms

11.08 Three considerations should be taken into account in deciding the positions of refrigerated stores and their compressor/condensing units:

(a) Access to the cold rooms from the goods entrance and preparation areas including the desirability of entry through an air lock to reduce temperature fluctuation.

(b) Temperature of surroundings and relative positions of cooking and other heat-producing equipment which may affect the performance of the plant. To reduce the refrigeration loading, cold stores should, where possible, be sited on the north or north-east side of the building.

(c) Problems arising from the equipment, eg. noise and heat and space occupied by the compressor unit. There may be advantages in siting the condenser outside the building to obtain better cooling. Because of the heat output, this equipment must not be located in a food store.

Construction of cold rooms

11.09 Cold rooms are generally square on plan to obtain the maximum area and access. The height is limited to about 2100 mm (7' 0") and shelving and hanging fittings are arranged to make the most use of the space. Walls, floors, ceilings and doors must be well insulated having a thermal transmittance ('U') value of about 0.341 to 0.454 W/m² °C (0.06 to 0.08 Btu/ft² hr °F) to minimize heat entry. The insulation is most commonly provided by expanded polystyrene in sheets approximately 100 mm (4") thick.

To avoid air entry and condensation within the structure the exterior must be sealed air tight and is usually surfaced with enamelled steel or asbestos cement sheeting. Inner surfaces must be proof against entry of condensate and moisture and must be capable of being easily cleaned. For this purpose enamelled or stainless steel sheeting is commonly used whilst preformed plastic linings are most suitable for small standard refrigerators. The floor of the cold room, to withstand traffic usually has a finish of tiles or granolithic cement and, to facilitate drainage, the floor surface must be laid with a fall to an odour

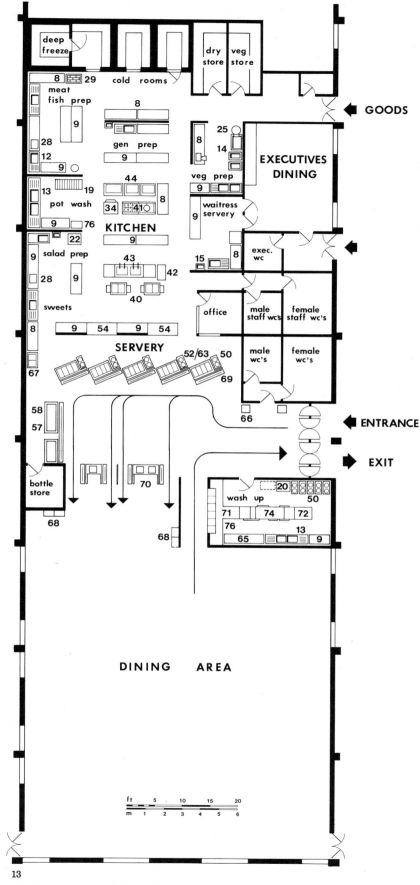

13

Staff catering facilities, The Plessey Co. Ltd., Portugal.
Equipment by Oliver Toms Ltd.
Plan showing the layout of a kitchen designed to supply 1000
meals over a period of 2 hours. To counter problems of food
storage in a hot climate, the installation includes a large pro-
portion of refrigerated storage space.

sealed outlet.

Doors to all refrigerated spaces must be close fitting with an airtight gasket fitted as an air seal. The doors to 'walk-in' type rooms must be openable from both outside and inside.

Equipment and fittings

11.10 All interior fittings, shelves and racks should be demountable, lightweight and easily removed for cleaning. Because of the contact with 'open food', interior fittings must be of non-absorbent materials such as stainless steel.

Lighting must be provided with suitable insulated fittings which are sealed against entry of moisture.

Cooling equipment

11.11 Two types of refrigeration equipment are in common use:

(a) *Vapour absorption system*, which has no moving parts and is operated by application of heat. This equipment is limited to small refrigerators up to about 0·23 m³ (8 cu ft) capacity.

(b) *Vapour compression system*. This is the normal equipment used for commercial plant and consists of four main parts:

1 A compressor driven by an electric motor which circulates and pressurizes the refrigerant.

2 A condenser in which the refrigerant loses heat to the outside air.

3 An expansion valve which regulates the pressure drop in the system.

4 An evaporator in which the refrigerant absorbs heat from the surrounding space in the cold room.

The compressor and condenser are sited outside the cold room and must have a good air circulation to dissipate the heat which is given off. Often the latter is exposed outside the building and, in large refrigeration plant, the condenser may be watercooled to improve heat transfer.

Inside the cold room, the evaporator is usually coupled with a fan to blow air over the coil surface and distribute the chilled air throughout the room.

Common refrigerants are dichlorodifluromethane and methylchloride and ammonia is also used in very large plant. Also on a large scale, indirect refrigeration is obtained by circulating calcium chloride or brine—which has been cooled by the evaporator—around the walls of the cold room.

'Deep freeze' refrigeration is essentially similar but the equipment has a higher capacity necessary to attain the lower temperatures required (−20°C (−4°F)).

Factors affecting performance of refrigerator

11.12 The duty of a refrigerator or cold room is based on the capacity of the equipment to maintain a stated interior temperature under normal operating conditions. This performance is liable to be affected by:

(1) *The quantity of food placed in the refrigerator and its initial temperature*. For calculation purposes in determining the necessary capacity of a cold room, the average density of loosely packed food is between 50–80 kg/m³ (3–5 lb/ft³) and its specific heat is assumed to be 3·77 kJ/kg °C (0·9 Btu/lb °F). For a 'reach in' type refrigerator, the average density is about 160 kg/m³ (10 lb/ft³).

(2) *Opening of the door*. Doors must be fitted with a closure device and seal. The 'well' type conservator is not affected to the same extent because the cold air is undisturbed. Entry through an annexe reduces temperature fluctuations.

(3) *Defrosting*. When a layer of ice builds up on the evaporator this acts as an insulant preventing air coming into contact with the colder metal surface. Defrosting should be done automatically—usually before the ice film is 3·0 mm thick—by various methods, eg heated cable, air or hot gas.

(4) *Siting of condenser* and its ability to disperse the heat.

Dehydration of food

11.13 Air coming into contact with the cold evaporator coil is locally cooled to such an extent that most of the water vapour in the air condenses out. This dehumidifying effect produces water and ice on the surface whilst leaving the air relatively dry.

The air circulating at a low relative humidity absorbs moisture from any exposed food surfaces causing dehydration, loss of weight, wilting and blackening—known as 'freezer burn'.

Dehydration of stored food can be minimized by maintaining the temperature of the evaporator only slightly below that of the ambient air, by providing a large cooling area and by avoiding overloading and wide variations in temperature of the contents. For prolonged food storage at low temperatures, food should be enclosed in impervious containers or wrappings to prevent moisture loss.

Odour contamination

11.14 Precautions must be taken against odour contamination of food in storage. Foods commonly responsible for tainting are fish, onions, potatoes, herbs and citrus fruits.

Other agencies, within and outside the building, which may cause odour contamination include smoke, fuels, offensive refuse and drains and various cleaning materials. Odours tend to persist even after removal of the source and can only be dispelled by thorough cleaning. The foods liable to absorb odours are meat, eggs, milk, butter, cheese and fats. To a lesser extent flour and other dried commodities may be affected.

Odour contamination can be reduced by:

1 Separation of storage.

2 Wrapping in vapour-proof material (eg polythene or aluminium foil).

3 Providing non-absorbent surfaces which can be easily cleaned after use.

4 Good ventilation.

Wrapping also serves the purposes of:

1 Reducing loss of moisture and drying out of the food (see 'dehydration' (11.13)).

2 Reducing oxidation of the surface.

12 MECHANICAL VENTILATION IN FOOD STORES

12.01 Natural ventilation of stores is frequently restricted by lack of external wall space or rendered unsuitable by the conditions outside the building—such as the proximity of refuse stores, drains, chimneys and other sources of contamination. In addition, it is difficult to ensure thorough air circulation in a large store divided by numerous storage racks and shelving.

Under these conditions, some form of mechanical ventilation is needed and this may be provided by plenum fan—either as a self-contained unit or connected to ducting—which may operate independently or as part of a balanced ventilating system.

Plenum system

12.02 Plenum ventilation provides a number of advantages in that the air entering the stores is under control and can be filtered, cooled and humidified to the correct temperature and condition. Entry of dust and pollutants through other openings is prevented and the distribution of air movement can be adjusted to ensure through circulation. Plenum systems include pressurized 'air curtains' used, in place of doors, to maintain conditions in cold stores and other rooms whilst permitting free entry for goods.

Extraction systems

12.03 Air extraction systems are generally not suitable for stores because of the lack of control over the inflow of air from outside and other areas. A balanced system—employing both plenum and extraction fans—would be used for large stores and rooms which have no external walls.

In cold stores and refrigerators, external ventilation must be restricted to minimize loss of cooled air and, except for the smaller cabinet refrigerators, air circulation within the space is provided by a fan unit blowing air over the cooling coil which comprises the evaporator of the refrigerating system.

13 HYGIENE IN FOOD STORES

13.01 Constructional requirements relating to hygiene in food stores are similar to those which apply to food rooms generally. In addition to providing for cleanliness and precautions against contamination of food—especially in those areas where food is liable to be exposed—particular attention must be given to preventing infestation of the food by rats, mice, and/or insects.

Insects

13.02 Insects commonly found in food stores may be grouped, broadly, into two kinds:
(a) Insects which are primarily scavengers and feed on a wide range of foods including garbage. These often enter the premises through ill-fitting and open doors, windows, ventilators, etc (eg housefly, cockroach, wasp).
(b) Those which infest specific foods and are usually brought into the premises with the food and remain confined to the storage areas (eg warehouse moth, larder beetle, flour mites).

Construction
Structural precautions against insects, as a summary, include:
1 *Floors, walls and ceilings*—Continuous smooth washable surfaces free from cracks and gaping joints. All junctions must be coved.
2 *Windows*—Close fitting with no gaps wider than 0·5 mm. Windows fixed unless protected by gauze.
3 *Doors*—Close fitting, metal edged, self closing.
4 *Open windows, ventilators*—Covered by flyproof gauze of copper, brass or galvanized steel (0·35 mm gauge mesh at 1 mm centres); removable for cleaning.
5 *Drains*—Drainage channels accessible, easily cleansed. Outlets sealed by traps.
6 *Shelf fittings, racks*—Accessible throughout and demountable for cleaning and redecoration. Kept 50 mm away from wall, unless mobile, and 200 mm (8″) clear of floor.
7 *Bins*—Metal or plastic bins for loose products (flour, sugar, cereals, dried fruit, etc) fitted with castors or wheel bases and hinged close fitting lids.
8 *Refuse*—Storage carefully positioned. Kept in enclosed bins or impermeable sacks with the stands raised at least 200 mm clear of ground. Surrounded by an impermeable drained area. Water and hosepipe provided for cleaning.

9 *General*—Adequate space and facilities with sufficient spare capacity to allow proper cleaning, separation of old and new stocks and easy inspection of stores.

Rats and mice

13.03 Rats and mice originate from harbourages in defective drains, rubbish heaps and derelict or neglected buildings, etc and are attracted by exposed food and refuse. They may be brought into the kitchen and stores in sacks of food, or enter through doors, open or broken windows and ventilators, defective drains or gaps in the structure —such as cavity walls and subfloor spaces. Rodents are able to penetrate wood, plasterboard, paper, sacking and most plastic materials by gnawing holes. Once established inside the building they form nests of chewed material in covered undisturbed places—often within the building structure.

Structural precautions against rats and mice
The methods used to prevent entry of insects also reduce risk of rodent infestation. Additional measures include:
1 *Holes* through walls (above or below ground), for pipes, cables, etc. must have any gaps filled with fine concrete, brickwork or wire mesh.
2 *Cavity walls*, hollow partitions and floors, pipe ducts and chases need to be stopped at each junction with wire mesh.
3 *External doors* should have a metal plate (0·9 mm gauge) 300 mm (12″) high fitted across the bottom and similar protection against gnawing should be given to the bottom of the door frames.
4 *Gratings, grilles, etc* should have openings less than 7 mm wide.
5 *Window sills* and other *climbing ledges* which might provide an entry route should be at least 1350 mm (4′ 6″) above the adjacent ground and, where possible, project 225 mm (9″) outwards from the wall face. This also applies to the boundary walls of any yard.
6 *External wall foundations* must extend to a depth of at least 600 mm (2′ 0″) to prevent entry by burrowing. This risk is further minimized by a concrete or tarmacadam path (at least 600 mm wide) around the perimeter of the building.
7 *Soil ventilating pipes and rainwater pipes* are required to have balloon guards fitted to prevent rats climbing out on to the roof. Where there is a risk of rats scaling up the outside, a rat guard (extending 225 mm (9″) outside the pipe) should be fitted.
8 *Floors*—particularly ground floors—should be of concrete construction.

14 MISCELLANEOUS STORES

Storage of cleaning materials

14.01 For immediate use, some materials—eg soap, detergent, cloths—are kept in a cupboard or on a shelf adjacent to each sink and washing machine. Cupboards used for this purpose must be well ventilated and fitted with impermeable shelves (eg laminated plastic, stainless steel) since cleaning materials are often put away wet. Reserves of cleaning materials and equipment are stored in a lockable room or cupboard which may be separate or form part of the room used by the cleaners. All cleaning materials must be kept apart from food and from utensils intended for food to avoid any risk of cross-contamination. Storage for cleaning reserves should include, at least, two bins for soap powders and shelves for cans of liquid detergent, block soap, scourers, bleaches, cloths and other items. Many of these are corrosive and, for safety, must be stored at a convenient reaching height (700 to 1400 mm) (2′ 3″ to 4′ 6″). Clear instructions regarding accidents should be posted with the first-aid facilities for the kitchen. Spare cleaning equipment is most compactly stored in a purposely designed cupboard or racks which can allow for the various sizes and shapes of the containers and utensils.

Facilities provided for cleaners range from a cupboard for mops, buckets, brooms and cleaning materials which would be appropriate for the smallest premises, to a fully equipped room containing a cleaner's sink and other fittings. To accommodate the variety of brooms, squeegees, scrubbers, mops and other items of equipment used in cleaning, cupboards or racks should be purposely designed and allow mechanical scrubbers and similar heavy equipment to be housed at floor level. It is also important to bear in mind the difficulties of negotiating steps and stairs with heavy mechanical equipment when the layout is being planned. There is usually a need to provide some separate cleaning facilities for the dining area.

Drying facilities

14.02 Drying facilities for wet towels and cloths are invariably required even if laundry work is done off the premises. The use of hot pipes and equipment in the kitchen for this purpose is not recommended and can be avoided by the provision of a small purposely designed drying cabinet. In large premises a domestic clothes washing machine may be installed in the cleaners' room as a supplement to the main laundry arrangements.

Servery store

14.03 Items such as crockery, cutlery and utensils used in the servery and dining room are largely returned—after being washed and dried—back into circulation, ie direct to the servery ready to be re-used. Temporary storage is needed to balance fluctuations in use, such as at the peak periods, and is best met by the use of portable trolleys to avoid double handling. Clean table items are also placed directly on shelves and trolleys ready for collection from the dining room.

Reserves of china, glassware and flatware, amounting to about 10 to 20 per cent of that in use, are usually kept in cupboards in or adjacent to the 'clean' section of the wash-up area. Larger reserves and bulk purchases are stored in a separate locked room.

Linen

14.04 A purposely designed linen store appropriate for large-scale catering will contain shelving for clean linen required in the dining area, towels, etc and racks and hangers for uniforms. Space should be provided for baskets and hampers receiving soiled linen and for sufficient corridor space, minimum 1200 mm (4′ 0″) wide, for distributing laundered items directly from baskets to the shelves. A table or bench is necessary for sorting and checking although this need not form a permanent feature unless it is also used for repair work.

The construction of linen stores must allow for easy cleaning and minimize dust and fluff harbourage. A warm temperature (15°C), good ventilation (providing at least 2 air changes per hour) and damp prevention are essential to avoid mildew or souring of damp linen. Precautions must also be taken against risk of staining by rust. Lighting should be sufficient to allow easy checking of items (200 lux 18·6 lumens/ft²) and, where sewing repair

work is also provided for in the room, a higher intensity of 400 lux 37·2 lumens/ft² is necessary. In each case the limiting Glare Index to avoid discomfort is 25.

In a small establishment, linen storage may be accommodated in drawers and/or fitted cupboards, but the essential requirements of ventilation and damp avoidance still apply.

General storage

14.05 Where dining facilities are intended for multi-purpose use—such as school meal halls, hotel banquet rooms and some canteen facilities—extensive storage space will usually be required for tables, chairs and other furniture, possibly including carpeting removed from the dining area. In this case, adaptability, stackability and portability are essential features of the furniture and transport is facilitated by the use of wheeled trolley bases.

17.02 Stores for this purpose must be sited near to and level with the dining room, be constructed to withstand heavy loading and possible scraping, etc, damage, and provide adequate space—including corridor and access areas—for the amount of furniture involved. A lighting intensity of 200 lux (18·6 lumens/ft²) is desirable, and the stores must be dry and well ventilated.

15 DRINK STORAGE

15.01 Requirements for storage of drink depend very much on the nature of the catering premises, its location and market. The facilities may range from the bulk storage and piped circulation of draught beer on a large scale—such as is typical of a public house—to the holding of a few bottled wines in the general food store. In the majority of licensed restaurants storage is provided for wines and other bottled and canned drinks.

Drink storage may include provision for:

Draught beer stored in a cellar.

Crates of beer, etc which may be kept in the same area or in a separate crate store.

Wines and Spirits in an area partitioned off from other drinks for security or in a separate locked room.

Location

15.02 The location of drink stores is determined by considerations of the needs of access for deliveries, of security and supervision, proximity to the serving area and constructional features such as requirements for temperature control. To meet these functional requirements, cellars for large-scale storage of beer are often most conveniently located at basement or semi-basement level whilst stores stores for bottled drinks are usually sited adjacent to the serving area.

Deliveries

15.03 Wines and spirits are normally delivered in cartons and an efficient system of recording must be employed to enable proper stock control. These stores will normally be kept locked and access should be through a supervised area. Crates may be carried by hand or trolley to the stores and hoists may be installed where the storage or areas of distribution are on other floors.

Special provisions need to be made for deliveries of large casks and barrels of beer which are rolled manually from the vehicle to the cellars and these facilities may include raised unloading bays (1200 mm (4′ 0″) high), inclined rolling ways and mechanical hoists. To some extent this is avoided by the use of bulk beer storage tanks which are filled by pipeline from a tanker vehicle but occasional access will be required for replacement of the tanks and equipment.

Unless the quantity of drink used is very small, vehicle access right up to the building is necessary. The doors leading to crate stores and wine stores should be 1000 mm (3′ 6″) wide or more and double doors, at least 1500 mm (5′ 0″) wide are needed for casks and barrels. Access to small drink stores may be through the general goods entrance to facilitate control and checking but it is usually necessary to provide separate access for delivery of draught beer.

Storage requirements

Cellars

15.04 Beer casks are stored off the floor supported on stillages, thrawls or mobile barrel tilters whilst kegs stand upright. Space in the vicinity is required for CO_2 or compressed air cylinders or pumping plant and shelves and hooks should be provided for buckets, filters and other equipment.

Beers are very sensitive to odours and facilities for good hygiene and controlled ventilation are essential. The optimum temperature for beer storage is 13 to 14°C (55 to 57°F) and, to avoid fluctuations, both cooling and heating equipment is usually required. Fan-coil units are commonly used for cooling with fan-heaters, controlled by thermostat, provided to maintain the correct temperature. The pipe supplying draught beer to the servery may also be chilled. Walls should be well insulated, giving a thermal transmittance value of 0·80 w/m² °C (0·14 Btu/ft²h °F) or less. A level of illumination of 200 lux (18·6 lumens/ft²) is required and, because of the humid atmosphere, light fittings should be of an enclosed moisture-proof type.

To allow for the heavy loading and frequent washing down, floors must be impervious with a resistant durable surface (eg quarry tiles or granolithic concrete), laid to falls and drained to gullies or channels which are covered by removable grating. If suspended, the floor should be designed for loadings up to 9·58 KN/m² (200 lb/ft²). Wall surfaces are also of smooth, hard, durable materials, such as cement rendering, with additional protection to reduce damage to exposed corners and openings. Ceilings are insulated to reduce condensation and plastered smooth for ease of decoration.

Hot and cold water supplies—suitably lagged—and a sink with drainer should be available for cleaning purposes.

Crate stores

15.05 The environmental and constructional requirements are similar to those for cellars. Crates are stacked up to 7 high (full) and 9 high (empty) in rows with passages between the stacks at least 900 mm (3′ 0″) wide for access. Trolleys may be needed for transportation and mobile plastic bins are frequently used to collect empty bottles from the servery. A suitable sack holder or bin should be available for broken bottles and, in larger premises, a bottle-crushing machine may also be installed.

A few crates are usually kept in the immediate vicinity of the servery for daily use. Facilities for bottle chilling are also provided in the servery.

Wine and spirits store

15.06 Wines are best stored in darkness with an even temperature free from draughts. The optimum storage temperatures are:

Red wines	14 to 16°C (57 to 61°F)
Sparkling and white wines	10 to 12°C (50 to 54°F)

If separate storage is not practicable, sparkling and white wines are confined to the lower rows of the storage racks with red and other wines above in order to utilize the natural temperature gradient in the room.

The wine bottles are stored horizontally in metal or wood racks—or bins—with a separated space for each bottle for easy location, inspection and removal without disturbing the others. Spirits are usually stored with wines and may be placed vertically on shelves or in bins.

The construction and servicing requirements for wine stores are similar to those for other drink storage whilst allowing for the fact that there is little risk of contamination of wine intact in bottles. Good artificial lighting is required for stock checking and for viewing bottles, including facilities for candle viewing where wine is to be decanted.

For all drink stores, particularly wine and spirit stores, features must be incorporated in the layout and construction to ensure security. External walls must be of substantial construction (equal to 290 mm (11″) brick cavity wall) and windows should be avoided. Where possible the entrance for deliveries, etc should be through an enclosure such as a yard and internal access should be through a supervised area. Doors need to be of industrial quality and secured by efficient bolts and dead locks. To a large extent, security requirements will be determined by the standards specified for insurance.

3 FOOD PREPARATION

1 PLANS

1.01 In preparing the layout plans for a kitchen it is invariably found that a number of alternatives are possible both in the type of catering facilities and equipment selected and in their arrangement in the premises. The merits and limitations of each scheme need to be considered in detail before a final layout can be determined to suit the particular situation and operating conditions. This work is greatly facilitated by the use of planning aids, examples of which are:

(a) Squared paper to scale.

(b) Sets of equipment templates on printed cardboard, etc also to scale, for superimposing on plans.

(c) Perforated templates of equipment in plastic or cardboard as an aid to drawing.

(d) Magnetized strips representing equipment, building walls, etc used with a metal base which serves as the basic plan.

2 FLOW ROUTES

2.01 Meal production may be considered as a production process with the food passing through a series of stages— described as flow routes—which follow in sequence from the supply of raw ingredients to the final assembly and service of meals. Careful planning of flow routes is necessary:

(a) to ensure that the correct facilities are available in their appropriate places and

(b) to reduce the risk of congestion and obstruction by avoiding routes crossing each other.

A simple flow route, appropriate for a small catering establishment, may be represented thus:

Goods entrance
⬇
Stores
⬇
Preparation
⬇
Cooking
⬇
Plating
⬇
Serving

As the size increases more specialization, both in equipment and concentration of work, becomes necessary and develops into a number of parallel flow routes:

Goods entrance

Vegetable store	Cold store	Dry goods store
Vegetable preparation	Fish preparation	Pastry and meat preparation
Wet equipment	Fish frying	Dry equipment

Plating
⬇
Serving

The sequence of operations is illustrated in the diagram shown above. In this simplified layout some cross flow cannot be avoided, eg steaming ovens will be used for puddings as well as for vegetables, and, where this occurs, the equipment must be carefully sited to allow for multi-purpose use.

Secondary circulation

2.02 Associated with the main flow of food there is a need to make provision for secondary developments such as the disposal of waste and the collection, washing and reuse of utensils. Waste and refuse are generally taken out through the goods entrance, ie in an opposite direction to the flow of food, but this depends on the means of removal. The use of waste-disposal units enables waste to be discharged at several points along the flow route. Secondary circulation of food utensils fall into two distinct areas:

Kitchen utensils
Preparation
⬇
Cooking   pan wash
⬇
Serving

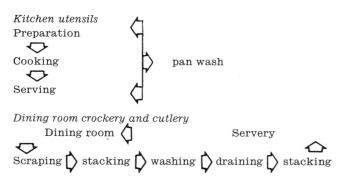

Dining room crockery and cutlery

Dining room ⬇   Servery

Scraping ▷ stacking ▷ washing ▷ draining ▷ stacking

In each case, utensils should be stored at the place where they are to be used. The efficiency of the operation will depend on the speed at which utensils are returned into use and the amount of handling involved.

Comparisons

2.03 Whilst comparisons between catering operations and simple line production processes are useful, in the initial stages of planning there are a number of significant differences. The preparation of a meal is not a continuous process but rather a series of independent processes, occuring in different sections, requiring different amounts of work, and taking different times to complete. Only in the final stage, when the meal is ready for service, are those various products brought together. To provide for these variations, equipment is required not only for preparation but also for accumulating, and temporarily holding, food in separate stages of preparation.

Work centres

2.04 The equipment and facilities used for related operations at each stage in the preparation of a meal are grouped together into 'work centres'. 'Work centres' are designed to provide the most convenient, compact and economical arrangement possible so that the minimum amount of effort and time is expended by the employees working in that area.

With a view to determining the optimum layout for any particular operation, a number of work study techniques have been devised and applied, with some success, to catering.

Work study in kitchens

The term work study encompasses two areas of examination; work measurement to evaluate the work content of a task and method study to improve the way in which work is done. The former is concerned primarily with measuring and comparing the output of individual workers and is used to establish standard times for different jobs, to compare outputs of kitchen staff, to determine incentive payments and to provide a basis for realistic costing of labour in catering.

Method study involves a critical examination of the methods and movements involved in carrying out kitchen operations in order to develop more convenient systems. Information revealed by studying existing methods of working is, therefore, of direct value in planning new catering facilities. The basic procedure in method study is to select a particular area of work, to record details such as the types of activity involved, distance travelled and/or time taken and to present these in a way which will enable deficiencies to be identified and improvements compared. Recording techniques usually fall into three categories:
· charts;
· diagrams and models and
· photographs.

In kitchen planning, reference is frequently made to process charts, time charts, travel and travel relationship charts, distance charts or string diagrams, meal sequence charts and photographic analyses. This last mentioned technique is used, particularly, in ergonomic studies and is a valuable aid to the efficient design of equipment and working areas.

Flow process charts

2.05 Details set out in a flow process chart record the work done in carrying out a particular operation, for instance, preparing an item of a meal using a particular kitchen layout. Each change in activity is listed in chronological order indicating the type of work performed, the distance —if any—travelled and the time taken. Types of work are usually classified into five groups each represented by a symbol:

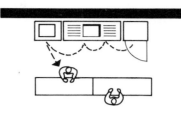

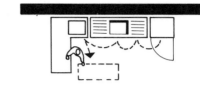

1

Work centres arranged in A—linear, B—parallel and C—right angled groupings and the effect on work movement.

○ operation — productive work
▷ transportation — travelling, carrying
□ inspection — verifying quality or quantity
D delay — waiting, queueing
▽ storage — holding, retaining.

By varying the original layout and sequence, changes in the work can be assessed and improvements introduced, for example, by reducing the extent of transportation and by eliminating delays where possible.

Flow process charts may record either the steps followed by a worker or the stages undergone by food materials and most standard charts are of the man/material type to allow this dual use. To reveal more information, the five classified groups of activity can be subdivided. For instance, transportation is frequently separated into laden and unladen travel in order to distinguish secondary journeys; the operation of a machine may be divided into productive and unproductive use, the latter including cleaning and assembly.

Outline process charts record only the main stages of operation and delay and are useful in planning multiple processes such as in the large scale production of meals. In another form an outline process chart may simply distinguish transportation from other types of activity and these details can then be represented on a travel or travel relationship chart.

Time charts

2.06 Charts showing comparisons in units of time are usually of the bar type and indicate the amounts of time expended on specified activities—expressed as absolute units, proportions or percentages. As with other methods of measurement, this can be related to workers, materials or the use of equipment.

Activity analysis generally involves sample studies carried out at different times of the working day to obtain aggregate totals. Various types of activity are identified and the time spent on each is determined and compared. The range of activities which can be measured is considerable and these are usually separated into three main groups having several subdivisions:

Examples of work study techniques

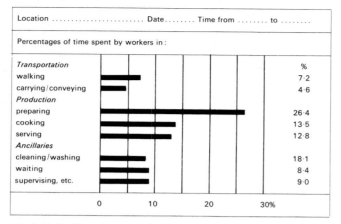

| Location .... Date .... Time from .... to .... | | | | | | | |
| Percentages of time spent by workers in : | | | | | | | |

							%
Transportation							
walking							7·2
carrying/conveying							4·6
Production							
preparing							26·4
cooking							13·5
serving							12·8
Ancillaries							
cleaning/washing							18·1
waiting							8·4
supervising, etc.							9·0

0 10 20 30%

(a) *Activity Sampling Analysis*

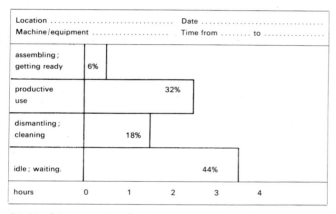

| Location .... Date .... | |
| Machine/equipment .... Time from .... to .... | |

assembling; getting ready	6%
productive use	32%
dismantling; cleaning	18%
idle; waiting.	44%
hours	0 1 2 3 4

(b) *Machine/operator chart*

MAN FLOW PROCESS CHART

Title ....
Chart begins .... ends ....

Distance (m)	Time (s)	Description
5		1▷ to pan rack
		① select pans; utensils
5		2▷ to boiling table
		② set out work area
8		3▷ to refrigerator
		③ measure out milk
8		4▷ to boiling table
	150	④ heat; put to one side
10		5▷ to store
		1☐ check fat and flour
		⑤ weigh out
10		6▷ to boiling table
	80	⑥ heat and melt fat
	400	⑦ blend in flour; cook
	300	⑧ stir in hot milk; simmer
7		7▷ to bain marie
		▽ hold until required

Summary

Time (total)	○ Operations	8
1100s	▷ Transportations	7
(0·3 hour)	☐ Inspections	1
Distance (total)	D Delays	0
53 m	▽ Storage	1

MATERIAL FLOW PROCESS CHART

Title ....
Chart begins .... ends ....

(*Note* showing comparative stages
undergone by the materials. The two charts must be separate.)

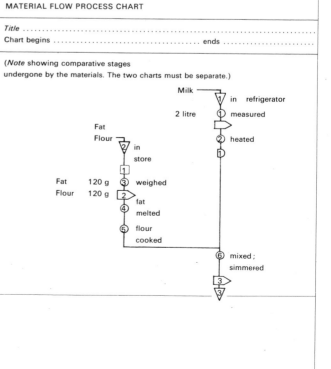

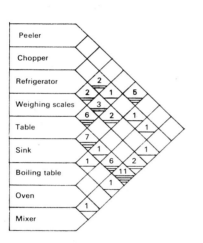

Number of movements from / Number movements to	Peeler	Chopper	Refrigerator	Weighing Scales	Table	Sink	Boiling table	Oven	Mixer
Peeler						2			
Chopper				1	1				
Refrigerator					1				1
Weighing scales		1	2		2				
Table			2	4		5		3	6
Sink	3		2		2				
Boiling table		1				1	1		
Oven		1			3				1
Mixer				1	5	1			

(d) *Cross travel Chart*

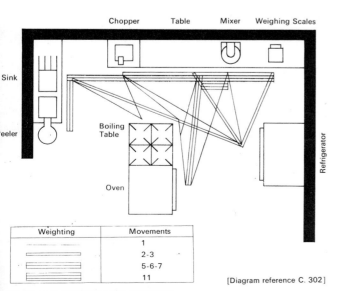

(e) *Travel Relationship Chart*

Chopper   Table   Mixer   Weighing Scales

Sink

Peeler

Boiling Table

Oven

Refrigerator

Weighting	Movements
	1
	2-3
	5-6-7
	11

[Diagram reference C. 302]

(f) *Travel Relationship Diagram*

- transportation — walking, carrying or conveying food and utensils;
- production — measuring, preparing, cooking and serving food;
- ancillaries — cleaning, waiting, talking, paper-work, etc.

Activity analyses show waste of time due to bad planning, for example, by excessive time spent in walking, carrying and cleaning and due to failings in organisation—such as the time spent in talking, waiting, etc.

Machine/operator charts record the use of a selected item of equipment throughout a working period. Aggregate totals of time are obtained for productive use, idle time and waiting time, cleaning, assembling, loading and other non-productive operations and these are represented to an appropriate scale on a bar chart. Charts of this type reveal deficiencies in the equipment (by the disproportionate amount of time spent in cleaning and non-productive operation), poor utilisation (from a large proportion of idle time) or lack of employee instruction.

Travel charts and diagrams

2.07 Information recorded from the movements and distances travelled by kitchen staff in the course of their work can be represented in a travel chart or on a scaled diagram of the work area. Travel charts may take several forms:

(a) frequency types record the number of movements between work centres such as benches, sinks and equipment;

(b) distance types show the distances between work centres and the accumulative distance travelled by one or several workers over a given period of time;

(c) proximity types indicate which centres should be close together because of the frequency of movement between them and for other reasons;

(d) multiple factor types take into account several aspects of location and can be given weights or degrees of importance in order to determine the most appropriate arrangement.

Apart from their obvious uses in the re-organisation of catering operations, travel charts and diagrams have many applications in the planning of new facilities. In this case, the travel movements have to be assumed from the analysis of typical menus and superimposed on the preliminary plans of the kitchen. The relative positions of the work centres are then re-arranged until the most convenient and economical layout is obtained.

The *cross travel chart* is an example of the frequency type and provides a summary of the movements to and from each work centre during a catering process. The numbers on a cross travel chart reveal those work centres—benches, sinks or equipment—which need to be located in a convenient central position and those which should be grouped close together. Further study of travel charts will often indicate patterns of sequence enabling work centres to be arranged in order of use.

A *travel relationship chart* summarises the information given on travel charts and simply gives—on diagonal intersections—the total movements between work centres, without distinguishing their directions. The frequency of moves clearly shows the best locations of work centres relative to each other and enables weightings of importance to be given to these relationships. Such information can be subsequently transferred to plans and diagrams of the kitchen layout.

2.08 Distance measurements are usually obtained from travel lines drawn on a scaled diagram of the kitchen.

Several movements between two centres can be represented by a number of parallel lines or by a single line drawn to different thicknesses. Long lengths of multiple or thick lines represent time and energy expended by workers travelling from one work area to another and the optimum layout is normally obtained by keeping the most frequently used travel routes as short as possible. There may, however, be other factors involved which prevent the relocation of, say, equipment or stores and, in these cases, a high frequency of travel suggests the need for improvements in transportation facilities for food or utensils, duplication of the work centres in other positions or/and re-organisation of the work.

String diagrams are used to measure the movements of a worker, which are traced from point to point on a scaled plan of the kitchen by means of a continuous length of string pinned to the drawing. Where more than one worker is involved, separate coloured strings are used to distinguish each individual. The total travel distance, in each case, is represented by the length of the string measured to the scale of the drawing.

String diagrams and other distance charts show the time and effort wasted in travelling unnecessarily backwards and forwards over long distances—a common problem in catering operations. They also indicate places where there is a risk of congestion due to the routes of workers crossing and show up the effects of obstructions or diversions to the main routes of circulation. By repeating the diagrams for modified layouts in the kitchen the most suitable positions for work centres can be determined.

Meal sequence charts

2.09 By combining outline process charts for the different items of a meal together into a master chart, the sequence of production for the whole meal can be represented. Meal sequence charts are a valuable aid in planning meals, particularly where these are to be produced in large quantities. The individual and total amounts of work and time are indicated on the charts and critical path analyses can be applied to determine the optimum sequence of work, amount of pre-preparation and provisions for temporary storage.

Analysis of work by photographs

2.10 As an alternative to describing worker movements, it is sometimes more significant to illustrate body actions by means of pictures. Camera studies are used, particularly, in the ergonomic design of equipment and fittings and include the following techniques:

Normal speed cine film provides an inexpensive way of recording and comparing the effects of change, for example, in layout, method of use and organisation of work.

Micromotion studies are based on a frame by frame analysis of a cine film to obtain a record of changes say, in movement, over short known intervals of time.

Menomotion techniques involve the acceleration of the speed of a cine film to a fraction of its original exposure time and this can be done by retarding the cine camera speed or by using a timing device to allow the exposure of single frames at predetermined intervals.

Stroboscopic pictures show several movements superimposed on the same picture.

Cyclegraphs record tracks of movement—usually by tracing a point of light attached to the wrist of a worker—at timed intervals of exposure.

In addition to films, cut-out paper manikins or jointed models representing typical or average body dimensions to correct scales are very useful in determining appropriate sizes and spaces, for instance, in the heights of work surfaces and shelves and in the positions and shapes of equipment.

Work centre planning

2.11 Arising from work study investigations, several factors are found to affect the efficient positioning of equipment in a work centre, namely:

· Compactness of layout
· arrangement of equipment
· limits of reach
· economy of movements
· multipurpose use of facilities
· mobility of equipment

In applying planning techniques to minimize physical effort, it is also necessary to consider the effects of environmental and psychological factors on fatigue, for example:

Environment—temperature, air movement, humidity, lighting, glare, noise.

Employment—hours of work, length of working day, weekly hours, number, frequency and duration of rest periods.

Psychological—monotony, frustration, dislike of job or supervisor, poor regard for value of job.

In catering operations it is often these secondary factors which are responsible for a low efficiency of work, high employee turnover and the difficulty of recruiting suitable workers.

Application

2.12 Direct application of theory in planning the layout of a kitchen is usually only possible when a new premises is being designed and, even then, restraints on space and arrangement are often imposed by structural and external conditions. Kitchens are, therefore, normally designed on an individual basis to take account of the different physical and operational requirements. This is particularly so in the case of alterations to existing premises which may necessitate the use of space which is small, awkwardly shaped and/or relatively inaccessible.

Within these limitations, however, it is usually possible to incorporate the principles of theoretical planning and several examples of kitchen designs are illustrated in this book. Ergonomic theory and work study findings have been interpreted into the practical details of catering design described in the following sections.

3 SPACE REQUIREMENTS

Insufficient space

3.01 In any particular kitchen there are two main demands on space. Part of the kitchen area will be physically occupied by equipment, utensils and workers and the aggregate of space needed for this purpose will depend, largely, on the amount of equipment installed. It is fairly common to find that overcrowding and congestion in catering premises has arisen from over-generous provision of equipment, from the retention of equipment which is obsolete or underutilized, or from additions to the equipment for which space was not originally allocated.

In addition to this occupied space there must be sufficient room for movement. Workers must be able to travel easily from one work area to another without having to wait or queue; there must be no obstruction to access or light; sufficiently wide passageways must be left for trolleys and mobile equipment, and free space is needed

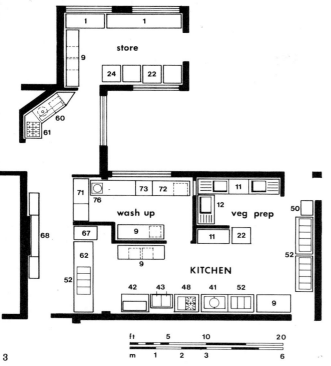

3

Thatchers Hotel, East Horsley. Equipment by Oliver Toms Ltd. This kitchen has been reconstructed within a confined space to allow flexibility in catering for an enlarged restaurant and new banqueting facilities. The latter is served from mobile counters independent of the restaurant service.

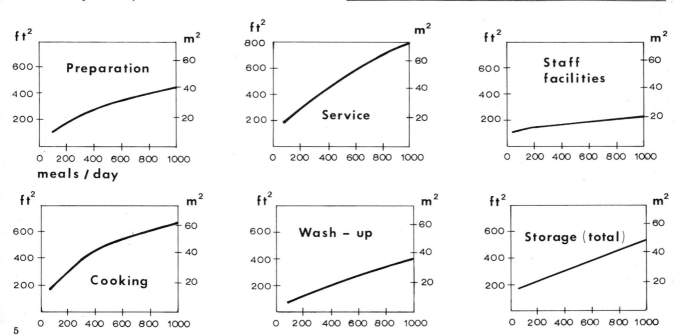

4

Areas required for storage kitchen, servery and staff facilities using conventional methods of food preparation.

Ratios of total area : meal served (average).

Number of meals prepared during one meal period	100	200	400	600	800	1000
Ratio of area required : meal						
(ft²)	9·20	6·25	4·60	3·80	3·55	3·05
(m²)	0·85	0·58	0·42	0·35	0·31	0·28

5

Individual space requirements for:
Storage, preparation, cooking and service of food, dishwashing and staff facilities.

for working, using utensils and operating machines.

A space which is too small for the output invariably generates problems of ventilation and temperature control. It is also difficult, under intensive conditions, to maintain standards of orderliness and hygiene and accidents are more likely to occur.

Overgenerous provision of space

3.02 Excessively large areas are not conducive to efficient catering operation. Time and energy are expended in walking and carrying items over long distances and the extended lines of communication tend to hamper supervision. There are increased costs in cleaning, heating, lighting and maintenance of the area and the capital cost invested in the kitchen will probably show a poor return if this space is greatly underutilized. In practice, it is found that excessive provision usually only applies to the working space in the kitchen—particularly as new

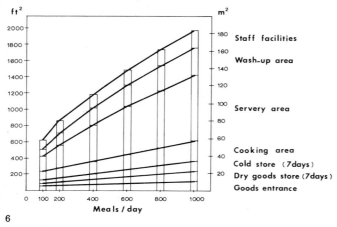

6

Areas required for finishing kitchens using mainly prepared frozen and chilled foods.

Ratios of total area: meal served (average).

Number of meals prepared during one meal period	100	200	400	600	800	1000
Ratio of area required: meal						
(ft²)	6·20	4·30	2·95	2·47	2·15	1·98
(m²)	0·58	0·40	0·27	0·23	0·20	0·18

techniques are tending to simplify preparation of meals. On the other hand, stores and serving arrangements are rarely oversized and often become inadequate in use.

4 DETERMINATION OF KITCHEN AREAS

Number of meals produced
4.01 The main determinant of space requirements in a kitchen is the maximum number of meals to be produced at any one time. In most catering establishments this will normally be for the mid-day meal period although, in some residential premises and high-class restaurants, the pattern of trade may create a greater demand in the evening.

For most purposes the size of the kitchen will be based on the total number of meals produced over this peak period and this is usually adopted as a convenient way of assessing the preliminary space requirements for a scheme. However, in modern kitchen design, a number of exceptions will apply to this rule and these modifications are considered in the following sections.

Type of meal
4.02 Less equipment and fewer staff are needed to produce a simple meal of only 1 or 2 courses without choice than for a more elaborate meal of, say, 3 or 4 courses offering a wide selection of dishes. In determining kitchen equipment and space requirements, allowances must be made for variations in the types of meals.

Type of catering establishment
4.03 Residential and commercial restaurants, such as in hotels, are normally in use over long periods of the day and evening necessitating more continuous working, more staff and greater space. In non-residential institutions (school meals, factory canteens, etc) the main bulk of the catering is in providing a hot mid-day meal. Much of this work can be prepared well in advance and, generally, there is less demand on space during the meal period.

Planning
4.04 Considerable economies can be obtained in the use of space by careful planning to ensure a more compact layout. The dimensions and shape of the kitchen and its relationship to other rooms will also affect the way in which the area can be used.

Equipment
4.05 Increases in the performances and capacities of modern cooking equipment allow fewer units of equipment to be used and, thereby, less space is occupied. Against this there is a tendency to use more equipment in areas of food preparation in order to save labour.

Convenience foods
4.06 One of the main objectives in using convenience foods is to save work and space in the kitchen where the food is made ready for serving. Finishing kitchens for convenience foods are simplified in design and reduced in area. Savings of up to 2/3rds are possible compared with traditional food preparation areas, although an increase in refrigerated storage capacity is usually required.

Service areas and ancillary rooms
4.07 There is some ambiguity in the way space for food service, store rooms and staff accommodation is allocated which tends to make comparisons difficult. For normal waitress service, the food service area is usually included in the general area of the kitchen. On the other hand, self service facilities are often quoted as part of the dining room space. Similarly, stores and staff rooms may, or may not, be included in estimates of kitchen space.

Average areas
4.08 Average floor areas required for a modern, well planned kitchen are shown in relation to the number of meals served during the main meal period each day.
The areas quoted are appreciably smaller than those which have previously been adopted for planning kitchens on traditional lines and presume that more efficient use will be made of the space with modern techniques and equipment.
In this context it is interesting to note that the Ministry of Education Bulletin No. 11, in 1955, recommended that school meal kitchens designed on the basis of work studies could occupy areas as little as 0·28 to 0·32 m² (3 to 3·5 sq ft) floor area/meal served per day compared with the much larger areas previously considered necessary.

Ratios of space
4.09 The ratio of space used for the dining area as compared with that occupied by the kitchen and ancillary areas (stores, offices, staff lavatories, etc) varies considerably from one type of operation to another and also with the frequency of use, ie 'turnover' rate, of the dining room. As an example, the ratio of revenue-earning to the total non-revenue-earning areas could be as high as 4:1 for a simple coffee shop cafeteria, and as low as 1:1 for a fast-service restaurant having a high 'turnover' rate of more expensive meals. In both cases the kitchen facilities are fully utilized but in the first this is achieved by economy of space whilst in the second the greater space is justified by the high output.
Where catering is provided for a more or less fixed number of meals, such as in an industrial or school canteen, the size of the dining room depends very much on the number of sittings during the main meal period, ie the peak demand for the dining room. If all the main meals are

served at once the size of the dining room needs to be disproportionately large and dining area:kitchen, etc area ratios are usually in the order of 3:1. On the other hand, when meals are taken in 2 to 3 sittings, the dining room may be considerably reduced in size to give ratios of about 1:1 or less compared with the kitchen area which is unchanged.

The ratio between the total kitchen area and those sub-areas occupied by the servery, stores, offices and staff sanitary facilities is about:

2:1 for conventional kitchens

to 1·5:1 for finishing kitchens using frozen precooked meals
With increase in size, the productive area of a kitchen is more efficiently used, representing an appreciable saving in the total space.

Within the kitchen area up to about 30 per cent of the floor space is occupied by equipment leaving rather more than 70 per cent free for work areas, traffic lanes and access. The aggregate work surface area of preparation tables, draining boards and benches, amounts to about 10 per cent of the kitchen area.

5 DIMENSIONS

5.01 Kitchen layouts are determined by two main sets of dimensions:

(a) the sizes of equipment and fittings and
(b) the spaces which must be left clear for access and movement.

Sizes of equipment

5.02 In deciding appropriate dimensions for equipment and work areas, account must be taken of the physical characteristics (anthropometric data) of the working population employed in the catering industry. By using representative body dimensions as a basis for design, suitable allowances can be made for working heights and limits of reach in various work situations.

Ergonomic theory is also being increasingly applied to the design of equipment and fittings, particularly to such features as the positions of handles and controls, the shapes of appliances and the sizes of utensils.

A third factor, which will play an even more important role in the future with the change-over to metric units, is the need for standardization of sizes and dimensions to facilitate interchange and replacement.

Typical dimensions for work benches, tables and shelves are illustrated in 7. The standard height for work tops is generally taken to be 865 mm (2' 10") but recent research indicates that a higher level is less likely to produce strain and backache with prolonged standing, and 900 mm (3'-0") is favoured by some designers. Sink tops are made to 865 and 900 mm heights—the latter being more common.

5.03 Wall benches are generally 600 to 750 mm (2' 0" to 2' 6") wide and island benches and tables are usually to a width of 900 mm or 1050 mm (3' 0" to 3' 6") to allow working on both sides. The length of a work area—such as a bench top—within convenient reach of one worker is about 1200 to 1800 mm (4' 0" to 6' 0") whilst a work top between 2400 and 3000 mm (8' 0" and 10' 0") would be suitable for 2 persons working side by side. In each case, the more concentrated work area is preferred unless space is required for utensils.

The heights of wall-mounted shelves are limited by the extent of forward reach required. In the interests of safety, shelves should not be fitted over hot equipment.

Mobile benches and trolleys are used extensively in modern kitchens to reduce unnecessary walking and carrying and seats may be provided in work centres where the work is repetitive and restricted in movement. The comfortable height of a work surface for a seated position (with a seat height of 430 mm (1' 5") is about 700 mm (2' 4"), which is lower than the normal bench top level and requires a special shelf or table. If a higher stool is provided it must be fitted with an appropriate foot rest.

6 GROUPING OF EQUIPMENT

6.01 The choice of alternative positions for equipment may be restricted by the shape and dimensions of the room but in most cases two types of grouping are possible:

(a) *Wall siting* with the cooking equipment arranged around the perimeter walls and work tables placed in the centre of the kitchen.

(b) *Island grouping* of the large cooking equipment in the centre of the room with the work benches and other equipment adjacent to the walls.

Wall grouping

6.02 Placing equipment against the walls allows considerable economies in the engineering services and this arrangement is usually adopted in smaller kitchens. The services are not only cheaper to install but also simpler and easier to maintain. For example, water pipes may run along the walls instead of over the ceiling or under the floor; waste pipes and channels can be kept short and discharge direct to outside gulleys; through the adjacent external walls and windows, convenient outlets for steam and fumes can be provided, as well as ventilators, enabling internal temperatures to be more easily controlled. With equipment arranged along the walls, the kitchen is less obstructed by canopies and pipes.

Back-bar equipment, used in snack bars and public houses, illustrates the development of a range of small equipment designed specifically for wall mounting.

Island grouping

6.03 In kitchens catering for larger numbers the wall space alone will probably be insufficient for all the equipment required unless the room is very long and narrow. Island groupings are, in any event, preferred in most cases because of the economy in floor space which can be achieved and to facilitate convenient arrangement of work centres around the equipment. Access for cleaning and maintenance is, generally, more easily provided when equipment is grouped away from the walls.

The positioning of work benches, etc around the perimeter walls also offers certain advantages in that the employees using the benches can be provided with natural light and ventilation and, possibly, a view through a window to improve their working environment.

With island siting of equipment, mechanical ventilation is essential and must include some form of canopy and ducting to confine and remove the steam and fumes. Canopies and ducts add considerably to costs and tend to be obstructive to light and view, in addition to creating extra cleaning difficulties both within the duct and on the outside exposed surfaces. Water services and waste pipes or channels are also extended further across the room and require more attention for cleaning and maintenance. Other factors which need to be taken into account in deciding the best positioning for equipment include:

(1) Lighting

6.04 All work areas require good lighting without excessive variation or obscuration of the light from one place to another. In particular, equipment such as ovens and boiling pans, etc need to be carefully positioned so as to allow light to show into the interiors without being obstructed by the opening of the doors or lids. Possible obstruction of light by canopies, ducting, beams or columns, throwing shadows over areas of equipment must also be considered. In most cases, this problem may be solved by either repositioning the equipment or by providing supplementary lighting—for example, within the canopy or space.

(2) *Sinks*

6.05 Regardless of the grouping of equipment, sinks are invariably positioned against a wall, both for support and to allow a short waste to extend through the wall to discharge over an external gulley.

(3) *'Wet' and 'dry' equipment*

6.06 Economies can be obtained by grouping together those items of equipment which use steam or water for cooking. This includes boiling pans, high and low pressure steamers and bains-marie, all of which require water connections and waste outlets or facilities nearby. In addition, provision must be made for removal of heat and steam and this can be most economically provided by grouping the equipment into one area.

From an operational point of view, the grouping is also most convenient since this type of equipment is used mainly for cooking vegetables and needs to be sited near to the vegetable preparation areas. At the same time, regard should be given to the possibility of using this or additional equipment of a similar nature for puddings, custards and other items prepared elsewhere in the kitchen. 'Dry' equipment includes that used for baking, roasting, grilling and frying processes and the associated boiling tops. The arrangement of this equipment is more flexible but grouping is used to confine heat and fumes and to enable siting near to the preparation areas for meat, fish and pastry.

Separation of cooking processes into 'wet' and 'dry' areas is generally only feasible in kitchens catering for more than 400 meals per day.

Aisle spaces between equipment

6.07 If groups of equipment in a kitchen are too widely spaced the area becomes uneconomically large, costs of services and cleaning are increased and the widespread nature of the work in the kitchen involves extra time and effort in transporting items from one place to another. Space must, however, be provided for persons working at equipment and benches whilst allowing sufficient room for others to pass by. For this, and for persons working back to back on opposite benches, a space width of 950 mm to 1050 mm (3′ 2″ to 3′ 6″) is regarded as the minimum.

Extra wide aisles—1400 mm to 1500 mm (4′ 6″ to 5′ 0″)—are required where mobile equipment or trolleys are used and additional space needs to be set aside for parking trolleys which are not in circulation.

Particular care must be taken to avoid congestion around hot equipment because of the greater risk of accidents where persons are stooping or handling hot, heavy dishes and to allow for the swing of opening doors. In this situation, clearances of 1250 mm to 1350 mm (4′ 0″ to 4′ 6″) are essential.

In each case, the two dimensions quoted represent the range between the absolute minimum width and the width which is normally recommended for design purposes.

Flexibility in planning

6.08 The nature of work in a kitchen is continually varying as different food materials are used and successive stages of preparation are reached. To facilitate these changes the equipment used in food preparation should be equally flexible in arrangement—by being movable and mobile. Tables can be fitted with wheels and locking brakes; preparation equipment and machines can be mounted on trolleys or wheel bases; mobile racks can be used for containers and utensils.

In addition, the use of mobile equipment permits easier stowage and storage when items are not in use, thus allowing economies in floor areas, facilitating cleaning and avoiding unnecessary handling and carrying when food is transferred from one section to another.

7 FOOD PREPARATION AREAS

7.01 Food preparation in a catering establishment is usually divided into four sections, partly because of the nature of the food and type of preparation which is involved, partly to facilitate the use of specialist equipment and staff. The areas concerned are:

Vegetable preparation
Meat and fish preparation
Pastry preparation
General preparation.

It is usually practicable to devote a section specifically to vegetable preparation even in a small kitchen catering for, say, 100 meals per day. The separation of areas exclusively for meat and fish preparation and for preparing pastry is generally warranted in a kitchen providing in excess of 200 meals per day, although there is considerable flexibility in these arrangements depending on the type of restaurant and degree of specialization amongst the cooking staff.

Division of preparation areas may be provided by:
(a) Separate rooms adjoining the main kitchen.
(b) Low walls (aproximately 1200 mm (4′ 0″) high) between the areas which are otherwise open to the kitchen; or
(c) The arrangement of benches and equipment into a specialist section within the main kitchen.

The 'open plan' arrangement outlined in (b) and (c) is usually preferred since this allows easier supervision and communication, requires less total floor space and enables all the cooking equipment to be grouped together in a central area of the kitchen.

As an exception, the pastry section is frequently kept in a separate room because of the delicate nature of this work and the specialist equipment which is needed. Vegetables are usually washed, peeled and trimmed in a separate area—which may form part of the vegetable store—in order to confine dirt and debris.

Where low walls are used as a means of separation (b) the cost of construction is increased not only in the walls themselves but also in complicating the floor drainage. Extra costs in cleaning and maintenance are also involved. The walls are, however, useful as a support for shelving, tool racks and appliances and they help to confine spillage to each area and to reduce reverberation of noise.

Physical separation of preparation sections is warranted in large-scale catering—such as in hospitals and large hotels—where a high degree of specialization is involved. In this case the cooking area is also divided into distinct sections.

8 VEGETABLE PREPARATION SECTION

8.01 Within this area the raw vegetables are prepared for cooking. Salad vegetables and fresh fruit may also be

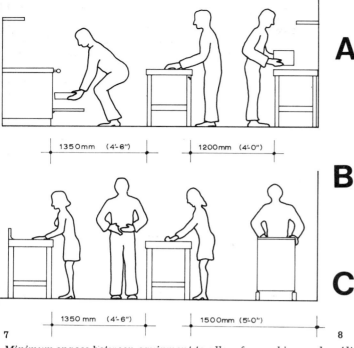

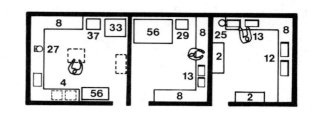

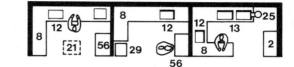

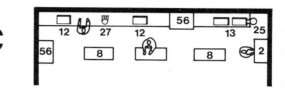

7

Minimum spaces between equipment to allow for working and circulation.

8

Alternative arrangements for preparation areas using
A—Separated rooms.   B—Bays.
C—Open plan kitchens.

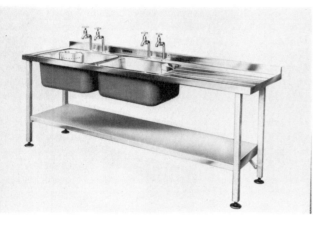

9

G. F. E. Bartlett and Son.
A double bowl stainless steel sink with one drainer supported by a galvanized stand which is adjustable in height. The perforated corner grids enclose waste outlets. Alternative models may have one bowl or two drainers.

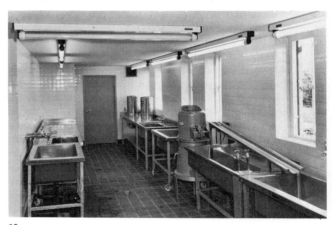

10

Vegetable preparation
An example of the layout of a vegetable preparation area showing potato peeling machine and associated sinks. The trough over the initial sink is to convey peeled root vegetables which have been trimmed and 'eyed' to a mobile sink.

initially cleaned and prepared here before being transferred to other sections for making up. The work in the vegetable preparing section generally falls into three areas which follow in sequence:

(a) Peeling or paring.
(b) Cleaning and removing 'eyes' and spots, etc.
(c) Trimming, cutting, shredding, dicing and other processes in preparing the vegetables for use.

Areas

8.02 The space required for vegetable preparation varies with the number of meals served, the number and variety of vegetable dishes included in each meal, the extent of pre-preparation—for instance, using frozen prepared vegetables—and the arrangement of the preparation area itself. If salads are included, the number of sinks and area of work surface need to be increased in this section.

Assuming vegetable storage is completely separate and that the space is used economically the following areas are a general guide:

Number of Meals served per day	Area For vegetable and salad preparation	
	metre²	feet²
Up to 100	3·7	40
„ „ 200	5·6	60
„ „ 400	8·4	90
„ „ 600	10·2	110
„ „ 800	12·1	130
„ „ 1000	13·9	150

Siting

8.03 Root vegetables such as potatoes are normally covered in soil and peeling, washing and trimming are essentially 'wet' processes which produce large quantities

11

Vegetable preparation area, General Foods Ltd., Banbury.
Equipment by G. F. E. Bartlett & Son Ltd.
View of the vegetable preparation area showing potato peeling
machine, sinks and benching.

of waste. This section should be sited, where possible, adjacent to the vegetable store and in a convenient position for disposal of refuse.

Working environment
8.04 Good lighting is essential in view of the need for speed and accuracy in work which tends to be unpleasant and monotonous. A suitable level of illumination is 400 lux (37.2 lumens/ft^2) with a limiting Glare Index of 25 and light fittings should be of a moisture-proof type.

Vegetable preparation usually involves standing or sitting at a sink or wet bench for long periods and some form of space heating must be provided to maintain the temperature above 15.6°C (60°F) and preferably at about 18.3°C (65°F). In many situations this requirement can be met by overhead fan heaters. Separate ventilation—ensuring about 3 air changes an hour—is also important to remove steam and water vapour and to minimize odours.

Construction
8.05 The walls must be smooth cement-rendered or ceramic tiled up to at least 1800 mm (6′ 0″) and all corners and junctions should be rounded or coved for easy cleaning. The vicinity of vegetable sinks, peeling machines and waste disposers is particularly vulnerable to splashing

and the sinks and drainers should have high moulded splashbacks.

Floors must be impervious and laid to falls to allow water, which may be spilled on the floor or used in cleaning, to drain to a grating-covered channel or trapped gulley. All the drainage must be accessible for cleaning and it may be necessary to install silt traps to retain soil and debris.

The most durable materials for flooring are quarry tiles but, as with all tiling, these must be set on an impervious base and pointed with acid-resisting cement mortar joints to avoid dislodgement.

To minimize risk of condensation the ceiling and external walls must be well insulated and sealed to prevent moisture penetration.

Windows are not essential in this area but, as in other working environments, the presence of a window provides a psychological benefit. If windows are provided they should be sited near the work bench area, with a sill height of at least 1050 mm (3′ 6″), unobstructed by equipment and accessible for cleaning.

Fittings and equipment
8.06 The basic equipment required in this section will include preparation tables and benches, sinks, waste

disposal units, mobile equipment and machines for potato peeling, potato chipping, potato mashing, and the shredding, dicing and slicing of vegetables.

Preparation tables and benches

8.07 Separate work surfaces are required for preparing vegetables before and after washing and these are provided on each side of the sinks in the form of draining boards. Work surfaces must be non-absorbent, durable and easily cleaned, and the most suitable materials for this purpose are stainless steel and hard laminated plastic such as melamine. The framework of tables and benches is usually of galvanized or enamelled iron work, and may be freestanding or supported clear of the floor by cantilevers fixed to the adjacent wall. The latter arrangement allows the floor to be clear of obstruction for cleaning, and is particularly suitable for fixed work benches and sink units. To allow flexibility in arrangement of work areas, tables should be easily movable.

Additional work tops—such as tables or mobile trolleys—are generally necessary for salad preparation. Mobility of equipment is particularly important where salad items have to be transferred to other areas for making up. Work benches are also used for mounting machinery and equipment at a convenient working height. In kitchens catering for up to 500 meals per day most of the equipment in this section is of the bench-mounted type whilst, in larger kitchens, space must be allowed for floor-standing machinery.

Cutting boards should be provided to reduce damage to the surface and blunting of knives and the materials for this purpose are usually of a plastic/rubber composition which is sufficiently resilient to withstand cutting without becoming absorbent or difficult to clean.

Potato peeling

8.08 The potato or vegetable peeling machine may be bench mounted or floor standing (pedestal type) and is used to remove the peel from some types of root vegetables such as potatoes, carrots and beetroots.

To reduce the length of carry, and confine dirt, the potato peeler should be sited adjacent to—and, in some cases, within—the store. It is also positioned so that the peeled vegetables can be discharged directly into a sink for washing prior to the removal of the 'eyes' and blemishes which are cut out by hand. When fitted above a sink of normal height (865 mm) the peeler is about 1500 mm (5′ 0″) high, and to allow easier charging of large machines, potatoes may be stored in elevated hoppers.

Alternatively, the peeling machine may be used with a low-level sink arranged so that workers are able to sit down whilst completing the hand work. To facilitate this a number of specially designed items of equipment are available including a combined sink and chute unit. Portable sinks are also used where space is restricted or where prepared potatoes have to be transported some distance to the cooking area.

Sinks

8.09 Double sink units are preferable allowing vegetables to be washed in one sink then transferred to the second to rinse and soak whilst awaiting use. Where the kitchen caters for less than, say, 100 meals per day this dual arrangement may not be warranted but a separate vegetable sink is essential, even in a small catering establishment, when raw vegetables are used.

Sinks are of pressed stainless steel construction manufactured to standard dimensions with single or double bowls ranging in size from 600 × 450 mm (24″ × 18″) to 750 × 500 mm (30″ × 20″) and 250 to 380 mm (10″ × 15″) deep. The unit may include single or double draining boards formed from the same sheet giving overall dimensions of 600 mm or 650 mm (2′ 0″ or 2′ 2″) width and lengths from 1200 (single drainer) up to 3050 mm (4′ 0″ to 10′ 0″). To provide a convenient working area for one person, the overall length of the sink and associated work surface should not exceed 1800 mm (6′ 0″). In washing fruit and vegetables a wire basket suspended in the sink is helpful and this can also be used as a means of transportation.

All fixed sinks should be supplied with both hot (at 60°C (140°F)) and cold water. The normal type of waste outlet to a vegetable sink must be protected by a sieve to reduce risk of blockage, and this is usually in the form of a removable grid fitted across the corner in which the outlet is situated.

Portable or mobile sinks—which consist of tanks on wheels—are sometimes used to provide greater flexibility in the arrangement of work areas and economy in space. These sinks are filled by hoses or standpipes and are fitted with waste outlets which can be emptied into a floor gulley.

Waste disposal

8.10 Machines, such as those used for peeling, have a filter or silt trap built into the equipment or connected nearby. The tendency in modern kitchen design is to discharge waste debris to the drainage system rather than to have to remove it by hand using conventional systems of refuse bins and sacks. In each case, however, the approval of the Local Authority must be obtained and restrictions may be imposed on the use of public sewers.

Powered waste disposal units (250 to 550 W) (0·3 to 0·7 HP) may be fitted below any sink outlet to macerate debris prior to discharge. Independent units (550 to 2250 W) (0·7 to 3 HP) are also used, fitted under hoppers—which are usually built into the work surface—and supplied with water for lubrication and cleaning.

Other preparation machines

8.11 Equipment for shredding, dicing, mashing and other finishing operations for vegetable preparation is positioned in the part nearest to the cooking area in order to maintain the flow pattern. This machinery is also potentially hazardous in use and must not be placed in a traffic area where the operator is liable to be bumped or have attention distracted.

Racks—preferably wall mounted—are required for the various attachments and a drawer or shelf under the bench is needed for blades and tools.

Most of this equipment requires to be mounted on benches but larger machines for shredding and dicing vegetables and for mashing potatoes are designed to stand on the floor. The positions of equipment need to be determined at the planning stage in order to ensure that space and services are provided.

Storage

8.12 In addition to storage for the tools and small equipment used in vegetable preparation, space should be allocated for parking mobile equipment such as trolleys when these are not in use. Daily supplies of vegetables may be kept in the preparation section and pots and pans may be transferred here, for storage, from the cooking area. In each case, to facilitate storage and transport, racks and other equipment should be mobile.

Schedule of equipment: vegetable and salad preparation

Equipment		Number of meals prepared per day—based on the main meal period.						
		50	100	200	400	600	800	1000
Benches/tables total area	(ft²)	8	16	24	34	42	50	56
	(m²)	0·7	1·5	2·2	3·2	3·9	4·7	5·2
Sinks—vegetables		1	1	2	2	3	3	4
typical size		24 × 18 × 15 ins 600 × 450 × 380 mm			27 × 20 × 15 ins 700 × 500 × 380 mm			
Sinks—salads		—	—	1	1	1	2	2
typical size				24 × 18 × 15 ins 600 × 450 × 380 mm	27 × 20 × 15 ins 700 × 500 × 380 mm			
Potato peeler		bench mounted				floor standing		
capacity		7 lb 3·2 kg		14 lb 6·4 kg		28 lb 12·7 kg		56 lb 25·4 kg
typical size		24 × 24 ins 600 × 600 mm				30 × 24 ins 750 × 600 mm		
Potato chipper		hand model		electric—bench or floor mounted				
typical size				24 × 18 ins 600 × 450 mm				
Shredder/slicer		bench mounted			floor standing			
typical size		24 × 15 ins 600 × 380 mm			30 × 18 ins 750 × 450 mm			
Potato masher		bench mounted			floor standing			
		27 × 18 ins 700 × 450 mm			30 × 18 ins 750 × 600 mm			
Refuse sack holders		1	2	2	2	3	3	3

Miscellaneous: Provision for adequate vegetable knives, peelers chopping boards and other small equipment

9 PASTRY PREPARATION SECTION

9.01 The range of work usually included in the pastry section includes:

(a) all hot sweets
(b) all cold sweets
(c) all pastry work
(d) all bakery items and
(e) certain finishing and post cooking work such as icing and decoration.

Arrangement and siting

9.02 Pastry work may be (1) prepared in a section of the kitchen and use the general cooking area or (2) form a self-contained unit having its own storage, preparation, cooking and, perhaps, wash-up facilities within the same area.

In the first case, the preparation area is located near to appropriate cooking equipment. Day-to-day requirements of the food ingredients are normally kept in, or adjacent to, the preparation area and, in this event, the relative position of the dry goods store is not important.

Where the pastry section is self contained it may be operated more or less independently and be sited some distance from the main kitchen provided suitable arrangements are made for transporting supplies and products (eg by lifts, conveyors or trolleys).

Food storage

9.03 Depending on size, other food commodities required for day-to-day use may be kept in cupboards and bins within the preparation section or in a kitchen store room adjacent.

Flour and other foods used in quantity are best kept in mobile bins which can be used for transportation and stored under a work bench. For small items such as flavourings, colourings and spices, wall cupboards are usually provided at about eye level—1500 mm (5′ 0″) high—fitted with adjustable shelves 150 to 300 mm (6″ to 12″) apart. For comfortable reach over a work bench the top shelf should be no higher than 1700 mm (5′ 6″).

Refrigerators

9.04 Storage of perishable food commodities may be centralized in a cold room or larder but some local refrigerated storage in the preparation area is an advantage. The size of the refrigerator is based on one day's requirements of dairy produces, fats, eggs, prepared mixes and should include space for made-up cold sweets.

Areas

9.05 For a pastry preparation section which forms part of a general kitchen the following areas are typical:

Number of meals served per day	Area of pastry preparation	
	m²	ft²
Up to 100	2·8	30
„ „ 200	3·7	40
„ „ 400	9·3	100

Number of meals served per day	Area of pastry preparation	
„ „ 600	11·2	120
„ „ 800	13·0	140
„ „ 1000	14·9	160

Space requirements are determined not only by the quantity but by the variety of food prepared in the pastry section.

Working environment
9.06 The pastry area should be kept reasonably cool and well ventilated. An ambient temperature up to 65°F (18·3°C) is suitable for working and for temporary storage of most items in course of preparation, but refrigeration must also be provided for perishable commodities.

Much of the work in this section involves bench preparation interspaced with the use of equipment for weighing, mixing, rolling, portioning, etc. Over the bench and equipment areas, the illumination level should be at least 400 lux (37·2 lumens/ft²) using blended natural light to obtain accurate colour discrimination. Light fittings must be positioned to avoid shadows on work areas—including shadows formed by the equipment and workers themselves—and a limiting Glare Index of 25 is recommended.

Construction
9.07 The general requirements for construction of kitchens apply to this area. Whilst the nature of the work is mainly 'dry' preparation, walls floors and equipment require frequent cleaning.

Fittings and equipment
9.08 Much of the work in the pastry preparation section is intricate, and normally done by hand but, with a large volume and variety of products, a whole range of specialist equipment may be used to simplify this work and also increase output.

The basic equipment will include tables and benches, sinks, weighing scales, machines for mixing, rolling and dividing pastry and dough, and tray racks, etc. Pastry ovens, boiling rings and other cooking equipment may be located in this section for convenience.

Tables and fittings
9.09 To be within convenient reach a working space of about 1200 mm (4' 0") length is allowed per worker and preparation tables are frequently 1800 to 2400 mm (6' 0" to 8' 0") long and 750 mm (2' 6") or 900 mm (3' 0") wide to allow multipurpose use, the latter being used in central positions where access is provided to both sides. The tables arranged against the walls may have raised kerbs to reduce spillage from the outer edges. A marble slab is often preferred for pastry making.

Equipment in continuous demand, such as weighing scales and the main mixing machine, must be located in a central position with working surfaces nearby. The tools and fittings, including measures, should be within reach and are best hung on racks or placed on open shelves for easy accessibility.

Considerable storage space is required for baking tins, trays and other containers which are usually kept on shelves. Mobile tiered tray racks are essential for transporting, receiving and cooling products as they come from the ovens. Storage for hand tools is provided on racks or in drawers under the work benches.

Sinks
9.10 At least one deep sink with hot and cold water should be provided in this area for use in preparation and for washing tools and equipment. If pan washing is done in this section, separate facilities should be provided specifically for this purpose.

Other equipment
9.11 In a kitchen catering for less than, say, 200 meals per day the mixing machine may be also used for general preparation and, in this case, should be sited centrally. Separate mixing facilities—which include beating and whisking—are warranted for pastry preparation in larger premises.

Other equipment for use in preparing pastry, bread and similar items include pastry rolling machines (hand or motor driven)—which roll out pastry or dough to a uniform thickness; and dough dividers—for cutting out a number of uniform pieces of set weight. Where bread and rolls are produced in large quantity, specialist bakery equipment, including proving ovens, will usually be required.

Pastry ovens
9.12 To provide the accurate and even temperature control required in baking, pastry ovens are designed very shallow and are usually stacked in tiers. Alternatively, convection ovens, which employ forced air circulation to distribute heat, may be used for this purpose. Pastry ovens may be sited within the preparation area or in an adjacent part of the cooking section. This also applies to boiling tables.

Schedule of equipment: pastry preparation

Equipment		Number of meals prepared per day—based on the main meal period.						
		50	100	200	400	600	800	1000
Benches/tables total area	(ft²)	6 (a)	10	18	30	40	46	50
	(m²)	0·6	0·9	1·7	2·8	3·7	4·3	4·6
Sinks		1 (a)	1	1	1	2	2	2
typical sizes		24 × 18 × 10 ins 600 × 450 × 250 mm			24 × 18 × 12 ins 600 × 450 × 300 mm			
Mixing machine		(a)	10 qt 11 litre		20 qt 24 litre	30 qt 34 litre	50 qt 57 litre	80 qt 91 litre
typical sizes		bench mounted			36 × 24 ins 900 × 600 mm			

Equipment		Number of meals prepared per day—based on the main meal period.						
		50	100	200	400	600	800	1000
Dough divider					bench mounted			
Pastry roller		hand				motor-bench mounted		
typical sizes		25 × 25 ins 650 × 650 mm				37 × 64 ins 950 × 1625 mm		
Pie machine		hand				motor-bench mounted		
Refrigerator	(ft³)	10	10	15	20	30	50	50
	(m³)	0·3	0·3	0·4	0·6	0·9	1·4	1·4
Pastry oven Number of decks		(a)	(a)	1	2	2	3	3
Shelf area	(ft²)			10	20	20	30	30
	(m²)			0·9	1·9	1·9	2·8	2·8
Proving oven					1	1	1	1
Boiling table Number of rings		(a)	(a)	(a)	2	2	4	4
Cooling rack tiered (mobile)		(a)	(a)	1	1	1	2	2
approx area					(oven tray size) 26 × 21 ins (Gastronorm) 650 × 530 mm			
Scales range		14 lb 6·4 kg			28 lb 12·7 kg			
Bins sugar		(b)	(b)	2	2	2	2	2
flour		(b)	(b)	1	1	1	2	2
Holders— waste sacks		1	1	2	2	2	2	2

Miscellaneous: Cupboard and drawer space for small tools, mixer attachments and bowls, measures, piping equipment, moulds, colanders, brushes, dishes, etc.

(a) Included in general cooking area.

(b) In dry good store only.

10 MEAT AND FISH PREPARATION

10.01 The range of work involved in preparing meat and fish items depends on:

(a) the size of the kitchen and the extent to which meat, etc is delivered ready prepared.

(b) the class of restaurant and variety of meat dishes offered.

In general terms, preparation facilities in this section may include:

· All forms of butchery and portioning of meat.

· Preparing poultry, game, offal.

· Slicing ham, bacon.

· Mincing and dicing meat.

· Meat processing, sausage making.

· Preparing cold meat dishes.

· Fish slicing, filleting.

· Preparing shell fish.

Areas

10.02 This area of preparation is extremely variable and the following figures represent only an approximate guide and assume that meat is delivered partly prepared.

Number of meals served per day	Area for meat and fish preparation	
	m²	ft²
Up to 100	4·6	50
„ „ 200	7·4	80
„ „ 400	9·3	100
„ „ 600	11·2	120
„ „ 800	12·1	130
„ „ 1000	13·0	140

Siting and arrangement

10.03 Meat and fish preparation must be located near the cold stores and 'dry' cooking area. Depending on size this section may be divided, by the arrangement of benches, into a number of separate work areas for:

(a) dressing poultry and game

(b) fish preparation

(c) raw meat and butchery items

(d) cooked meats and preparation of cold dishes.

Environment and construction

10.04 Cool conditions, with the temperature maintained below 15·6°C (60°F), are desirable and good lighting, particularly over the work tops and machines where sharp tools are used. A suitable standard is 400 lux (37·2 lumens/ft²).

The walls should, preferably, be glazed tiled at least up to 1800 mm (6′ 0″) height and floors must be non-slip, durable and resistant to grease and fat spillage. Frequent washing down is necessary, particularly behind sinks and machinery, and junctions between the floor and walls should be coved for easy cleaning. The floor must have a suitable fall for drainage.

Tables and fittings

10.05 To avoid risk of cross-contamination, separate tables should be provided for each of the four main areas indicated. If space does not allow this, fish preparation may be confined to a portable worktop or slab, but a separate work surface is always essential for cold prepared meats.

12
Sandwich preparation. Equipment by Stotts of Oldham
A specially designed sandwich preparation area built into a large industrial installation. Features include refrigerated cupboards, handy containers for sandwich ingredients, bread-buttering machine and cutting board.

13

The kitchens, York Post House. Trust Houses Forte Ltd.
Equipment by Moorwood-Vulcan Ltd.
Details of the equipment and layout to the kitchens of a modern hotel.

Work surfaces are normally of stainless steel although marble or slate slabs are often preferred for fish preparation and composition materials are now used for cutting boards and chopping blocks as a substitute for wood.

To accommodate the large number of knives and hand tools used in this section, storage racks, drawers and cupboards should be provided. Meat trays and dishes are usually stored on shelves or runners fitted under the benches or kept in portable racks. Mobile storage bins are often used for meat scraps, waste fat and bones.

Where extensive butchery work is involved—eg catering for over 500 meals per day—meat-hanging rails, hooks, power saws and other specialist equipment should be provided.

Sinks are required for washing meat and fish and for cleaning equipment and utensils. For the latter, deep sinks (basins 380 mm deep) are most suitable and the use of double sinks enables both operations to be carried out in the same area.

Equipment

10.06 *Mincing machine.* In a small kitchen (up to 150 meals per day) mincing attachments may be used with the mixing machine provided this is sited in a central position. A separate mincing machine—usually bench mounted— is warranted in larger premises.

Slicing machine. This is used for a variety of meats and should be located near the cold meat area.

Other equipment used in this section includes meat tenderizers, dicing machines and bowl cutters. A refrigerator may also be available for temporary storage of meat, etc in course of preparation.

Schedule of equipment: meat and fish preparation

Equipment		Number of meals prepared per day—based on the main meal period.						
		50	100	200	400	600	800	1000
Benches/tables total area.	(ft²)	8	12	20	30	40	48	54
	(m²)	0·7	1·1	1·9	2·8	3·7	4·5	5·0
Sinks		1	1	1	1	2	2	2
typical sizes		24 × 18 × 10 ins 600 × 450 × 250 mm			24 × 18 × 12 ins 600 × 450 × 300 mm			
Chopping boards		table board			floor standing block			
typical sizes					24 × 24 ins 600 × 600 mm		48 × 24 ins 1200 × 600 mm	
Cold slab length— fish preparation		24 ins 600 mm			30 ins 750 mm		2 × 30 ins 2 × 750 mm	
Meat saw		hand			electric			
Mincing machine		bench mounted			floor standing			
typical sizes		12 × 10 ins 300 × 250 mm				24 × 18 ins 600 × 500 mm		
Slicing machine typical sizes		20 × 18 ins 500 × 450 mm			24 × 18 ins 600 × 500 mm			
Cold store in preparation area	(ft³)	—	10	10	15	15	20	20
	(m³)	—	0·3	0·3	0·4	0·4	0·6	0·6

Miscellaneous: Knife racks, cutting knives, sharpening steels, choppers, waste sack holders

11 GENERAL PREPARATION SECTION

11.01 The need for an area of general preparation depends on the extent of specialization in the three main areas considered. Within this general area, food dishes are assembled and made ready for cooking and certain post-cooking operations are carried out, such as sieving and mashing. The work involved can be most conveniently carried out on tables spaced around the cooking equipment.

11.02 A separate section may be needed for preparing cold dishes, sandwiches and other items which do not require cooking, and this must be located near the servery.

Schedule of equipment: general preparation

Equipment	Number of meals prepared per day.						
	50	100	200	400	600	800	1000
Hand-wash basin, soap, nail brush, etc	1	1	1	1	1	1	1
				(legal requirement)			
Towel dispenser	1	1	1	1	1	1	1
Pan rack length	2′ 0″	3′ 0″	4′ 0″	2 × 3′ 0″		2 × 4′ 0″	
	0·6 m	0·9 m	1·2 m	2 × 9·0 m		2 × 1·2 m	
Meat slicer			1	1	1	1	1

Miscellaneous: soup sieve, mashing machine, cupboards and racks for small serving equipment, etc.

4 FOOD COOKING AND EQUIPMENT

1 SELECTION OF EQUIPMENT

1.01 Equipment is often obtained in advance of a detailed examination of its proposed use and, as a result, it is not uncommon to find valuable kitchen space occupied by items of equipment which are underutilized and, in many cases, unnecessary and obstructive.

In selecting any item of equipment, certain criteria must be applied to establish, in the first instance, the purpose behind the requirement and whether such equipment is, in fact, needed at all and secondly the suitability of possible alternatives. Only as a third stage should comparisons be made of individual performances, capacities, sizes and other features.

1.02 The various purposes for which equipment may be required can be summarized under five main headings:
· To produce meals in sufficient quantity.
· To provide an adequate variety of food.
· To ensure a suitable quality of food product.
· To facilitate preparation and cooking within a reasonable time.
· To reduce costs of food production either directly or by reducing the labour involved.

A preliminary assessment of the basic equipment needed for food preparation, cooking and serving, and for ancillary areas such as the washing-up of dishes, can be made from the size and nature of the proposed catering operation but some rationalization must also be applied to modify the initial selection by taking into account:

(a) The possibility of equipment serving more than one purpose, particularly where it is likely to be used only infrequently.

(b) The cost of the equipment, including the labour and attendance associated with its use, compared with the advantages gained over other methods.

(c) The use of alternative arrangements which could make the equipment unnecessary, such as the use of prepared convenience foods instead of ordinary market produce.

Evaluation of equipment

1.03 Characteristics of equipment can be evaluated and comparisons made between similar items supplied from different manufacturers by examining both the particulars provided by the manufacturer and by making enquiries concerning other features. The various matters which have a bearing on the suitability or otherwise of catering equipment are summarized below. All of these will be significant to some extent but certain features may be more critical in particular circumstances and

questions of size, capacity, cost and delivery are usually uppermost at the initial stage of selection.

Capacity—not only the nominal capacity but that part which can be effectively used.

Size—taking into account clearances for doors, handles and other projections which will determine the dimensions of the space occupied.

Weight—in relation to bench or floor loading.

Mobility—which may be important in facilitating multi-purpose use.

Module—allowing standardization and interchangeability with other units.

Internal dimensions—with regard to the use of standard containers.

Ergonomic considerations—extent of reaching, bending and lifting required and the weights involved.

Performance—rating of appliance, efficiency and performance characteristics as shown by tests.

Quality of construction—including electrical and mechanical safety, as compared with British Standard and other approved specifications.

Operation—facility of control and accuracy of adjustment.

Hygiene—ease of cleaning, including the means of access for cleaning, resistance to deterioration, scratching and damage during use.

Maintenance—accessibility for replacement of components, availability of spares and servicing arrangements.

Delivery period—which may delay or interrupt the installation programme and result in subsequent loss of business.

Depreciation—estimated life of components and of the equipment as a whole. A seven- or ten-year cycle is frequently adopted for large appliances although certain equipment with heavy maintenance costs may be written off in a shorter period.

Costs—the costs of using equipment (cost-in-use) are compounded from the initial outlay divided by the anticipated useful life of the equipment together with the annual running expenses. The cost-in-use should take account of:

(1) *Initial cost* of the basic appliance.

(2) *Additional costs* of trays and other items used with the appliance.

(3) *Installation costs* including charges for building in work, connections for gas, electricity, water and drainage services and any delivery and handling charges.

(4) *Depreciation* period having regard to the nature of the

equipment and cost of maintenance.

(5) *The annual charge* represented by $\dfrac{(1) + (2) + (3)}{4}$ together with an allowance for percentage interest on the capital employed.

(6) *Maintenance charges* for equipment servicing plus replacement of components.

(7) *Insurance*.

(8) *Costs of cleaning* and routine maintenance carried out by catering staff.

(9) *Running expenses* in respect of gas, electricity and/or fuel consumed during average annual period of use.

Standards

1.04 As a guide to quality of catering equipment a number of standards are available in the UK.

Gas Council. Lists of tested and approved gas catering appliances, issued each year.

Showrooms: 139, Tottenham Court Road, London W1P 9LN.

BS2512:1963 (under review): 'Gas heated catering equipment'.

BS4104:1967: 'Catering equipment burning liquified petroleum gas'.

Electricity Council. Publications on catering equipment for various types of catering.

Showrooms: 45, St Martins Lane, London SW1.

BS4147 (in 12 parts 1967–1971): 'Electrically heated catering equipment'.

British Standard Specifications lay down requirements for quality of finish, construction and insulation; resistance to corrosion and damage; safety from sharp edges, flame failure, electrical shock or other dangers in use; limits on overheating of the outer casing and risks of fire; performance requirements and endurance tests.

Dimensions

1.05 At the present time there are no universal standards for sizes and dimensions of British manufactured catering equipment. Whilst each manufacturer usually has adopted a modular unit to allow convenient grouping of his own appliances, these are generally not interchangeable with similar equipment from other suppliers.

1

Module sizes for Gastro-norm containers.

2

Cooking equipment suite. Glynwed Foundries Ltd.
An example of the layout of modern modular equipment arranged in a suite. The central spine encloses pipe work and connections.

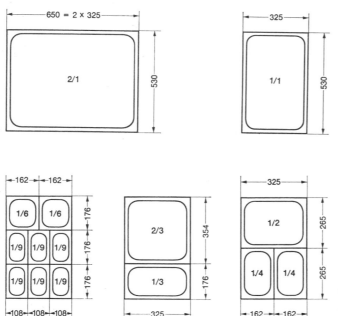

3

Counter service. Equipment by Glynwed Foundries Ltd.
An example of a modern counter of modular units suitable for gastronorm containers incorporating heated, unheated and refrigerated sections. Two grillers are mounted on the back wall.

With the introduction of metric dimensions an opportunity has been afforded for some rationalization of sizes and the European Catering Equipment Manufacturers Association favours the use of the Swiss 'Gastro-norm' system which is widely used on the European Continent. This is now drafted as a recommended specification by the British Standards Institute. The 'Gastro-norm' is essentially a series of insert dimensions for pans and trays but the same unit sizes can be used for all kinds of equipment from the trolleys conveying the containers to the interior spaces provided in refrigerators, ovens, cupboards bains-marie and serving counters. Using such a standard system confers many advantages in simplicity, easy transference of food with the minimum of handling and economy in the use of containers and in the space required for their stacking and storage.

The trend in equipment design is towards standard matching units having interchangeable basic components —such as boiling tops, ovens and stands—which can be assembled in a variety of combinations. Such modular units may then be butted close together to form a suite of equipment having neat simple lines, a continuous worktop and façade and hidden service connections.

The design of matching modular units not only gives a good appearance but also makes for greater simplicity and safety when working and easier cleaning and maintenance is possible with deliberate provision being made for access.

Materials

1.06 Materials used for catering equipment must be strong, corrosion proof, resistant to damage by heat or impact and scratching, and easily cleaned. The most common materials are steel and ironwork protected from rust by surface treatment or as stainless steel alloys. Aluminium is also used to some extent but mainly for containers. Copper utensils are also common, the copper usually being protected internally by a film of tin.

As a summary, the main applications for iron and steel work in catering equipment are:

(a) *Wrought iron*

Tubular or angle wrought iron is often welded to form the framework of cabinets, tables, etc. The iron is protected by galvanizing with a layer of zinc to BS729.

(b) *Cast iron*

Used for forming appliances and utensils of various shapes. Exposed surfaces are given a vitreous or porcelain enamelled finish which is often white or mottled grey colour.

(c) *Mild steel*

Forms the sheeting used on the sides of the cabinets, etc and may also be pressed into various forms. Vitreous enamelling is used as a finish for working areas whilst other surfaces are often galvanized for protection. BS3831 relates to vitreous enamel finishes for catering appliances.

(d) *Stainless steel*

The most common material, used in sheet form for external surfaces and interior linings, for table tops, pressed sinks and containers, stainless steel is inherently resistant to corrosion and meets all practical requirements.

Surfaces coming into contact with food should have a dull polished finish whilst other surface finishes may be matt or grained. The thicknesses of stainless steel recommended for various uses are as follows:

Situation	mm	SW gauge
Worktops and elevated shelving	2·0	14
Sinks and under shelving	1·6	16
Body panels, box-type doors / Covering over mild steel tops	1·2	18
Domestic sinks	0·9	20
Containers	0·7	22

2 EQUIPMENT REQUIREMENTS

2.01 In examining the requirements for equipment, consideration must, initially, be given to the output demanded of the kitchen. The maximum quantity of food which must be produced at any one time will indicate the greatest pressures on the equipment whilst the period over which the main meal is taken, compared with the cooking times involved, represents the amount of re-use which can be obtained from each appliance. Variety of choice in the meal will determine the degree of separation

needed in food preparation, cooking and service and, following from this, the optimum sizes of equipment. A third, equally important, feature is the type of catering and a decision, for example, to use only frozen convenience foods will have a considerable bearing on both the amount and type of equipment required for this more specialized use.

Output of equipment

2.02 Guidance on the selection of equipment should, where possible, be obtained from the chef or cook who will ultimately take charge of the kitchen since much depends on the practical interpretation of meal requirements. In general, two alternative approaches can be used to assess the output of catering equipment, either:

(a) by calculating the number of portions which can be obtained from a particular size of appliance in the time required to produce a meal and comparing this with the output demanded of the kitchen; or

(b) by adopting an average figure based on a space allowance (area or volume as appropriate) per meal produced.

The latter method, being relatively simple, is useful in preliminary estimates but both methods of calculation must be used to obtain more accurate information.

Equipment loadings

2.03 Electrical power requirements for equipment are indicated in kilowatts (kW). For gas supplies the Gas Council recommends a direct conversion of heat rate (power) from the traditional units of British thermal units/hour (Btu/h) to megajoules/hour (MJ/h) with the value in kilowatts in brackets, eg MJ/h (kW).

The relationship of the units is as follows:

Btu/h	Horsepower	Megajoules/h	Kilowatts
1000	0·3930	1·055	0·2931
2545	1·0	2·685	0·7457
947·8	0·3725	1·0	0·2778
3412	1·341	3·600	1·0

3 OVENS

3.01 An oven is essentially an enclosed space in which food is cooked by application of heat or energy. Ovens are also used for reheating—or regenerating—frozen and other prepared foods.

In the case of ovens which employ 'dry heat' for roasting and baking processes, the heat may be applied:

(1) externally, by circulating hot gases, high-pressure steam or hot oil in flues, ducts or similar passages around the outside surfaces or

(2) internally, using gas burners or electric heating elements which may be exposed or enclosed within the oven space.

The microwave oven, in contrast to other methods, employs electromagnetic waves of high frequency (2450 Megacycles/second or 2450 MHz) to transfer energy to the food.

Cooking by 'moist heat' is provided in steam ovens which may be designed to operate at atmospheric pressure or at higher pressures which permit higher temperatures to be attained. Steaming has a number of advantages compared with boiling in water and, in particular, is less liable to produce disintegration of the food and leaching of its soluble constituents.

High-pressure steam cooking compares with other baking processes in that the rate of cooking is accelerated but without moisture loss from the food product.

4

Stotts of Oldham.
LASMEC Mark 2 Combined roasting and steaming oven.
The roasting section (top) is a convection oven.

5

Modular cooking equipment. Stotts of Oldham.
Modular equipment arranged in an island suite. The illustration also shows the grease filters fitted in the extraction canopy.

6

Equipment by Zoppas Ltd.
The cooking range illustrated has an open boiling top over an oven. With module units, a variety of combinations can be obtained using different under units and tops to meet a wide range of requirements.

7

An electric single oven range.

Standards

3.02 Electrically heated ovens should comply with British Standard Specification 4167, 'Electrically heated catering equipment', Part 1, 1967 (ovens) or Part 5, 1969 (steaming ovens).

Requirements for gas heated ovens are specified in BS2512:1963 'Gas heated catering equipment', Parts 1 (general), 2 (ovens) and 6 (steamers). Similar provisions are contained in BS4104:1967 for catering equipment burning liquified petroleum gas.

Performance tests

3.03 To comply with the British Standards, the time taken for the centre of the oven to reach 177°C (350°F) above ambient should not exceed:

Electric ovens	Time (mins)	Gas ovens	Time (mins)
General purpose			
Under 0·25 m³ (8·83 ft³)	40	*Normal duty*	30
Over 0·25 m³	70	*Heavy duty*	50
Pastry			
Steel sole type	70	*Roasting*	70
Tile sole type	90	*Pastry*	70

In addition, the ovens must satisfy four practical cooking tests designed to check:
(a) High-temperature cooking performances (scones).
(b) Heat distribution (small cakes).
(c) Low-temperature cooking (slab cake).
(d) Roasting (Yorkshire puddings)—does not apply to pastry ovens.

Steam ovens

3.04 Steam ovens should be capable of raising the water to boiling temperature within 30 minutes (with automatic water supply) or 45 minutes (if manually filled). Cooking tests designed to check the working performance include:
(a) Steam cooking of a full load of potatoes within 60 minutes.
(b) Cooking of steamed pudding (with standard ingredients) within 2 hours.

Oven range

3.05 The oven range is used for general purposes and consists of two main components, an oven or ovens used for baking and roasting, and a boiling top for operations such as boiling, stewing, steaming or frying.
The boiling top may be in the form of:
(a) Individual electric plates or open gas burners of various sizes;
(b) a solid top having fast heat in the centre reducing to simmer heat at the edges; or
(c) a griddle plate for direct cooking and shallow frying.
Oven usage depends on the cooking times required for different dishes and the number of shelves and trays which can be accommodated. Although ovens are usually quoted in cubic capacity the most critical measurement is the usable shelf area which, for most purposes, relates to shelves separated by a clear space of 150 mm. For general catering purposes an average of 0·0155 m² (24 sq inches) of usable shelf area is normally required per meal with an increase or reduction of 25 per cent depending on the type of catering.

3.06 Typical sizes of ranges

Oven capacity	Internal size	External dimensions	Total loading
4 cu ft 0·113 m³	21″ × 18″ × 18″ 530 × 460 × 460 mm	30″ × 32″ × 34″ 760 × 810 × 870 mm	11–14 kW
5 cu ft 0·142 m³	24″ × 24″ × 15″ 600 × 600 × 400 mm	36″ × 34″ × 34″ 910 × 870 × 870 mm	12–15 kW

Ovens of 0·178 m³ (7 cu ft) capacity are also available.

General purpose oven

3.07 In large kitchens it is often more convenient to separate ovens from the boiling tops. The ovens may then be mounted on stands at a convenient working height or stacked one above the other in tiers of two to save floor space. Dimensions are similar to those for ranges and loadings, for the ovens only, are approximately:

Oven capacity		Total load
cu ft	m³	kilowatts
4	0·113	5
5	0·142	6
7	0·198	7

Working capacities of ovens may be calculated from the following food densities:

Meats:	130–160 kg/m³	(8–10 lb/cu ft)
Poultry:	110–130 kg/m³	(7–8 lb/cu ft)
Trayed up dishes:	65–75 kg/m³	(4½ lb/cu ft)

Forced-air convection ovens

3.08 The use of a fan to circulate hot air enables heat to be transferred more rapidly and more evenly distributed than in ovens of conventional design. As a result, shelves may be placed nearer together giving greater batch loadings and reductions of up to 40 per cent in conventional cooking times can be obtained.
In primary cooking, the convection oven can be used for a wide range of purposes—roasting, frying, grilling, baking, etc—and this oven is also particularly suitable for fast end cooking and reheating of frozen food. For the latter purpose the normal reheat time is 25 minutes.
In larger sizes the oven is usually mounted on a stand at a convenient height whereas small units may be bench mounted. Tiered units are also manufactured to standard or special designs:

Capacity	External dimension w × d × h	Loading
4 cu ft (0·113 m³)	32″ × 32″ × 34″ 810 × 810 × 870 mm	8 kW
7 cu ft (0·198 m³)	40″ × 36″ × 54″ 1020 × 910 × 1370 mm	10–12 kW
10 cu ft (0·283 m³)	44″ × 46″ × 62″ 1120 × 1170 × 1580 mm	13–15 kW

2 cu ft (0·057 m³) ovens with a loading of 4 kW are also available.

2 cubic ft (0·057 m³) ovens with a loading of 4 kW are also available.

Pastry oven

3.09 To minimize temperature variations within the oven space, pastry ovens are shallow (300 mm or less) and have special facilities for the accurate temperature control necessary for baking operations. The units are usually arranged in tiers.
Pastry ovens are installed where the production quantities of cakes and pastries warrant this special provision. To a large extent, this work is tending to become centralized whilst, in other cases, the convection oven is increasingly used for pastry work.

Decks	Oven size	External dimensions	Loading
1	30″ × 24″ × 9″ 760 × 610 × 230 mm	38″ × 43″ × 54″ 960 × 1090 × 1380 mm	5 kW
2	30″ × 36″ × 9″ 760 × 910 × 230 mm	50″ × 43″ × 66″ 1270 × 1090 × 1680 mm	14·4 kW

Where pastry ovens are used in conjunction with general purpose ovens, approximately 0·0039 m² of shelf area/meal (6 sq ins) is required.

8

Oliver Toms Ltd.
An example of a modern forced-air convection oven showing the external appearance with double glazed doors for viewing the cooking process,[8] *the ease of access to the controls provided by a sliding carriage*[9] *and method of bulk loading direct from trolleys with the minimum of handling and delay.*[10]

10

11

G. F. E. Bartlett and Son, Ltd.
The simplicity of design and controls of new catering equipment are shown in this 4 cu ft (0·12 m³) forced-air convection oven.

9

Roasting cabinet

3.10 Consisting of an insulated cabinet having large doors, adjustable sliding shelves and a drip tray at the base, this oven is purposely designed for meat roasting and would be appropriate for use in, say, a speciality restaurant based on roast dishes. Variations include ovens for spit roasting of small joints and poultry.

Typical sizes

Capacity	Oven size	External dimensions w × d × h	Overall loading
17 cu ft 0·48 m³	24″ × 26″ × 48″ 610 × 660 × 1220 mm	46″ × 36″ × 63″ 1170 × 910 × 1600 mm	8·5 kW
30 cu ft 0·85 m³	33″ × 30″ × 52″ 840 × 760 × 1320 mm	55″ × 40″ × 66″ 1400 × 1020 × 1680 mm	12·0 kW

Rotary or reel ovens

3.11 To ensure even heating the reel oven incorporates rotating shelves which travel round vertically through the oven space averaging out any temperature variations between the upper and lower regions.

Microwave oven

3.12 In the microwave oven energy is supplied to the food by electromagnetic waves of high frequency which cause an increase in molecular motion resulting in heat generation within the material. The electromagnetic spectrum producing this effect covers the frequencies from 300 to 300 000 megahertz (M.Hz) but the frequency used in cooking is controlled in the UK by the Post Office at 2450 M.Hz which corresponds to a wave length of about 0·12 m. Similar control over the use of microwaves for cooking and electrotherapy purposes is exercised in the USA by the Federal Communications Commission and, of the 5 frequencies allowed, 2450 M.Hz is most commonly used although microwaves of 915 M.Hz are also employed in some apparatus.

Properties

Microwaves are reflected by metallic surfaces whereas good dielectric materials such as glass, plastics, ceramics and air transmit the waves with little energy absorption. Materials that are successful subjects for *microwave heating* are those possessing polar molecules—of which water is the most important example being present in practically all foods. The configuration of the electric charges in these molecules form electric dipoles which can be rotated into alignment by an applied electrical field and the work done in overcoming the internal resistance of the dipole moment causes a loss in electromagnetic energy which appears as heat. Although the heat generated over each AC cycle is small, this is greatly amplified by microwaves alternating at high frequencies—2450 million times each second.

The energy conversion or heating power per unit volume of a food material (W/m³) can be expressed in fairly precise terms and will depend on the value of the applied electric field (V/m²), the frequency of the waves (Hz), the dielectric constant of the material at that frequency and the loss tangent. For a particular oven condition only the last two parameters will vary and their product is described as the loss factor. It follows that the more a material absorbs microwaves the smaller will be the penetration. Absorption is increased with shorter wavelengths (2450 M.Hz) but

longer waves (915 M.Hz) penetrate to a greater depth—although their heating effects tend to be more irregular. Rise in temperature of a material being heated will also vary according to its specific heat and density and food products of a mixed composition may be difficult to heat uniformly. Since microwaves are much more readily absorbed by water than dry organic polymers, this property can be used in the drying of food products.

Drying and heating processes can also be carried out with *dielectric heating* apparatus in which the oscillation of molecular dipoles is produced by an alternating electrical field between two plate capacitors. Such equipment tends to be bulky and is generally limited to line processing of food and other products which are of regular composition and uniform thickness.

In contrast to the direct heating of food and water, an oscillating magnetic field can also be used to heat the vessels in which food is placed—by a process known as *induction heating*. In this case, heating results from the resistance of the material to rapidly changing eddy currents induced in it by an induction coil through which an alternating current is flowing. Steel and iron based vessels are most suitable for this purpose, having sufficient inherent resistance to give a full range of cooking heats. On the other hand the resistance of glass and ceramic materials is so high that they are unaffected by the current flow and can be used as cool surfaces on which the cooking takes place.

Cooking with microwaves

In penetrating into a food material there is a gradual decrease in energy and a uniform food thickness of 20–25 mm, optimum (¾–1″), is normally adopted to ensure even heating throughout. Wave penetration into larger masses may be improved by indentation or by creating air spaces within the material.

Other factors which influence cooking times are: the initial temperature of the food (lower temperature—longer time), the density of the food material and the quantity of food cooked in the same batch (greater density and quantity—longer times). Irregularity of cooking may arise from the shape of the food or its variable composition, from the containers or from defects in the apparatus. Typical cooking times for most items of raw food range from 45–60 seconds.

The cooking process by microwaves is essentially one of penetration heating of the whole mass compared with other processes which initially heat the outside. Hence in microwave cooking there is little difference in texture or flavour between the outer layers and the interior and, to create this contrast, a number of supplementary processes may be used, eg:
· Steaks, etc may be initially seared on a grill or griddle.
· Pastries may be subsequently crisped off in an infra-red oven.
· The microwave oven may incorporate infra-red or forced convection heating.

Reheating of pre-cooked frozen food

One of the main uses for microwave ovens is in reheating food which has been fully or partly precooked. However, the ice crystals in frozen food, which are not homogeneous, have a much lower absorbency rate than water and tend to form cold spots whilst other areas become overheated and dehydrated. Alternative ways of overcoming this problem include:

(a) Defrosting prior to microwave heating.

(b) Exposure to microwaves for a short period followed by standing to allow heat distribution prior to further heating.

(c) Pulses of microwave energy interspaced with thawing periods.

Food containers

Suitable materials for the containers used in microwave cooking include:

Material	Comments
China and glass	Thick containers tend to absorb a high proportion of the energy
High-density polyethylene	Temperature range 15·5 to 121°C (60–250°F). Comparatively expensive.
Polypropolene	−7 to 143°C (20–290°F)
Paper laminated with plastic surfaces	Increasingly used for disposable containers

Materials which are unsuitable for the containers used in microwave cooking include:

Material	Comments
Waxed paper	Wax absorbs microwaves and melts
Polystyrene	Starts to soften and distort at 80–90°C. May be treated with heat-resistant laquer
Metals	Reflect the waves preventing penetration and producing uneven heating effects

Engineering features

Compared with conventional methods of cooking the power requirements for microwave ovens are small and most operate with an electrical loading of 2·5 kW single phase supply. There are, basically, three components:

(a) *The supply unit* which transforms and rectifies the mains voltage.

(b) *The magnetron* generates very high frequency electromagnetic waves which are then beamed into the oven.

(c) *The oven* itself incorporates a slowly rotating agitator which has metal reflecting blades to disperse the waves over the space and the metal enclosure of the oven is designed to ensure even heating.

Whilst only about half of the electrical energy supplied is transmitted, most of the microwave energy in an oven is absorbed and the overall efficiency of the equipment is high. The performance does, however, greatly depend on the correct distribution of waves by multiple reflection and defects in the oven or the insertion of metal objects can set up standing wave patterns and wave interferences which cause irregular heating, arcing and possible damage to the magnetron.

To ensure safety, doors are fitted with metal perforated panels, interlock devices which switch off the power automatically when the door is opened and grooved seals around the edges. The US Department of Health, Education and Welfare specifies that leakages from microwave apparatus in normal use must not exceed 5 milliwatt/cm² (50 W/m²) measured 50 mm (2 in) from the surface whilst the standard in Britain to comply with the 'Safety precautions relating to intense radio frequency radiation',

issued by the Post Office is, at the present time, an upper limit of 10 milliwatt/cm² (100 W/m²) for leakage measured 50 mm from the surface.

Microwave ovens require frequent servicing and testing to check performance and leakage—particularly around the doors. Although the initial cost and subsequent maintenance and depreciation charges are high, microwave ovens have a wide range of uses for fast reheating of prepared foods to short order, in vending machines, snack service and mobile units. It would, generally, be uneconomic to consider the microwave as a substitute for other methods of cooking but it may be a useful supplement in certain types of operation.

Infra-red oven

3.13 Cooking processes in infra-red and quartz ovens rely primarily on intense radiation of infra-red waves, mainly in the waveband 1·5 to 5·0 μm, which are emitted by heating elements at temperatures of about 790°C (1450°F) The heaters are usually coiled tungsten filaments enclosed in quartz tubes of $\frac{1}{2}$ to 1 kW loading and these are fitted in rows of six or more between food compartments. This allows radiant heat to be emitted directly on the food below and to the shelves and trays above in order to provide indirect heating by conduction and hot air convection. To prevent the surface of food overheating, cooling air is drawn by fan across the compartment and some models—such as the 'Recon plus'—incorporate refrigeration facilities which also permits dual use of the oven for temporary cold storage.

Temperature regulation is, therefore, provided by air flow and by varying the intensity of heating over the shelves giving typical ranges of:

air temperature 95 to 285°C (200 to 500°F)

shelf temperature 120 to 325°C (245 to 625°F).

The advantages of the infra-red oven lie in the speed at which high temperatures can be attained, enabling the oven to be brought into use quickly; high capacities and versatility in the range of cooking processes which are possible—roasting, grilling, poaching, baking, reheating, etc—by adjustment of the shelf and air temperatures. Infra-red ovens are available as bench or stand mounted models and the larger floor units are designed to allow direct loading with food trolleys.

Steaming ovens

3.14 The supply of steam may be provided from a separate generator or boiler and regulated by valve or be generated within the appliance. The temperature of the steam is determined by its pressure and steam ovens may be grouped into:

(a) atmospheric pressure type (100°C);

(b) semi-pressure type operating automatically at a slightly higher pressure of 3·45 k N/m² ($\frac{1}{2}$ lb/sq inch) giving temperatures of about 102°C (215°F);

(c) pressure steamers in which high pressures of the order 34·48 kN/m² (5 lb/sq inch) are used with temperatures of 108°C (227°F) enabling rapid heating and cooking of food.

The water level in the reservoir supplying steam is normally regulated by a float valve and the rate of steam generation is controlled by thermostat. Capacities of steam ovens range from 0·08 to 0·17 m³ (3 to 10 cubic ft) with loadings of approximately 3 to 12 kW (1 kW per cubic foot).

The box-type oven is the most common and is fitted with baskets and shelves on runners. An alternative design—

12
Legumier boiling pan. Oliver Toms Ltd.
Showing the interior and arrangement of baskets in a boiling pan for green vegetables.

the multideck steamer—is made up from a series of circular pans arranged in a tier in which each pan can be swivelled sideways for access in loading and unloading. Pressure steamers range from small counter models suitable for 100 meals operation to larger 2–3 compartment models with integral steam generating equipment and have loadings from 12 to 24 kW. A safety device must be fitted to ensure that the door cannot be opened whilst the steam cock is turned on.

High-pressure steamers are used extensively for cooking raw and prepared frozen vegetables, for steaming fish, meat and poultry, and cooking puddings. The 'Jet Cooker' is a small pressure cooker operating at higher pressures (103 kN/m^2 or 15 lbs/sq inch) used specifically for fast heating of frozen foods.

Typical dimensions of atmospheric type steaming oven

Capacity	Shelves	Internal w × d	External dimensions w × d × h	Loading
6 cu ft	6	17″ × 21″	30″ × 33″ × 60″	6 kW
0·17 m³		450 × 530 mm	770 × 840 × 1520 mm	

Approximately $0{\cdot}0077 \text{ m}^2$ of shelf area (12 sq ins) is required per meal or, alternatively, steam oven capacities may be calculated from:

Root vegetables 320–380 kg/m³ (20–24 lb/cu ft)
Fish   80 kg/m³ (5 lb/cu ft)
Puddings   320 kg/m³ (20 lb/cu ft)

13
The Plessey Co. Ltd., Staff Catering facilities. Equipment by Oliver Toms.
Examples of steam ovens.

14

Stotts of Oldham.
LASMEC Mark 2 boiling table.

15

Stotts of Oldham
LASMEC Mark 2 boiling pan.

4 BOILING EQUIPMENT

Boiling tables

4.01 The space required for boiling generally exceeds the top areas available on ranges and supplementary boiling tables may be provided to extend these areas.

Boiling and simmering burners and plates are available in various sizes and combinations or in the form of solid tops. The table is supported on a stand which usually incorporates storage space for pans and pots.

Recent developments in cook-freeze systems, necessitating the use of convection and similar high-speed ovens, has also led to a resurgence in the use of separate boiling tables for supplementary items such as reconstituted soups and 'Boil in the bag' products.

4.02 Loadings vary from 6·5 to 30·5 kW according to the number of individual boiling plates required.

Typical sizes

External dimensions w × d × h	Loading
48″ × 30″ × 34″ 1220 × 760 × 860 mm	12·4 kW
66″ × 30″ × 34″ 1680 × 760 × 860 mm	21·2 kW
84″ × 30″ × 34″ 2130 × 760 × 860 mm	30·2 kW

Boiling tables should comply with BS4167 Part 2: 1968, for electrically-heated catering equipment, which includes performance tests with both hot and cold starting, and BS2512 Part 3: 1963, for gas boiler burners. In addition to meeting thermal efficiency requirements gas burners must satisfy combustion sampling tests.

About 0·013 m² (20 sq ins) of boiling top area per meal is suitable for all boiling, shallow frying, etc operations. Where boiling pans are used, a 90 litre (20 gallon) boiling pan has a similar output and size to a boiling table of 0·6 m² (6 sq ft) area.

16

Equipment by Zoppas Ltd.
An example of a pressure jacket boiling pan. Water is supplied to the pan through the swivel arm on the left.

Boiling pans

4.03 The maximum size of saucepan for convenient handling is about 14 litres (3 gallons) and, for larger quantities, purposely designed equipment is required. Boiling pans are jacketed containers heated directly by gas or electricity or—more commonly—indirectly by air, water or steam to allow boiling of vegetables or cooking of thick liquids without danger of sticking or burning. The rate of heating can be regulated from vigorous boiling to gentle simmering. In recent models, the jacketed space is evacuated and can be filled with steam from a small heated reservoir giving very sensitive temperature control. The boiling pans in a large installation may be supplied by steam from a central boiler or generator.

Boiling pans are supplied with water from a direct connection or through a swivel arm arrangement. The pan may be emptied through a stopcock or through a pouring lip by tilting on pivots, in each case over a channel or waste outlet, to facilitate washing out. A wire basket, which may be suspended on a swivel crane, is used for removing vegetables. To allow easy access for stirring or cleaning, the rim should not be above 1000 mm high and lids are hinged and usually counterbalanced. Electric stirring equipment may also be incorporated.

Capacities range from 45 litres (10 gallons) up to 455 litres (100 gallons) but the most common range is from 45 to 137 litres (10 to 30 gallons) with ratings of 6 to 13·5 kW representing about 0·1 kW per litre capacity (0·5 kW per gallon).

Most boiling pans are cylindrical in shape but rectangular units based on modular sizes of 900 × 900 × 870 mm for grouping with other cooking units are now available.

The *tilting kettle* is a small compact boiling pan of 41 litres (9 gallon) capacity having a steam jacket heated by an immersion heater (7·5 kW).

4.04 To comply with BS4167 Part 9: 1969, 'Electrically-heated catering equipment', boiling pans should satisfy the following tests:

Heating up

Litres capacity	Time (minutes)
Up to 100	60
Up to 100–150	70
Over 150	80

Draining

Up to 65	5
Over 65	Rate of 15 litres/min

BS2512 Part 7: 1963, lays down standards for the heating up of gas-fired boiling pans.

Typical dimensions

Capacity	External dimensions w × d × h	Loading kW
10 gal 45 litres	36″ × 39″ × 31″ 910 × 990 × 790 mm	7·0
20 gal 90 litres	41″ × 44″ × 33″ 1040 × 1120 × 840 mm	11·0
30 gal 135 litres	44″ × 49″ × 34″ 1190 × 1240 × 860 mm	14·2
40 gal 180 litres	47″ × 51″ × 36″ 1190 × 1300 × 910 mm	16·5
Tilting kettle 9 gal 40 litres	30″ × 20″ × 34″ 760 × 510 × 860 mm	7·5

The output of boiling equipment will depend on the type of material cooked, the portion sizes and on the extent of re-use of the equipment during the main meal period. As a guide, a 45 litre (10 gallon) boiling pan will, on average, give the following portions: potatoes or root vegetables (100–150 meals), bulky green vegetables (40–80), soups

(150–200), custards (400–500), gravies, garnishes or sauces (400–600), porridge (250–350).

For general purposes 1 litre of boiling capacity is adequate for 1·5 to 2·0 meals.

Stockpot stand

4.05 This is a small boiling table having one high-capacity burner or element, on a stand 450–600 mm (18–24″) high which is used exclusively for heating a large vessel for soup or stock production.

5 FRYING EQUIPMENT

5.01 In processes of frying, food is heated either partially

17

Stotts of Oldham

LASMEC Mark 2 Fryer with storage compartment below and a new slide over device for transfer of baskets from hob to pan and back.

18

Stotts of Oldham.

Deep fat fryer with double compartment.

19
The Plessey Co. Ltd. Equipment by Oliver Toms.
Deep fat fryers installed in a modern kitchen of a factory canteen.

20
Equipment by Zoppas Ltd.
The Bratt pan has a wide variety of uses and is emptied by tilting.

21
Zoppas Ltd.
A gas fired fry-top or griddle plate on stand which is also available as a twin unit. With the adoption of module dimensions, this unit can be combined with an oven base.

or fully immersed in fat at temperatures between 150 and 200°C (300 to 400°F).

Shallow fat frying is carried out in a pan or on a fixed or mobile frying surface known as a griddle. The frying process is a rapid one and can be used repeatedly during the meal period and to supply food to order.

For deep fat frying, food is immersed in 100 to 150 mm (4 to 6″) depth of fat. Although portable vessels can be used, purposely designed units are almost always installed because of the risk of fire and the need to confine oil splashing and fumes.

5.02 Standards for deep fat fryers

BS	Type	Time to raise oil temperature through 153°C (300°F)
4167 : Part 4 1970	Electric heated immersion type	20 mins
	External heated	35 mins
2512 : Part 5 1963	Gas heated	30 mins

In addition, the cooking time for a standard batch of chipped potatoes must not exceed 10 minutes.

In the case of griddles, BS4167: Part 8: 1969, specifies that an electrically heated plate must be uniformly heated up to a temperature of at least 220°C with no variation over the surfaces greater than 15°C. For gas burning appliances, BS2512 requires a griddle plate to attain a temperature rise of 171°C (340°F) within 20 minutes.

Deep fat fryers must be provided with wire trays and stands for draining off fat. Modern designs incorporate a cool zone, in which sediment can collect without charring, and provision for draining off the fat. Rapid heat recovery and sensitive thermostat controls are important operating features. Fumes may be confined by means of a lid or removed through extract ducting, the latter being fitted with grease filters. In addition, side and back panels are desirable to confine splashing of oil during use.

Typical dimensions

	w × d × h	Loading kW
Single unit	36″ × 32″ × 35″ 910 × 810 × 880 mm	15·8
Double unit	72″ × 32″ × 35″ 1830 × 810 × 880 mm	31·5

The output of a single unit is generally in the order of 18·27 kg (40–60 lb) chipped potatoes/hour.

Shallow tilting frypans (Bratt pans)

5.03 This appliance is widely used on the Continent and is becoming increasingly popular in the UK for multi-purpose use in deep or shallow frying, boiling, stewing or braising. The pan is square or rectangular 150 to 250 mm (6 to 10″) deep fitted with heating elements in the base and mounted on trunnions for tilting to empty.

Typical dimensions

Overall dimensions w × d × h	Loading kW
46″ × 32″ × 36″ 1180 × 820 × 930 mm	12

6 GRILLING EQUIPMENT

6.01 The process of grilling is reliant on radiant heat obtained from an intensive source such as red hot tiles, plates or wires or incandescent charcoal. Heating may be applied from above (salamandering), below or on both sides as in toasting. The area need not be enclosed and is generally mounted at a convenient height between shoulder and bench level (900 to 1400 mm). Grillers may also be incorporated under the tops of ranges.

Typical sizes

Grilling area	Overall dimensions	Loading kW
16″ × 15″ × 9″ 410 × 380 × 230 mm	24″ × 20″ × 20″ 610 × 510 × 510 mm	4
22″ × 15″ × 9″ 560 × 380 × 230 mm	30″ × 20″ × 20″ 760 × 510 × 510 mm	5
30″ × 15″ × 9″ 760 × 380 × 230 mm	33″ × 22″ × 20″ 840 × 560 × 510 mm	7

6.02 The area generally required for grilling is approximately 0·001 m²/meal (1·5 sq ins) but is dependent on the size of dishes and the extent to which grilled items feature in the menu.

Grillers and toasters should comply with BS4167: Part 3: 1969, for electrically heated catering equipment which stipulates that the time taken to reach operating temperature should not exceed 10 minutes. In the case of gas

22

Griller units. Glynwed Foundries Ltd.
An example of a grill unit on floor stand.

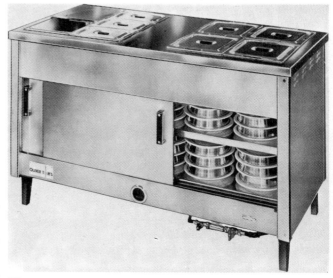

23

Hot cupboard. Oliver Toms Ltd.
A rear view of a counter hot cupboard unit with a heated bain-marie top. These units may also be used unheated for cold dishes.

24

Equipment by Zoppas Ltd.
The open bain-marie is used in the kitchen for holding containers of food at a regulated temperature.

fired equipment, a simple toasting test is used to check the intensity and uniformity of the grill heat.

7 HOLDING UNITS

Hot cupboard

7.01 Cabinets used to keep food warm and to heat receptacles and plates prior to service are collectively described as hot cupboards. The internal temperature is maintained at about 76 to 88°C (170 to 190°F) to avoid damage to crockery and excessive drying of food. Heat may be applied to the bottom, sides or shelves to meet the following standards:

Specification	Temperature rise	Time
BS4167 : Pt 11 : 1970 (Electric heated)	65°C (Internal temperature variations less than 10°C)	45 mins
BS2512 : Pt 10 : 1963 (Gas heated)	120°F above room temperature	45 mins

The standard hot cupboard has sliding doors on one side only but 'pass-through' units, with doors on opposite sides, are used between the kitchen and servery. Mobile units are increasingly used for convenient handling, eg:
(a) Heated lowerators for plates.
(b) Mobile trolleys with hot and cold compartments. Cupboards in the servery and kitchen may also be refrigerated for storage of cold items.

Bains-marie

7.02 This equipment usually occupies the top of the hot cupboard, forming an integral unit, but may be separate.

It consists of a heated well into which vessels containing cooked food are placed ready for service. The well may be 'open' or have a frame for fitted vessels and may be filled with heated water or warmed air, the temperature of which is regulated by thermostat. Vessels should be based on Gastro-norm sizes to facilitate easy interchange and other standards for bains-marie are contained in BS4167: Part 12: 1971 (electrically heated equipment) and BS2512: Part 10: 1963 (gas heated equipment).

Similar arrangements are used for refrigerated cabinets and wells or dole plates which are used to serve chilled yoghurt and cream dishes and for salads. The refrigerator unit is normally housed under the counter as a purposely designed fitting.

Typical dimensions for hot cupboards and other related counter cabinets range from 600 to 900 mm (2′ 0″ to 3′ 0″) counter depth and, in width, from 600 to 2400 mm (2′ 0″ to 8′ 0″). Most units are now produced in modular sizes to allow easy interchange and combination of different cabinets to form continuous counters. The standard height of a serving counter is usually between 865 and 900 mm (2′ 10″ and 3′ 0″) and the counter legs are normally adjustable to allow for variations in floor levels during assembly.

Cabinet type hot cupboards are up to 1700 mm (5′ 6″) high and are used for reserve storage behind the counter and in situations, such as for banquets, where there is an intensive short period of service. A variation of the cabinet type of cupboard has doors in both the front and rear faces and can be mounted in the wall between the kitchen and the servery as a 'pass-through' unit. Meals placed in the cabinet from the kitchen are stored there until required in the servery. 'Pass-through' cabinets may be heated or refrigerated, have large or several small and separate compartments and may have glass doors to serve as a display case for the food.

In estimating hot cupboard requirements, calculations may be based on a standard 1200 mm (4′ 0″) cupboard which will hold about 300 plates—ie equal to 150 two-course meals.

8 BEVERAGE-MAKING EQUIPMENT

8.01 Equipment for making beverages includes various types of water boilers, urns and café sets and vending machines. Water boilers may be of the bulk type for producing large quantities of boiling water at a particular time such as in a short tea interval, or of the instantaneous type for a smaller but more continuous supply. The latter operate automatically by expansion of water on boiling or by the pressure generated during the formation of steam.

8.02 The capacity of boilers is normally quoted in litres (gallons) or litres/hour (pints/hour) output and, as an approximate allowance, 4 to 5 cups per litre (18–20 cups/gallon) may be assumed.

Bulk water heaters should comply with BS4167: Part 6: 1969, for electrically-heated catering equipment which requires heating up times from 21°C to 100°C as follows:

Capacity	Time
litres	minutes
Up to 90	60
91 to 135	80
Over 135	90

BS2512: Parts 8 and 9, relate to gas heated water boiling equipment and contain specific provisions for safety.

Insulated urns are used in conjunction with water boilers and are frequently fitted on tea service trolleys.

The combination of instantaneous boilers with milk and coffee urns is used in café sets for mounting on counters. Beverage-vending machines also incorporate instantaneous water heaters together with reservoirs and feeding devices for milk, coffee and tea in powdered form.

9 PAN WASHING FACILITIES

9.01 Special facilities for washing the pots and pans used in the kitchen and servery are generally necessary where over 200 to 300 meals per day are produced and this is normally a manual process requiring deep sinks—preferably double sinks with separate washing and rinsing/sterilizing bowls. The size of sink appropriate will be determined by the size of utensils used in the kitchen, bain-marie containers, etc and the standard range is from 750 × 500 × 380 mm deep (30″ × 20″ × 15″) to 1500 × 750 × 600 mm deep (60″ × 30″ × 24″) with rim heights normally fixed 865 mm (34″) above floor level. With a large sink capacity it may be necessary to provide local heating to maintain a suitable water temperature.

Draining boards must be provided on both sides of the bowl to receive dirty utensils and allow drainage following rinsing. Some splashing is unavoidable and the area around the wash-up area must be tiled or protected by an impervious splashback. Sink outlets and overflows must be easily accessible and, where possible, removable for cleaning.

Mechanised pot washing facilities are available in the form of special wash-up machines and rotary pan scrubbers, the latter being installed for use with sinks.

9.02 The pan wash should be sited conveniently near both the cooking area and servery and, in smaller establishments, it is an advantage to locate the pan washing sink immediately adjacent to the main wash-up area so that it can be used to supplement the latter, for example, if

25

The near view of a beverage counter showing the under counter boiler and cup trays.
Beverage-making equipment. Oliver Toms Ltd.

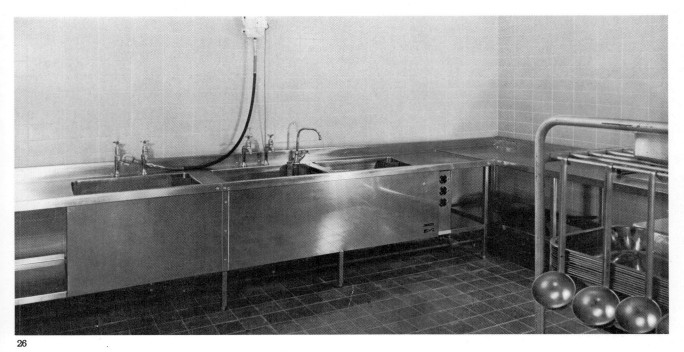

26

Staff Catering facilities, British Steel Corporation. Equipment by Stotts of Oldham.
The pan wash-up area with a triple sink unit. A pan scourer is fitted on the adjacent wall.

the wash-up machine is out of action. Pan storage racks are sited nearby and, to minimize handling, mobile racks are usually more convenient than fixtures.

Pan washing facilities are not normally required in a finishing kitchen in which food is mainly supplied ready prepared. In general, the trend in catering is towards the use of disposable containers—such as light-weight aluminium trays—in order to reduce labour in cleaning. At the other extreme of scale, more use is being made of small fixed appliances, such as boiling kettles and brat pans, instead of portable pans.

10 LAYOUT OF COOKING EQUIPMENT

Island grouping

10.01 Central island grouping of cooking appliances is generally practicable (a) where the least dimension of the kitchen is about 6·5 m (21′ 0″) and (b) when more than 100–150 main meals are prepared at any one time. The positioning of the cooking equipment must take into account the flow lines of food through the kitchen, as illustrated, with boiling and steaming appliances associated mainly with the vegetable preparation area whilst ranges and ovens are positioned near the meat and pastry preparation. Because of their repeated use during the meal period, deep fat fryers and grillers are best arranged at one end of the island or line conveniently near the servery to minimize travelling and, in catering for extensive call order service, this equipment may be grouped to form a separate section adjacent to the servery.

10.02 If the width of the kitchen is 9·5 m (31′ 0″) or more and the meal output in excess of, say, 400 to 500 main meals per day, travel distance and congestion of movement around the island site can be reduced by separation of the 'wet' equipment, ie steaming and boiling appliances used mainly for vegetable cooking from the ranges, ovens, grillers, etc comprising the 'dry equipment' for meat and pastry. Some overlap, such as the use of steamers for puddings and boiling pans for custards and other sweets, is unavoidable but this can be minimized by careful location of those units which are intended for multiple use.

With island grouping the appliances are served by central gas, electricity and water services; an extraction hood is usually positioned over the island area to confine and draw off steam and fumes and a grating covered channel is often provided around the equipment for spillage and drainage.

To facilitate the transfer of food to and from the cooking equipment, tables should be provided (a) between islands and (b) between the cooking island(s) and servery, the latter tables also being used for plating up meals.

27

Employee catering facilities, BOAC maintenance and service hangar. Equipment by Glynwed Foundries Ltd.
Falcon double oven range with open burners and solid top, steamers, fryers, griddle plate and boiling plate and boiling pans comprising a central island grouping. Drainage is through individual waste pipes.

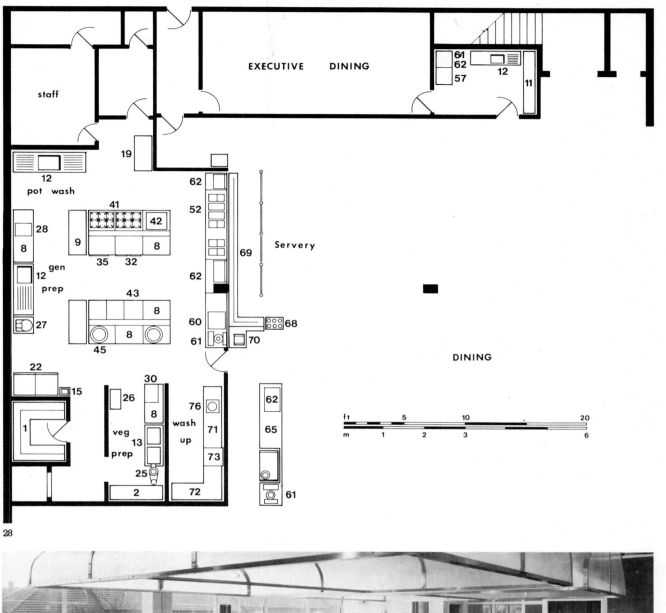

28

29

Staff catering facilities, David Brown Ltd. Equipment by Stotts of Oldham.

Example of two Module 36 suites of equipment arranged in island groupings.

30

Suite of 5 LASMEC boiling pans backing on to 3 three-tier steaming ovens. At the left is a mobile sink.

31

3 three-tier LASMEC steaming ovens.

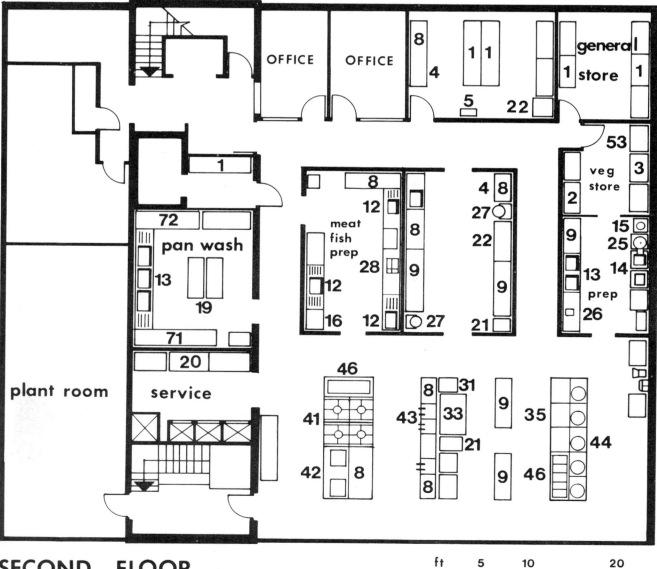

SECOND FLOOR

32

Staff Catering facilities, Special Steels Division, British Steel Corporation. Equipment by Stotts of Oldham.
Catering equipment worth more than £30,000 installed in the kitchen and serveries of a new three-storey dining block.

33
Stotts of Oldham.
A call order counter unit.

34
Back-bar equipment. Adams and Son Ltd.
Typical examples of back-bar equipment from the 'Barline'
range including a griddle plate, bain-marie and deep fat
fryers all to module dimensions.

Wall siting

10.03 Positioning of cooking appliances against walls is most suited to small kitchens particularly where the amount of food preparation is reduced to a minimum. With wall grouping there is a need to limit travel distances between work areas and these are usually arranged on each side of an aisle.

11 BACK-BAR UNITS

11.01 The tendency towards quick meal service, together with the need for economy in kitchen space, has led to the development of small back-bar units which can be mounted immediately behind the serving area to provide visual cooking. The units are usually mounted on top of cupboards, etc and must be manufactured to a standard module size for making up an appropriate group. Module dimensions recently adopted by one manufacturer—which are typical of the unit sizes—are 350×500 mm, 500×500 mm and 700×500 mm.

Examples of equipment used in back-bar catering are deep fat fryers, shallow fat fryers (80 mm deep), grillers with or without griddle plates or boiling rings, bains-marie, convection ovens and microwave ovens.

Standard units are also used for the understructure and include heated, unheated and chilled cupboards, warming drawers, chip scuttles, refuse chutes and open type shelving.

12 ACCELERATED COOKING

12.01 With increasing acceptance of frozen and chilled prepared food in catering, the trend is towards the use of fast reheating and end cooking equipment. Such facilities are generally required in small commercial

35
Staff Catering, Kodak Head Office. Equipment by G. F. E.
Bartlett and Son, Ltd.
A general view of a kitchen installed late 1971 which serves up
to 800 meals per day in a restaurant having flexible self service,

waitress service and snack bar sections which can be adjusted
in seating to meet daily requirements.
The equipment is grouped into islands, separated by tables, and
is arranged so that the units are at a convenient working height.

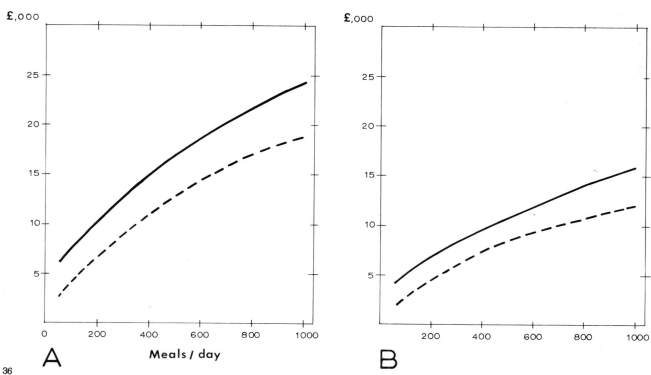

Comparisons of capital costs of buildings and equipment for:
A—Conventional kitchens.
B—Finishing kitchens using mainly prepared frozen and
chilled foods. (Based on 1972 prices.)

Staff catering facilities, The Plessey Co. Ltd., Ilford. Equipment
by Oliver Toms Ltd.
A range of modern convection ovens in which forced-air
circulation is used within the oven space to ensure even heat
distribution.

38

Recon Plus. Foster Refrigeration Co. Ltd.
An illustration of the bench-mounted model of the Recon Plus equipment for fast reheating of chilled and frozen food using high intensity infra-red and convection heat.

restaurants where kitchen space is restricted and for the finishing kitchens of large catering organizations which enable the preparation and primary cooking of food to be economically grouped into central kitchens or commissaries.

The range of cooking equipment used for this purpose includes:

Microwave oven

12.02 Speed of reheating or cooking will be affected by several factors—density, thickness, shape, quantity and initial temperature of the food and the type of containers —but typical timetables are:

Defrosted frozen foods   15–60 seconds.
Cooking items of raw food   45–60 seconds.

Water has a higher absorbency rate than ice and direct heating of frozen food by microwaves may result in uneven temperatures (cold spots). To allow for the delay during absorption of latent heat, frozen food may be heated in stages either by initially defrosting or by the use of pulsometer microwave equipment. Microwave heating may also be combined with forced convection of hot air or radiant heat to provide surface browning.

Forced convection ovens

12.03 The convection oven may be used for prime cooking, giving reductions of up to 40 per cent in time compared with traditional ovens, or in the finishing stage. Independent shelving arrangements in the form of trolley racks can be pre-loaded with frozen food to allow quick loading and maximum use of the oven. End cooking times for frozen food are normally based on a cycle of 25 minutes.

High-pressure steam cookers

12.04 This equipment is particularly suitable for end cooking of frozen vegetables, puddings, stews and other items which require a hot moist atmosphere. The 'Jet' cooker operating at higher pressures (103 kN/m^2 or 15 lb/ins^2) with 'dry' steam is used for reheating a wide variety of frozen foods where weight loss is an important consideration.

High-speed infra-red ovens

12.05 Intense radiant and infra-red heat is used to cook and reconstitute food and also to heat the shelves on which the food rests. At the same time, cooling air is drawn across the food to prevent overheating of the surfaces and reduce loss of moisture and flavour by dehydration. A variation of this equipment includes freezing facilities for storage of frozen food prior to use of the equipment. Frozen food can be reconstituted direct from −18°C (0°F) to serving temperature in the following times:

60 minutes—76 mm (3″) thick
20 minutes—25 mm (1″) thick.

High-pressure deep fat frying

12.06 This is a new development in which food is cooked in fat or oil under pressure with the oil temperature controlled by thermostat. As a result of the surrounding pressure, the moisture in the food is able to rise to higher boiling temperatures, giving rapid cooking in the centre, whilst the outside is crisped by contact with the hot oil.

Finishing kitchens for pre-cooked frozen meals:

Area	Equipment		Meals served per day—based on main meal period						
			50	100	200	400	600	800	1000
Goods entry	Scales capacity	lbs	28	28	56	56	56	56	56
		kg	12·5	12·5	25·5	25·5	25·5	25·5	25·5
	Trolleys for frozen meal trays and general use		2	2	3	4	5	6	7
Cold stores	Deep freeze room	ft^3	44	88	175	350	525	700	875
		m^3	1·3	2·5	5·0	10·0	15·0	20·0	22·0
	(based on 7 day stock)								
	Normal cold room	ft^3	12	18	30	42	54	66	78
		m^3	0·3	0·5	0·9	1·2	1·5	1·9	2·2
	(based on daily delivery of dairy produce, otherwise 3 deliveries per week)								
Dry stores	Shelving—width 450 mm (18″) length	ft	20	30	50	70	90	110	130
		m	6·1	9·1	15·2	21·3	27·4	33·5	39·6
	(for canned and dried items, 3 deliveries per week)								

Area	Equipment		Meals served per day—based on main meal period						
			50	100	200	400	600	800	1000
Kitchen	Convection oven capacity	ft³	3·25	6·5	13	26	39	52	65
		m³	0·09	0·18	0·37	1·02	1·10	1·47	1·84

(based on reheating all frozen meals in 1 hour, ie 2 reheatings of average 30 minutes each)

Boiling tank or
pressure steamer
(for 'boil-in-the-bag' food where this is to be used. Provision depends on type of equipment, eg rotating boiling tank 1000 mm (40'') diameter produces a total of 120 bags/hour in 4 reheatings of approximately 15 minutes each)

	Microwave oven 2 kilowatt units		1	1	1	1	2	2	3

(depends on number of snacks required and availability of alternative call-order equipment. Based on 30 second cycle of reheating with 4 snack items/loading)

Supplementary equipment

	Griller	ft²	2	2	3	4	6	8	10
		m²	0·2	0·2	0·3	0·4	0·6	0·7	0·9

(for call order grills and toast. Based on surface area)

	Griddle	ft²	2	3	4	5	7	9	11
		m²	0·2	0·3	0·4	0·5	0·7	0·8	1·0

(for snack catering, particularly at breakfast)

	Fryer	lbs/hr	25	50	100	200	300	400	500
		kg/hr	10	25	45	90	135	180	225

(for 'flashing off' blanched frozen meals. Based on 15 minutes use before and 15 minutes during meal period)

	Boiling rings	No	2	2	3	4	5	6	7

(for reheating of canned vegetables, soups, etc)

Wash-up (crockery, cutlery, etc)	Wash-sterilizing unit length for dishwashing	ft	9' 0''	11' 0''	12' 0''				
		m	2·7	3·4	3·7				
	Capacity of machine	Pieces/hr			1200	2400	3600	4800	6000
	Sink for serving dishes, etc (length)	ins	24	24	30	36	42	48	48
		mm	600	600	750	900	1050	1200	1200
	Burnishing machine		—	—	—	hand	hand	hand	hand
	Waste disposal units		1	1	1	1	2	2	2

(based on 550 W (0·75 hp) machines assuming part refuse collection. For complete waste disposal 2230 W (3 hp) units employed)

Source : Paper by D. J. Cottam given to Catering Teachers Association Annual Conference Wolverhampton, October 1969.   Based on equipment by Stotts of Oldham.

5 CONSTRUCTION AND SERVICES

1 CONSTRUCTION OF KITCHENS

Ceiling heights

1.01 The taller the ceiling the greater the difficulties and costs of cleaning and redecoration, the problems of access to services and the noise from reverberation. On the other hand, a low ceiling is liable to create a sense of oppression, to be stained and to increase difficulties of ventilation and light distribution. Typical ceiling heights to module dimensions are:

3600 to 4200 mm (12′ to 14′) for large production kitchens;
3000 to 3600 mm (10′ to 12′) for small finishing kitchens;
2400 to 3000 mm (8′ to 10′) for stores, etc.

Controlling dimensions

1.02 Details of preferred sizes for building units are contained in BS4011:1966, 'Basic sizes for building components and assemblies'. With the view to rationalizing the variety of sizes of building components and to introduce modular dimensions into building plans, it is recommended that units should, as a first preference, be in increments of 300 mm with 100 mm as the second preference. For smaller dimensions up to a maximum of 300 mm, units of 50 mm and 25 mm are the third and fourth preferences respectively.

These preferences for sizes are embodied in BS4330:1968, 'Recommendations for the co-ordination of dimensions in building: Controlling dimensions' (metric units). Further information on metric dimensions in buildings is contained in the *A J Metric Handbook*.

Walls

The walls of a kitchen may be considered in two parts:

1.03 (a) *The lower part* up to a height of about 1800 mm (6′ 0″) must withstand frequent splashing and cleaning with water, grease, alkalis, acids and scouring agents and remain easy to clean. In addition, areas of the wall may be subject to scraping or impact and to uneven heating and cooling due to the proximity of appliances and pipes, etc.

Finishes which satisfy most of these requirements are glazed tiles—with acid resisting joints—or a hard gloss paint applied on a dense, smooth rendered surface. However, over a large area, a hard cement rendering is susceptible to cracking.

1.04 (b) *The upper part* of the walls is less liable to damage and should be constructed to prevent condensation and provide some degree of sound absorption. For an external

wall the thermal transmittance ('U' value) should not exceed 1.14 W/m^2 °C ($0.2 \text{ Btu/ft}^2\text{h}$ °F). If a porous absorbent lining or plaster finish is used, the surface must be vapour sealed with an impervious washable paint. In the interests of hygiene, light distribution and appearance, white or light colours are preferable.

Splashbacks

1.05 Areas of walls behind sinks and washbasins and behind stoves and grillers require special protection against water, steam, grease and heat. As alternatives to glazed tiles, special sheet materials such as stainless steel, enamelled steel or glass may be used for this purpose.

Partitions

1.06 Partitions are frequently used to provide a physical barrier to noise, view, steam, fumes, etc and to separate areas such as the chef's office. Where a partition is not required to carry weight, the construction may be based on a lightweight metal frame, covered by sheets of laminated plastic, stainless steel or anodized aluminium, or by hardboard which is sealed and faced with plastic film or ceramic tiles. Partitions separating the kitchen and servery combine functional purposes with decorative requirements. The screening to wash-up areas and offices in the kitchen is often constructed of transparent perspex or glass to facilitate supervision.

Where possible, partitions should be demountable to allow rearrangement and access for alterations.

Partition walls required to support wall-hung equipment and shelving must be formed from a heavy metal framework or be constructed with brickwork or concrete blocks suitably finished with hard, durable surfaces. The former may facilitate a certain amount of prefabrication work, particularly in locating and installing the engineering services.

Ceilings

1.07 The ceiling finish should not harbour dirt nor be liable to cracking or flaking but must be easy to clean and redecorate. To reduce risk of condensation, a ceiling and roof construction should provide thermal transmittance value of less than 0.97 W/m^2 °C ($0.17 \text{ Btu/ft}^2\text{h}$ °F), and to prevent interstitial condensation, the surface should be vapour sealed with an impervious paint film. Alternatively, a vapour seal may be incorporated in the construction and, in this event, the exposed finish may be absorbent provided the porous material is inert to moisture. Where possible, kitchen ceilings are also designed with a view to reducing noise but the acoustic treatment must not be affected by moisture nor add to fire hazard.

Canopies and extractors at ceiling level reduce the risk of steam drifting to other areas and condensing on surfaces which might become stained and damaged.

Floors

1.08 The floor of a kitchen should be easy to clean, able to withstand hard wear, water, grease, oil, acids, alkalis and cleaning agents and variations in temperature. At the same time it is desirable that the floor is not cold to the feet, nor excessively hard and noisy. Materials in common use are quarry tiles and mosaic tiles laid in impervious acid-resisting cement which meets most requirements except noise reduction and resilience. The floor temperature can be maintained by providing insulation or floor heating in the subfloor. Terrazzo and granolithic screeds incorporating carborundum and similar surface finishes may be used as alternatives.

To facilitate washing, all floors must be laid to falls (1 in 120 slope) to drainage outlets in the form of channels or gulleys which are covered by removable gratings. Drainage channels are frequently provided around islands of equipment to serve the duel purpose of floor drainage and of receiving drainage from the appliances following cleaning.

All junctions between floors and walls must be coved, preferably in the flooring material. To avoid risk of accidents there must be no sudden change in floor level within the kitchen area or its approaches.

Floor structures must also be capable of supporting the heavy weights of equipment which are superimposed and, because of the grouping of cooking appliances, etc it is not reasonable to average floor loading values. As a guide, typical laden weights of individual cooking appliances are in the order of 150–300 kg (3–6 cwt) per unit for medium duty equipment and 200–400 kg (4–8 cwt) or more for each heavy duty unit.

Doors and windows

1.09 Where possible doors and windows should be of simple design and flush with the adjacent interior surfaces. Windows should be positioned to provide uniform natural light over work areas, but with a sufficiently high sill height—minimum 1100 mm (3′ 7″)—to be clear of benches and equipment. To avoid risk of oil and steam condensation and difficulties of access for cleaning, windows should not be provided in walls adjacent to cooking appliances. All windows in the kitchen area, particularly roof lights, should be provided with drip channels and drainage outlets and, to ensure that moisture runs away down the glass, the angle of roof windows should be no less than 30° to the horizontal. Opening windows must be sufficiently high and, preferably, baffled to avoid draughts at working level.

1.10 If external doors open directly into the kitchen the inrush of cold air is liable to create problems of ventilation and burner control and access to the kitchen should be through a draught lobby or intervening area. The doors should be sufficiently wide for trolleys and equipment, and double doors with leaves of unequal width are usually most convenient. To reduce maintenance, doors should be fitted with finger plates and kickplates. Internal doors for the use of waiters and waitresses are usually

arranged for one-way traffic but where double swing doors are provided these must be fitted with a glass or transparent perspex window at eye level.

Precautions against insect entry are detailed in Chapter 2 (Hygiene in Food stores).

2 HYGIENE

2.01 Requirements for hygiene are contained in the Food and Drugs (General) Regulations, 1970. In relation to the construction of food premises, the Regulations require that any article or equipment with which food comes into contact must

(a) be capable of being thoroughly cleaned;

(b) be non-absorbent;

(c) prevent risk of food contamination.

This applies to the construction, materials, condition and state of repair of all work surfaces and equipment. The walls, floors, doors, windows, ceiling, woodwork and parts of the structure must also be in a condition which will enable them to be kept clean and prevent risk of infestation by rats, mice or insects (see Chapter 2).

2.02 Food rooms must not communicate directly with a sanitary convenience or sleeping place and, in planning the layout, suitable space must be allowed for removal and proper storage of waste food and refuse and the proper location of sanitary conveniences.

A clean and wholesome supply of hot and cold water must be provided together with sinks and other facilities for washing food and equipment. Separate wash-hand basins with appropriate washing and drying facilities, locker accommodation—for outdoor or other clothing and footwear—and first aid facilities must be provided for personnel handling food. Under the Offices, Shops and Railway Premises Act, 1963, and related Regulations, suitable and sufficient sanitary accommodation and other staff facilities must be available for persons employed in kitchens, restaurants and associated premises. Similar statutory provisions apply to factories in which food products are manufactured on a larger scale.

2.03 The Food Hygiene Regulations also require that suitable and sufficient means of lighting and ventilation must be provided in food rooms and stipulate the temperatures at which certain foods (those which are commonly involved in food poisoning) must be kept whilst awaiting serving, namely:

above 62·7°C (145°F)

or below 10°C (50°F).

Food hygiene requirements are enforced by the public health inspectors employed by Local Authorities and advice on these matters should be sought in the first instance.

3 LIGHTING

3.01 Good lighting is essential in a kitchen:

(a) to ensure cleanliness of the premises and equipment;

(b) in checking food for quality and extraneous matter;

(c) for skilled operations in preparing, decorating and serving food;

(d) for the comfort of employees allowing faster and more accurate working with reduced physical and mental strain and irritation;

(e) to reduce excessive contrasts and risk of accidents;

(f) in serving food to provide an attractive display.

3.02 The levels of illumination recommended under the Illuminating Engineering Society (IES) Code are as follows:

Situation	Minimum service illumination		Limiting Glare Index
	Lux	Lumens/ft²	
General area of kitchen	200	19	22
Food preparation sections	400	37	
Cooking section	400	37	
Washing-up area	400	37	
Serving counters	400	37	
Stores	200	19	25

These standards should be regarded as the minima and where a high degree of precision is involved, such as in cake decoration and inspection, an illumination of 600 lux is warranted. With older workers higher levels of lighting (50 to 100 per cent more) are usually necessary to compensate for less sharp vision.

3.03 Under standard sky conditions (5000 to 6000 lux or 500 lumens/sq ft) a daylight factor of at least 4 per cent is required over the kitchen area and up to 8 per cent over work areas. Unless there are windows on more than one side this is usually not attainable without creating strong contrasts and shadows. High-level windows and roof lights provide good light distribution but must be positioned or screened to avoid direct entry of sunlight and balanced by light entering through lower windows to prevent shadows forming around the walls. Sill heights are determined to a large extent by the height of work-tops (870 mm) and the need for some splashback protection.

Artificial lighting

3.04 Light fittings should be of the anti-corrosive type and preferably recessed flush with the ceiling. Fluorescent tubular lamps are almost universally installed because of their efficacy, low heat output, long life, and availability in a useful range of wattages and 'colour' variations. In addition, the lower concentration of brightness of a tubular lamp is less likely to produce glare. 40 mm diameter lamps 1200 mm or longer have a nominal life of 7500 hours, assuming they are switched on not more frequently than 3 hourly intervals.

For general kitchen use of BS colours, 'White' (100), 'Warmwhite' (100) and 'Daylight' (95) are most common because of their higher efficiences but these lights tend to emphasize yellow-green colours whilst being weak in red. For better colour rendering, as in inspection areas, 'Northlight' (65) and 'Natural' (75) are preferable whilst for display use 'Deluxe natural' (55) is particularly suitable because it emphasizes the red colours of meat, etc.

Light fittings are arranged to give a suitable general level of illumination over the whole area together with greater concentration over work areas. To avoid excessive ceiling shadows additional light fittings may be necessary around or within ventilator hoods.

3.05 Calculation of lighting requirements to give the desired level of illumination must take into account the proportion of light from the fittings which reaches the worktop level (coefficient of utilization) and the extent of obscuration due to dirt on the fittings themselves (maintenance factor). The coefficient of utilization depends on:
· the type and height of the light fitting
· the height and size of the room
· the reflectance values of the ceiling and walls

and for general diffused lighting in a kitchen is usually in the order 0·4 to 0·6. As an approximate guide, the lighting loads required to give required levels of illumination using diffusing light fittings are as follows:

Illumination	Total wattage required per square metre		
	Incandescent (200W)	Fluorescent	
		White (65W)	De luxe Warm White (65W)
200 lux	35	10	16
400 lux	70	20	32
600 lux	—	30	48

In addition to considering light intensities regard should be given to
(a) *Contrast*—sufficient directional variation of light to appreciate depth and texture.
(b) *Glare*—avoidance of excessively bright areas (exposed lights, and light reflecting surfaces) within field of vision whilst working. Matt paint and dull polished surfaces are preferable.
(c) *Shadow*—sufficient background lighting to minimize dark shadows forming around equipment, etc.

4 ACOUSTICS

4.01 A considerable amount of noise is generated in the kitchen by machinery, water, steam and gas burner jets, impact noises and resonance of metallic surfaces, and other sources including the workers themselves. The noise level is accentuated by reverberation within the room, ie the prolongation of sounds due to their multiple relection from the surrounding surfaces, and this is a feature of the relatively large volume of a kitchen and the preponderance of hard reflecting surfaces. It is desirable to keep the noise level in the kitchen down to about 55–60 dB to avoid excessive interference with speech and communication and to reduce the irritating and tiring effects of prolonged exposure to loud background noise, particularly in the middle frequency range. In addition some provision should be made for sound baffling and insulation between the kitchen and dining area. A special case arises when the latter is used, even occasionally, for after-dinner speeches and other functions and, to achieve these quiet conditions, a noise reduction of up to 45 dB is desirable.

4.02 To reduce sound levels, the main sources of noise must be confined. This includes the wash-up plant and some form of screening should be provided around this area. Partition walls separating preparation areas help to divide up the volume of the room and the lengths of sound paths. Similarly a low ceiling will reduce the reverberation time of sounds but is also liable to create problems in ventilation and lighting.

Sound absorbing materials are essentially porous and their use is limited to ceilings and the upper part of walls in the kitchen. To allow easy cleaning and redecoration, the exposed face may be of hard durable material perforated to allow sound waves to penetrate through to the more porous backing. The latter must be inert to water vapour and oily fumes and, preferably, be water repellent. Typical ceiling constructions include perforated metal trays and plastic or asbestos based tiles with glass or mineral wool backing.

As a new development, acrylic fibre carpets have been used

in some cafeterias and kitchens to reduce noise and improve comfort in standing. The carpeting is completely washable, inert to moisture and can be both vacuum cleaned or scrubbed.

4.03 To confine kitchen noises, partition screening is generally considered desirable between:
(a) the kitchen and serving counter; or
(b) the serving counter and dining area.

In the latter case, the screen may be both decorative and noise reducing whilst partitions between the kitchen and servery are generally functional, providing a support for appliances and utensils or space for cupboards. Noise insulation is best achieved by ensuring there is no opening through which airborne sounds from the kitchen can pass directly to the dining area. This necessitates the use of self-closing doors, and/or some form of screening in front of the opening to baffle the sound. The screens and partitions should be of reasonably heavy construction or, if of hollow panelling, must be lined with resilient material to dampen resonance.

As a precaution against noise nuisance, the selection of equipment and engineering plant should take account of its noise-generating characteristics.

5 VENTILATION AND HEATING

5.01 The ventilation system of a kitchen is designed to meet a number of requirements:
(a) to remove steam, heat, fumes and oil droplets in order to prevent condensation, smells, staining and the build up of high temperatures and humidities in the room;
(b) to control the inflow of fresh air to ensure proper air distribution and to prevent draughts causing discomfort to employees working in the area.

These conditions must be under control at the peak periods of activity and, as far as possible, be independent of outside weather conditions. Natural ventilation of kitchens is suitable only for small-scale catering (say up to 100 meals per day) and, even then, is only likely to be effective where there are high level outlets—such as lantern lights or roof ventilators—to allow escape of rising hot steam and air. In most situations mechanical ventilation is required to ensure deliberate movement of air and the withdrawal of impurities.

5.02 Condensation of water vapour and oil fumes is most effectively controlled by confining these to the production area and removing them by extraction of the air in this vicinity. Various arrangements used for this purpose include canopies over cooking appliances, air funnels over the top of deep fat fryers and enclosures around dish washing machines fitted with extract connections.

The velocity of the air flow must be sufficient to ensure that the particles remain entrained in the air stream and is partly determined by the design of the canopy and is also dependent on the amount of air extracted. For steam and fume removal, velocities of 0·02 to 0·05 m/s (40–100 ft/min) are necessary at the face of a canopy or hood but excessively high velocities are liable to cool off the cooking surfaces and to interfere with burners and pilot lights.

5.03 Standards of ventilation may be based on the number of air changes per hour in the kitchen or on a rate of air removal for each of the various appliances.

Under no circumstances may the kitchen extraction system be used for the ventilation of staff or public sanitary conveniences and, in the case of a large building, the exhaust air from the kitchen is normally kept separate from that which is recirculated for air conditioning.

Design standards

Area	Temperature*		Air changes/ hour	Notes
	°C	°F		
Cooking section	—	—	20–60	Where the heat output is large in relation to the volume of the kitchen the higher rate of air change is necessary.
Vegetable preparation	15·6	60	2–3	Local supplementary heating usually required.
Pastry preparation	15·6	60	2–3	Preparation areas included in the same room as cooking appliances require 20–25 air changes/hour.
Meat and fish preparation	15·6	60	4–6	
Servery	15·6	60	5–10	Mechanical ventilation necessary unless adjacent to external wall.
Pan wash and manual wash-up	15·6	60	6	Large automatic dish-washers require individual steam exhaust outlets.
Staff rooms and offices	18·3	65	1½–2	Separate natural ventilation preferable.
	18·3	65	4–6	For internal rooms mechanically ventilated.

* Temperature requirements based on an outside temperature of −1·1 °C (30 °F).

Air inflow

5.04 Air inflow to the kitchen may enter through natural inlets such as ventilator openings. These must be carefully positioned to prevent draughts causing discomfort to workers and to avoid short circuiting the air flow across the room. Air velocities through non-mechanical ventilators should not exceed about 1·0 m/s (200 ft/min).

In a large building the inflow of air is usually mechanically distributed by means of a plenum fan and ducting system to selected positions in the work areas, and the air entering the kitchen can be regulated, filtered, heated and conditioned to provide optimum conditions.

To avoid the drift of steam and cooking smells into the dining area, it is important that between 10 and 20 per cent more air is extracted from the kitchen than the inlet system provides and this unbalance must be maintained under all operating conditions.

Ventilating ducts and canopies

5.05 Canopies may be constructed of stainless steel, anodized aluminium, galvanized steel or translucent panels of reinforced glass or fibreglass. The area of a canopy will be determined by its height and extraction rate but, typically extends about 150 mm (6″) outside the cooking area. Where grilling or frying is included the inlet to the ventilating duct must be fitted with grease filters and automatic dampers should be incorporated as a fire precaution. Some filtration and/or condensate removal is desirable in every case to minimize risk of staining and leakage from the ducting, and all filter units must be easily accessible.

Unless carefully designed, canopies and ducting tend to interfere with light distribution and create unsightly obstructions which add to cleaning work and to the heat radiated into the kitchen. The sizes of exhaust ducts are normally based on velocities of about 7·7 to 10·2 m/s (1500 to 2000 ft/min) to reduce settlement of dirt and grease whilst minimizing the tendency to vibration noise which occurs at higher velocities. The area across the filters is increased to limit the velocity to about 1·5 to 2·0 m/s (300–400 ft/min). Where possible the ducting should be incorporated in the ceiling space and the canopy sited in a position which will permit a short direct line to the outlet terminal.

5.06 In selecting the extraction fan and associated equipment, consideration should be given to:

(a) the need to satisfy varying conditions, eg by regulating the rate of extraction or part recirculation of air;

(b) avoidance of overloading, excessive noise, vibration, corrosion and the build up of grease and dirt;

(c) access for maintenance and

(d) the need for duplication of fan machinery for servicing and repairs.

Temperature

5.07 Regulation of the temperature in a kitchen is mainly a matter of ventilation, ie of removing the heat generated and released into this space from cooking appliances, hot cupboards, dish washing, refrigerators, and other equipment and from the occupants themselves. Extremes of temperature over about 25°C (77°F), begin to cause increasing discomfort and physical and mental exhaustion and these effects are aggravated by high humidities which restrict the evaporation of perspiration and self-regulation of body temperature. In addition, high ambient temperatures accelerate food decomposition and the growth of food poisoning organisms.

On the other hand, the temperature in the kitchen and ancillary areas must not fall so low, for example in winter, as to cause discomfort to workers, the tendency to misting on cold surfaces and risk of water freezing in pipes and appliances. The main cooking and preparation sections will require little or no supplementary heating during working hours but ancillary rooms and other working areas—offices, cloakrooms, vegetable preparation, butchery and wash-up sections—must be provided with space heating facilities. This may be in the form of unit heaters or a central heating system, preferably arranged near the external walls or mounted at a high level to warm incoming ventilating air. In addition, provision may be made in the ventilation system for part of the exhaust air to be recirculated into the kitchen to provide fast initial heating at the start of the working day.

6 HOT AND COLD WATER SUPPLY

6.01 Large quantities of both cold and domestic hot water are used in a kitchen and the probability of water being drawn off simultaneously at a number of points necessitates generous pipe sizes. To minimize cost of pipework, the cold water storage cistern and calorifier or water heater should be sited as close as possible to the kitchen. The main hot and cold pipes may be enclosed in a duct or chase but each must be well insulated to reduce transfer of heat from one pipe to the other. Stop cocks and drainage points must be provided for each main section and, as far as possible, the mains pipework should form a closed network rather than long isolated branches.

6.02 Water supplies are normally required at the following points:

Connection	Cold water	Domestic hot water
Drinking water points	√*	
Vegetable preparation sink	√*	√
Other food preparation sinks	√*	√
Boiling pans	√*	
Water boilers and café sets	√*	
Steaming ovens	√	
Potato peeler	√	
Waste-disposal unit	√	
Pan wash	√	√
Wash-up sinks	√	√
Rinsing/sterilizing sink	√	√**
Dishwashing machine	√	√**
Cleaners sink	√	√
Lavatory basins in cloakrooms and kitchen	√	√
Water closets	√	
Tap and hose for refuse bins	√	

Notes

* Water supplies for drinking and for washing food, etc should be taken direct from the service pipe. All other cold water supplies are connected to the distribution network.

** Hot water used for rinsing and sterilizing should be supplied at a temperature of 82°C (180°F). This may be obtained by locally boosting the temperature of the hot water normally distributed or through an independent supply.

The normal temperature of hot water supplied to sinks is 55–60°C (130–140°F). Where possible washbasins should be supplied with water at a slightly lower temperature—about 50°C (120°F)—and water for hand washing may be conveniently supplied through a mixing valve at a suitable temperature for use with a spray.

Quantity

6.03 The total quantity of water required per main meal varies from about 7 litres (1½ gals) up to 18 litres (4 gals) depending on the type and size of catering involved. In particular, dishwashing machines, waste-disposal units and vegetable preparation account for a large proportion of the water usage and the latter figure includes staff toilets and wash basins.

Water supply authorities generally require a full day's supply of water to be stored in the premises. The peak demand for cold water is likely to produce flow rates of up to 7 litres/hour (1½ gals/hour) for each main meal prepared. Demand for hot water is mainly concentrated into the short periods coinciding with the service of the meals and immediately following when washing up takes place. Hot water storage, based on a 2 hour recovery period, is approximately 2·7 litres/meal (0·6 gals/meal).

Drainage

6.04 Discharge of waste from cooking appliances grouped into an island arrangement may be into open channels which also serve for floor drainage. The channels are usually constructed of semicircular glazed units laid to falls and covered by grating which must be removable for cleaning.

Although this method provides for economy and flexibility, open channels conveying hot water are liable to emit steam and the gratings tend to harbour dirt. An alternative arrangement is to discharge the waste and cleaning wash from each appliance to an individual waste pipe extending under the floor to a suitable trapped gulley, situated, where possible, outside the building.

Sinks, potato peelers, dishwashing machines, waste-disposal units and similar appliances producing waste with a high proportion of solids must be discharged direct to individual waste pipes and, for this reason, are best sited adjacent to the external walls of the kitchen. The individual waste connections to appliances are generally 38 mm ($1\frac{1}{2}$ ins) diameter but long lengths of waste pipe extending under the floor are larger to reduce risk of blockage and siphonage.

6.05 Waste pipes must be constructed of strong, corrosion resisting materials with gas-tight joints. Copper, galvanized iron and, in larger sizes, bitumen-coated cast iron pipes are generally used and polyvinyl chloride (p.v.c.) may be suitable in certain situations where the temperature is not excessive. The pipes must be laid in straight lines at an even gradient (minimum 1 in 48, or $1\frac{1}{4}°$) between access points and provision must be made for proper ventilation, support, expansion movements and protection. Waste pipes must be sealed to prevent escape of odour by providing a trap which is usually fitted immediately below each appliance. In addition, the waste pipes normally discharge to trapped and ventilated gulleys before entering the drainage system.

Specially designed gulleys, or interceptors, are usually required to arrest silting debris and/or grease as a condition for connection to a public sewer and this waste may have to be removed by hand although some authorities permit solidified grease, etc to be broken up and flushed into the sewerage system. In all cases it is desirable that gulleys and interceptors should be sited outside the building but, where this is not practicable, the fitting must be provided with a sealed airtight cover and ventilated through a pipe extending outside the building. It is illegal for any drain ventilating pipe to open into a food room.

Although the quantity of water used in a kitchen is considerable, 100 mm (4″) diameter drains are generally adequate for separate foul water drainage increasing to 150 mm (6″) diameter for very large premises.

The slope of drains—which for 100 mm diameter pipes should not be less than 1 in 50—is important to ensure that silt does not accumulate and provision may be made for automatic flushing at intervals. To ensure access for inspection and rodding, all drains must run in straight lines between inspection chambers, and the main junctions are formed within the chambers.

Surface water is invariably collected in a separate system of pipes and the quantities of water running off an extensive impermeable area, such as a carpark, will often necessitate drains of 150 mm, 230 mm (6″, 9″) or larger diameters.

7 HEAT AND POWER SUPPLIES

7.01 The demands for heat and power in a kitchen depend on many factors and will vary throughout the day according to the intensity of use. Calculations of loadings may be based on:
(a) the numbers of meals prepared/day and, particularly, during the peak period; and
(b) the types of equipment used.

As an indication of gas or electrical consumption the following allowances may be used in preliminary estimates:

Number of meals served	Quantity of gas/meal*		Units of electricity/meal
	m³	ft³	kW/h
(a) Backbar or call order service			
—100 meals	0·23	8	0·5
(b) Traditional cooking equipment			
—100 meals	0·34	12	1·4
—500 meals	0·25	9	0·8
—1000 meals	0·20	7	0·6

* Based on a gas calorific value of 500 Btu/ft³ (18·6 MJ/m³).

Gas and electricity services must be designed to meet the peak demand on the assumption that all the equipment may be in use at the same time. In order that the loadings can be accurately calculated and provided for, the kitchen plans should show details of:
(a) the positions of all the cooking equipment and power operated appliances, socket outlets, etc.;
(b) the maximum electricity loading or gas consumption of each appliance, etc.;
(c) descriptions of each appliance and the mode of connection including any special provisions.
Individual details of typical terms of equipment are given in Chapter 4.

Gas services

7.02 It is advisable to consult the Gas Board on new installations and major extensions which may involve the substitution of a larger service pipe. The main governor, control valve and meter are fitted near the point of entry in a dry ventilated cupboard which should have full width doors to allow easy access.

In extending the gas supply from the meter to the kitchen, pipe sizes should be related to the lengths of pipe run and gas ratings of the particular appliances rather than to the size of their gas connections. Preferably, the piping should be housed in channels sunk in the floor with a standpipe coming up to connect to each appliance and some of the modern modular units have hollow plinths to accommodate and conceal the connections and associated equipment.

Almost all appliances now have integral governors to regulate the gas pressure at the burners and are fitted with individual stop taps for isolating during servicing, etc.

Electrical services

7.03 In planning the electrical installation, appliance connections must be arranged so as to balance the phases of supply and be of adequate capacity to meet the simultaneous demand without overloading any section. Details identifying the types of equipment and their electrical loadings are usually listed in schedules and the positions of switches, lighting points, socket outlets, etc.—which are represented by standard symbols—should be shown on the kitchen plans.

To ensure a good standard of design, materials and workmanship, compliance with the Institution of Electrical Engineers regulations is normally specified and, in particular, attention should be drawn to the following specific requirements:
(i) A mains switch to isolate all equipment—except the refrigerators and cold stores—should be provided both for emergency use and to enable the building to be turned off at night and during holidays, etc. The main switch board or room should be located near the entrance to the kitchen.

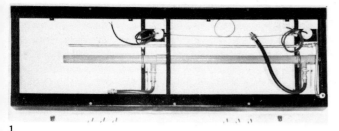

1
LASMEC Mark 2 prefabricated plinth to house all the pipe-work, cables and services.

3
Stotts of Oldham.
Interior of gas heated forced-air convection oven showing equipment components.

H—fan switch
J—automatic ignition and
    flame failure device
K—electric thermostat

L—spark ignition device
M—combined solenoid/
    governor
P—fan unit

2
Stotts of Oldham.
Electrically heated forced-air convection ovens arranged in tiers.

4
Stotts of Oldham
Constructional details of an electric forced-air convection oven.

A—counterbalanced door
B—door seal
C—stainless steel interior
D—slide-out top and
    bottom panels
E—fan with sealed bearings

F—one-piece insulation
    mattress
G—insulated component
    sub-panel, single or
    three phase supply, with
    terminal connectors for
    additional units.

(ii) Individual isolation controls must be on a common moisture-proof panel mounted on a wall in the kitchen in a position which is not likely to be affected by heat or moisture.

(iii) The electrical wiring should be sunk in ducting or conduit in the floor to rise up into the control panels of the individual items or equipment. The point at which the service connection leaves the floor must be properly sealed.

(iv) the wiring to control boxes which are liable to have a high internal temperature should be in suitable cable and all exposed wiring to high-level fittings must be protected by conduit.

(v) Lighting points, socket outlets and switches must not be sited directly over hot surfaces nor in positions exposed to wetting or steam. Fittings must be corrosion resistant and, where necessary, of a sealed type.

(vi) In the interests of safety, the earth continuity resistance, insulation resistance and polarity of all parts of the electrical installation must be tested on completion of any new work or alterations.

Steam

7.04 Steam for use in cooking processes may be obtained from local boiling units which generate the steam, as required, at a suitable pressure for use. The generating units may be integral with the equipment or provided as separate boilers serving a number of appliances.

Efficiencies of steam generators are high—generally in excess of 75 per cent—and may be approaching 100 per cent in boiler-steamers and hot cupboards providing the steam traps and valves are in good order.

Steam from a mains supply is usually an economical

source of heat in larger kitchens serving 1000–2000 meals daily. The steam must be clean and may be employed to heat steam ovens, boiling pans, waterboilers, sterilizing sinks, dishwashers, hot cupboards and serving counters, etc. Where mains steam is used, provision must be made for draining back the condensate to the boiler.

High-temperature hot water and hot oil
7.05 Water at high temperatures—regulated by the pressure—may be used as a heating medium. The cooking equipment must be specially designed to allow for circulation of the hot fluid which is supplied from a central heating unit and is also connected to calorifiers for heating water for other purposes.

8 MOBILITY AND TRANSPORTATION
8.01 Progressive changes in catering technology, together with a growing awareness of the need to obtain greater utilization of equipment and productivity in catering operations, have led to two main developments in layout planning, namely:
(a) the tendency to concentrate related activities into compact work centres; and
(b) the possibility of separating food preparation and cooking from the point of meal service.
These changes are facilitated by the use of mobile units, of which there are a wide variety, ranging from vehicles to trolleys and specialized portable equipment, and by the installation of various forms of food conveyor systems.

Standard trolleys
8.02 A standard trolley is normally about 600 × 900 × 900 mm high (2′ × 3′ × 3′) constructed of a tubular frame of stainless or stove enamelled steel or polished aluminium with three or more shelves which may be supplied with trays or drop sides. The castors are an important feature and must be fully or half swivelling (depending on purpose), quiet in use, resistant to corrosion and damage, as large as practicable, fitted with ball bearings, preferably sprung and provided with a wheel lock if intended as a work top.
Trolleys are used for a variety of purposes serving as additional work surfaces or for temporarily holding and transporting food ingredients, utensils, plated meals and crockery—including dirty crockery.
8.03 Smaller fully swivelling trolleys approximately 500 mm (1′ 8″) square and 1350 mm (4′ 6″) tall are convenient for stacking trays and can be fitted with linen shelves, replacement cutlery and table items and a waste bin for use in the dining room. As other variations, this type of trolley can form the base for a mobile beverage dispensing unit or as a mobile hot cupboard using interchangeable insulated food containers with built-in elements.

Specialized mobile units
8.04 With the introduction of pre-portioning, freezing and accelerated cooking systems, purposely designed mobile racks frequently form an essential part of the food handling process. The racks must be fully interchangeable for preloading in the food preparation area and, subsequently, transferring to freezing, cooking and chilled or heated holding cabinets ready for service.
Hot cupboards, bains-marie units and cooking appliances are often made mobile to facilitate extension and re-arrangement of the kitchen and servery layout to meet changing requirements, for example when catering for banquets and special functions. This flexibility is also a desirable feature in finishing or peripheral kitchens.

Trolley parking and cleaning
8.05 The convenience of mobile units is often offset by the congestion which arises when inadequate space has been allowed for passageways and for parking. A width of 1500 mm (5′ 0″) is required for trolleys to pass persons working on one side of the aisle increasing to 2000 mm (6′ 6″) to allow for workers on both sides. When not in use, trolleys may be parked under shelving, along walls or in spaces provided near to the work area.
Provision must be made for washing down mobile units and, to facilitate cleaning, it is an advantage if the trays, containers and other components are removable. In large-scale catering, purposely designed trolley wash areas with water/steam cleaning and drainage should be provided whilst, in other cases, facilities will be required for hand washing.

Food conveying systems
8.06 Mechanical conveying systems may be necessary in a number of situations:

Use	Type of conveyor
(a) for transporting food supplies in bulk to and from stores, etc and for movement of food trolleys, furniture, etc from one floor to another.	Goods lifts
(b) To facilitate the plating of meals in large catering units, eg hospitals, centralized transport and industrial catering operations.	Belt conveyors
(c) For vertical movement of prepared meals and dirty crockery between kitchens, wash-up areas and serving floors (using removable trays).	Trayveyors and Dumb waiters
(d) For transportation of prepared food to and from preparation, cooking and freezing sections in different parts of the kitchen and on different floors.	Belt conveyor and elevator systems
(e) In food service and for collecting dirty crockery.	Carousel and rotary turntables
(f) In food cooking such as spit roasting, rotisseries, reel ovens, etc and in large continuous grilling and cooking equipment.	Rotating shelves and support bars; horizontal chain or platform conveyors
(g) To convey dirty crockery from a convenient receiving point to the wash-up area.	Conveyor belt systems
(h) In transporting dirty crockery, etc through large dishwashing machines.	Chain or link conveyors

8.07 Apart from manually controlled goods lifts, food conveyors operate automatically moving continuously at a preset speed which may be fixed or adjustable and in one direction or reversible. All parts liable to come into contact with food must be readily accessible, resistant to damage and spillage and easily maintained in a clean hygienic condition. In addition the positioning and accessibility of the machinery, and the noise generated, are important considerations.
In determining the position and space requirements for a conveyor system, regard must be given to the relative positions of associated work centres and support equipment since the effectiveness of this system depends on its continuous use.
For plating systems, independent heated or refrigerated trolleys are positioned in series on each side of the moving belt and, as trays pass along, food items are added from the trolleys to make up the composite meal. Support equipment must be located nearby and space provided for the replacement trolleys which can then be brought into the line as required.
Similar arrangements apply to food assembly processes in which mobile work benches and trolleys are used to concentrate the work alongside the conveyor system.

5

G. F. E. Bartlett and Son.

An example of a stainless steel, general purpose trolley available in 2 or 3 tiers.

7

Staff Catering facilities, British Steel Corporation. Equipment by Stotts of Oldham.

Special stainless steel tubular trolleys designed to convey heated bain-marie containers by lift from the top floor kitchen to the two serveries on other floors.

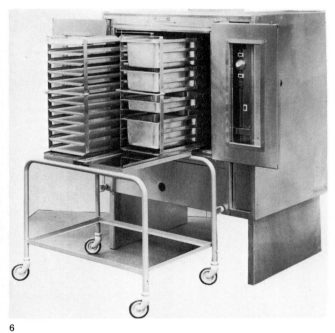

6

G. F. E. Bartlett and Son.

Showing a method of loading the convection oven using mobile carriers and racks.

8

Part of the vegetable preparation area showing the use of two of the 4 mobile sinks.

9 DISHWASHING

9.01 Dishwashing facilities may be separated into three categories according to their purpose and position:

(a) *Pot and pan wash*—which includes the washing up of all cooking utensils and food containers used in the kitchen and servery (see Chapter 4, Pan washing facilities).

(b) *Servery wash-up*—small service counters for snacks and beverages are often provided with their own wash-up facilities unless grouped close to the main wash-up area. This also applies to bar counters which normally have local equipment specifically for washing glasses.

(c) *Wash-up for tableware*—the correct siting and layout of the main wash-up area comprise important features of catering design since bad planning or inadequate provision of dishwashing facilities is liable to affect the proper functioning of both the dining room and the servery. Public awareness of bad hygiene—due to disorganization or otherwise—is a factor which no restaurateur can afford to overlook.

Servery wash-up facilities

9.02 Handwashing, using a double sink with washing and

rinsing/sterilizing bowls, can cope with the crockery, etc. from between 60 to 80 snack type meals per hour but, at this rate, will occupy one employee full time during the meal period. Adequate space must be allowed on one side—preferably on the left—for the accumulation of stacked dirty tableware (minimum length 900 mm (3′ 0″)) and for a draining surface of at least 1200 mm (4′ 0″) on the other side to allow rinsed, sterilized crockery to drain and dry. Unless the clean crockery can be unloaded direct from the sterilizing baskets to the storage shelves or trolley, an additional 600 mm (2′ 0″) of space is needed for stacking prior to removal.

This space should preferably be provided on draining boards which are moulded or seamed to form a continuous unit with the sink bowls, but in larger units separate sections of benching may be required. Bowl sizes for catering sinks are usually 600 mm × 400 mm in area (24″ × 15″) and 250 or 300 mm deep (10″ or 12″).

The temperature of hot water for washing purposes should be supplied at about 60°C (140°F) but sterilizing water needs to be at a higher temperature 82°C (180°F) to ensure effective sterilization and rapid air drying following a short immersion of $1\frac{1}{2}$ to 2 mins. This can be obtained by circulating hot water at the higher temperature to sterilizing point or—more commonly—by boosting the temperature locally with individual heating units fitted below the sinks. To allow immersion without risk of hand scalding the crockery and cutlery items are first stacked in baskets and remain in the baskets for subsequent draining and drying.

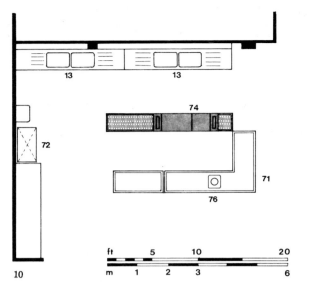

10

Typical arrangement for dishwashing facilities using an island layout to facilitate access.

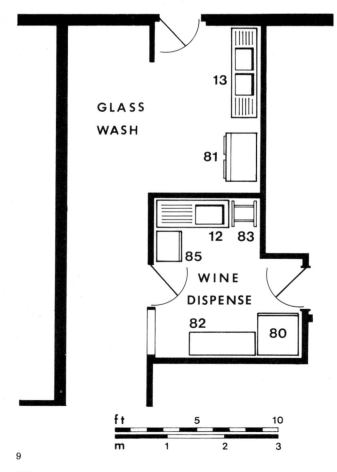

9

Plans of glass wash and wine dispense areas, Post House, Leicester. Trust Houses Forte Ltd.
The equipment includes an electrically heated glass washer and racking for wine and glasses.

Glass washing

9.03 Glasses are usually washed separately from other tableware because of their greater fragility and risk of cracking by sudden changes in heat. In addition, separate handling avoids the risk of heavy soiling from grease and food transfer from plates.

Glass washing machines are broadly grouped into three types:

(a) *Small hand-operated machines* which are suitable for use in small bars and are designed to wash one glass at a time. This machine is bench or counter mounted and relies on the action of rotating rubber wipers assisted by small jets or surges of water which contains appropriate cleansing and antibacterial solution.

(b) *Under-counter units* each consist of a cabinet fitted with a watertight door which is loaded with glasses in a rack. The washing process follows a cycle in which jets of hot water initially wash then rinse and sterilize and finally rinse with cold water to allow immediate use on unloading. A rinse aid solution is often added to provide more rapid drainage and drying. A typical size of under-counter unit is 660 × 500 × 760 mm (26″ × 20″ × 30″) capable of washing about 500 glasses per hour.

(c) *Spray-type glass washing machines* are employed in the largest premises and enable the glasses to be transported mechanically on a rotary conveyor through a series of washing, rinsing and sterilizing spray chambers. The capacity of a spray machine, which is about 1100 mm (3′ 6″) long overall, is in the order of 30 glasses per minute.

Collection of used tableware

9.04 Arrangements for collecting dirty tableware depend on the type and size of establishment and, with minor variations to suit particular circumstances, include the following alternatives:

(1) *Waiter or waitress collection* from the table with the tableware taken direct to the wash-up area or to a trolley or tray which is usually screened from the dining area so that scraping and stacking can be carried out discreetly.

(2) *Collection on to trolleys* taken round to the tables by staff employed specifically for table clearance duties. This method is used with meal self-service arrangements.

(3) *Self clearance* by the diner returning the tableware after use to a suitable collection point—trolley, hatch or conveyor. Self clearance is facilitated if the meal is eaten off

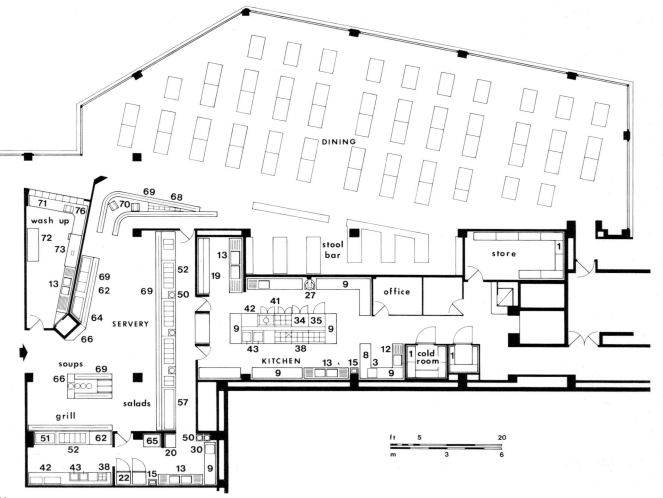

11

London Weekend Television. Concorde Catering Equipment
Co. Ltd.
*This self-service restaurant, based on a 'free flow' system, is
designed to serve up to 700 people over a 2 hour lunch period.
The dining room and servery are arranged so that they do not
overlook each other. Maximum use of the seating area, and the
elimination of unsightly trolleys, is obtained by using a self*

*clearing system where the diners remove their dishes to a hatch
on leaving the restaurant. Siting the dishwashing area in an
island position reduces cross traffic.
Hot beverages are served in a coffee lounge on the floor above—
supplied by hoist—and this helps to give an increased turnover
of the dining seats.*

tableware which remains on the serving tray and various
tray systems, eg the 'Warwick' tray, have been developed
to aid this dual use.
Variations apply where disposable tableware is used which
does not need to be scraped, stacked and returned to a
central wash-up area but is collected as refuse.

Self clearance

9.05 Where self clearance of tableware is intended, the
location and design of the receiving area for dirty crockery
are critical features of the operation. The receiving area
must be situated *en route* to the exit, conspicuous but
preferably sufficiently screened from the dining area to
avoid unsightliness and noise. It must be completely
separated from the servery and the circulation routes must
not cross even when the same entrance/exit is used.
To enable the trays, crockery, cutlery and other items of
tableware to be conveniently removed, scraped, and stacked or loaded directly for washing with the minimum of
handling or carrying, the receiving area must be immediately adjacent to the wash-up. If this is not possible,
mobile trolleys must be provided, preferably designed for

this purpose with multiple shelves (usually six high) of
tray size and having sufficient clearance to receive a tray
plus the height of the tallest item of tableware used
(usually the water glass).
9.06 Receiving points for dirty tableware may be designed
as a single table top or as a series of shelves. The former is
suitable for individual dishes as used in school meals service but is wasteful of space whereas the multi-shelf
arrangement is purposely for tray systems. As in trolleys,
each shelf is designed to receive a tray and contents and is
accessible from both sides enabling the tray to be inserted
in one side and removed from the other. If a uniform tray
size is used, the shelves may be omitted and the trays
inserted directly into runners or supporting slots. Such
arrangements are particularly suitable for the type of tray
which has an overlapping edge ('Warwick' trays) but, in
any event, the shelves should be removable for access and
cleaning. For convenience in use without excessive stooping or stretching, shelf assemblies should be kept between
900 mm and 1500 mm (3' 0" and 5' 0") height.
9.07 Single bench tops are used with waiter/waitress service and are suitable for self clearing systems provided

the trays and crockery are removed practically as fast as they are deposited. The maximum width of reach across the receiving top is 900 mm (3′ 0″) and runs of benching are normally made 750 mm (2′ 6″) wide with workers on one side or 1200 to 1350 mm (4′ 0″ to 4′ 6″) when both sides are used. The area required depends essentially on:

(a) the rate at which meals are served—since this also influences the rate of completion of meals; and

(b) the speed at which the tableware is removed, scraped and transferred to the dishwashing machine or sink.

In practice some accumulation is usually unavoidable during the peak periods and an allowance of 1·00 m² (10 sq ft) per 100 served is a reasonable minimum requirement. Some economy in space may be achieved by providing a shelf above the benching as a second tier.

Conveyor systems

9.08 Dirty tableware and trays may be mechanically conveyed from the receiving point through a small port to the wash-up area by means of a rotary turntable (carousel) or circulating conveyor belt system. Such an arrangement provides better screening and separation of the clearing and wash-up areas from the dining room, improving appearance and reducing noise in the customer areas. It also reduces the effort of reaching for dishes, etc since these are transported to the worker in the loading area, but demands continuous attention to ensure the dirty crockery is removed as fast as the machine operates. Both rotary and conveyor belt systems are also used in conjunction with waiter/waitress service to make more effective use of space and easier separation of the wash-up area from the servery.

Trolley collecting arrangements

9.09 Where tableware is collected in the dining room on to trolleys, adequate space must be allowed for trolley circulation and tables are generally best placed end to end in straight lines so that the diners back on to the trolley aisles. Such a layout permits trolley collection with the minimum of awareness or interruption.

Trolleys are provided with a bag or container for scrapings, separate trays for cutlery, shelves for trays and stacked crockery and facilities for wiping table tops. The trolley enables dirty tableware to be transferred direct to the wash-up area.

10 MAIN WASH-UP AREA

10.01 As indicated in the last section, the siting of the main wash-up area is an important aspect of planning and must take account of the following requirements:

(i) Where self clearing of tables is intended, the receiving area for trays of dirty crockery, etc. must be conveniently and conspicuously near the exit. This must not be adjacent to nor involve persons crossing the route from the entrance to the serving counter.

(ii) If waiter or waitress service is used, the circulation route must provide for deposit of used tableware at one end of the service line before reaching the food counter. The area for receiving dirty dishes, etc should be screened from the food counter to avoid risk of contamination.

(iii) The wash-up should be sited near the servery so that the tableware can be returned directly into use after washing with the minimum of handling and duplicated storage. Alternatively, clean dishes may be placed directly on trolleys for transportation to the servery and kitchen. For large establishments, and where distant collection of dirty crockery is unavoidable, such as in hospitals, auto-

matic conveyor systems should be used.

(iv) In a smaller premises it is desirable that the dishwashing facilities are located near, and accessible to, the pan wash in the kitchen in order that the latter can be utilized in emergency should, for instance, the dishwashing machine be out of action.

(v) The arrangements for receiving and washing dishes must ensure the minimum of unsightliness, congestion, confusion and noise.

Plate scraping

10.02 Near the point of collection provision should be made for disposal of food scraps and other residues prior to stacking or loading the dishes, etc into racks for washing. The usual arrangement consists of a hopper set in the benching over a metal or plastic bin or disposable impervious sack which is removed when full. Alternatively, the hopper may lead to a waste-disposal unit which macerates and discharges the solids directly into the drainage system. This requires continuously running water whilst the machine is operating and must, therefore, be connected to the water supply system. The electric motor used to drive the rotating impeller in this type of machine may range from 552 to 2238 W (¾–3 hp). In small installations, waste-disposal units may be fitted below the sink. Waste disposal by water carriage is a convenient, economical and hygienic method but its use may be restricted by the local drainage authority on account of difficulties of sewage conveyance and treatment. Difficulties may also arise from careless use causing blockage or damage and, in selecting a waste-disposal unit, consideration must be given to its accessibility and ease of clearing.

An alternative method is to employ direct incineration but this process presents economic and practical difficulties due to the high moisture content of food waste.

Pre-rinsing

10.03 Pre-rinsing is incorporated in most medium and large spray-type machines and is a desirable preliminary to other methods of dishwashing. The rinse water washes off the bulk of the food debris and softens any which has become hardened on the plates thus keeping the main wash-up water cleaner and more effective. Pre-rinse arrangements for manual washing can be combined with plate scraping using a small hand-controlled spray to wash the food debris into the funnel of a waste-disposal unit. In other cases, the pre-rinsing can be carried out after the crockery has been placed in baskets by passing the baskets through a shower chamber before loading the dishwashing machine.

In each case, the working surface must be drained away from the wash up sink or dishwashing machine to a separate waste outlet and be provided with a raised rim to prevent spillage.

Stacking and placing in racks

10.04 Before washing by hand or brush-type machine, tableware must be sorted and stacked conveniently adjacent to the sink or tank. Similarly, space must be provided for loading crockery and cutlery in baskets or racks prior to entering a dishwashing machine of the spray or agitated water type.

After the washing and sterilizing stages, the crockery and cutlery must be first allowed to drain and dry with sufficient space provided for this purpose in addition to that required for later emptying the racks and baskets.

12

Dishwashing facilities, BOAC maintenance and service hangar, Employee catering. Equipment by Glynwed Foundries Ltd.
View of wash-up section showing conveyor belt for return of *used dishes from the dining room to the 'flight'-type dishwashing machine. Dishes are also brought to this area by the elevator shown in the background.*

13

Wash-up area, Employee catering services, Ford Motor company, Essex. Equipment by Hobart Ltd.
A view of the collecting area for dirty dishes brought by conveyor belt from the canteen. In the centre of the tabling are *hoppers for scraping debris from the plates which are then loaded into the 'flight'-type dishwashing machine shown in the background.*

10.05 Typical space allowances are tabulated below for intermittent use whilst, for continuously operating dishwashing machines, the area taken up by the machine includes loading and unloading sections of conveyor.

Collection area for unsorted tableware prior to sorting and scraping	600 mm length (24″) per 10 meals (1) Minimum 900 mm (3′ 0″) Maximum 2400 mm (8′ 0″)
Stacking area for tableware sorted and stacked for manual washing	300 mm length (12″) per 10 meals (2) Minimum 900 mm (3′ 0″) Maximum 3600 mm (12′ 0″)
Loading into racks for machine washing	Depends on rack/basket size. Minimum 1000 mm (3′ 6″)
Draining and drying in racks or baskets after washing and sterilizing	Manual process and brush type machines : *Minimum* 1200 *mm* (4′ 0″) Conveyor or spray type machines up to 3600 (12′ 0″)
Unloading baskets and racks for clean crockery awaiting removal	100 mm length (4″) per 10 meals Minimum 600 mm (2′ 0″) Maximum 2400 mm (8′ 0″)
Spray-type machines with mechanized conveyor systems Rotary conveyor type (600–1000 meals/hour)	Space occupied by machine plus conveyor system *Width* *Length* 1500 mm 3900 to 4800 mm (5′ 0″) (13′ 0″ to 16′ 0″)
Flight type escalator conveyor (over 1000 meals/hour)	750 to 1200 mm 3900 to 7900 mm (2′ 6″ to 4′ 0″) (13′ 0″ to 26′ 0″)

Notes: (1) Based on self clearance. Smaller areas suitable where part stacking is provided.
(2) Assumes some accumulation of dishes whilst awaiting washing up.
The lengths relate to tabling 750mm (2′ 6″) wide.

Layout planning

10.06 The work in the wash-up area, even where elaborate dishwashing machines are used, involves a high labour content in handling, sorting, stacking and placing various items of tableware. To facilitate these operations, the layout of the benching and equipment must be carefully planned to take account of ergonomics and work study.
Aspects of bad planning, such as congestion and overloading, extended reach, awkward motion, loss of rhythm and miscalculation of position, are liable not only to reduce output and efficiency but also to give rise to an increase in breakages, improper cleaning and poor hygiene.
10.07 The layout must follow the sequence of operations so that there is a definite flow pattern of work. For manual washing, or the use of a small dishwashing machine, a straight run of benching is appropriate up to about 3600 mm (12′ 0″) but for larger installations it is preferable to arrange the benching in a U-shape to minimize travelling. Large spray-type dishwashing machines should be centrally placed to allow access to both sides of the loading and unloading benches or conveyors and also to facilitate maintenance of the machine.

Manual washing of tableware

10.08 This is described in the section 9.02 and is appropriate for a turn-over of up to 50 to 70 main meals per hour. Even on a small scale, manual washing is expensive in that it occupies an employee continuously whereas the use of a dishwashing machine frees the operator part of the time for other work such as table clearing. When spray- or brush-type machines are used it is necessary to have sinks available nearby in the kitchen for emergency use in the event of machine breakdown.

Dishwashing machines

10.09 Capacities of machines may be stated in:
(a) Numbers of pieces of crockery and cutlery washed per

Staff catering facilities, British Steel Corporation. Equipment by Stotts of Oldham.
One of the two dishwashing pantries with Hobart equipment

and including a calorifier, waste-disposal unit and glass washing sinks. A roller conveyor automatically returns the racks to the 'dirties' section for refilling.

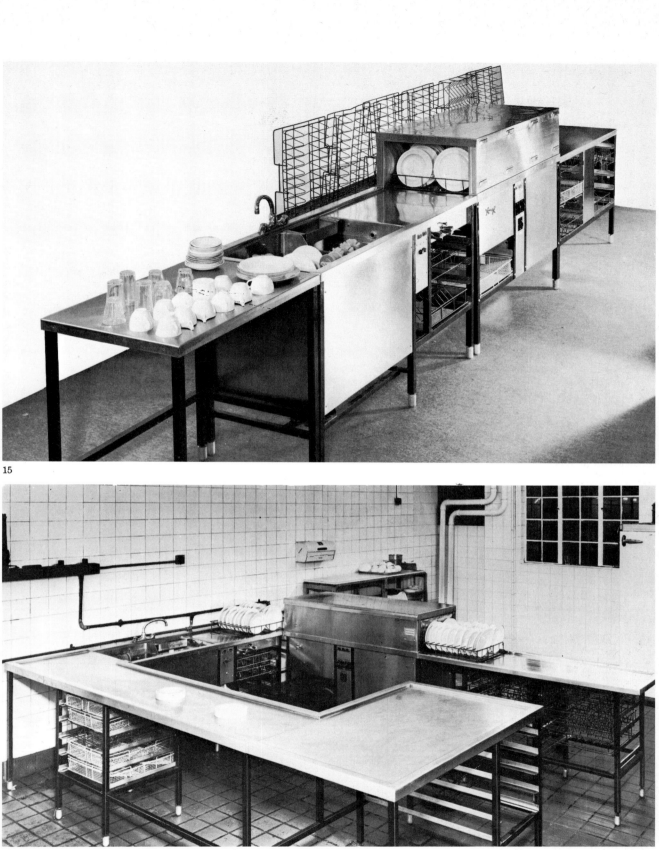

15

16

Dishwashing equipment. Staines Kitchen Equipment Co. Ltd.
Simple layouts for rotating brush-type dishwashing machines
followed by an enclosed sterilizing chamber through which the
dishes are conveyed in racks.

hour or
(b) number of meals coped with per hour. Normally 5 pieces
of crockery and 5 items of cutlery are taken as representing one meal.
Washing machines may also be described as being manually operated, semi-automatic or fully automatic depend-

ing on the extent of manual loading and regulation required.

Brush-type machines
10.10 Machines of this type have a series of motor driven
rotating nylon brushes which are fitted into a tank filled
with hot water and detergent. Articles are washed by hold-

ing them between or over the brushes and are then placed in a basket for immersion in a heated sterilizing tank of clean water.

Brush-type machines may also be designed to deal separately with cups, saucers, plates and glasses and are very effective in removing hard and greasy deposits. The washing process, filling with water and addition of detergents, are all manually operated and, in this respect, the process is similar to hand washing. Such machines range in size from models capable of handling tableware from 25–40 meals per hour up to 250 meals per hour or more.

Agitated water machines

10.11 This type of machine relies on the turbulence of the water for an effective washing action and consists of open tanks filled with water which, in the washing section, is agitated by motor driven impellers fitted behind a protective mesh screen. The tableware is placed in long-handled baskets for immersion in the tanks and one model has one washtank (at 60°C (140°F)) and one heated sterilizing tank (at 88°C (190°F)) whilst another has two washtanks with a third for sterilizing. Detergent may be added automatically with the wash water and an advantage of this machine is its availability for use as a simple sink should the agitator motor fail. The capacity of these machines vary from the equivalent of 100 to 300 meals per hour.

Spray-type machines

Spray-type dishwashing machines utilize the scrubbing action of high pressure jets of water directed at the tableware which is placed into racks prior to loading the machine. The washing process varies with the design and size of the machines which are in four main groups:

10.12 *Small spray-type machines* are built into a run of benching and consist of a single chamber which is loaded

17
Centre Airport Hotel, London Airport. Equipment by Hobart Ltd.
An example of a small dishwashing machine located in a corner position.

and emptied by hand with one rack at a time. The jets are directed at the contents through lower and upper arms which may each be fixed or oscillating to provide greater scouring effect. The operation is described as semi-automatic in that wash water at 60°C (140°F) is initially used with a regulated amount of detergent added automatically or manually and then, by operating a control, sterilizing water at about 88°C (190°F) is injected. The sterilizing water is usually recycled by pump action for use in subsequent washes.

Intermittent machines of this type can cope with the tableware from 100 to 300 meals per hour and may be left- or right-hand feed. Some models may have doors in adjacent sides for fitting into a corner site when wall space is restricted.

10.13 *Medium-size automatic conveyor type* dishwashing machines have multiple compartments through which the tableware is conveyed in racks undergoing washing followed by rinsing/sterilizing as separate stages. The conveyor and washing/sterilizing operations are carried out automatically. Such machines can be built into benching and are appropriate for 400 to 500 meals per hour.

Larger machines of this type, capable of handling up to 1000 meals per day, have an additional compartment which may serve as a pre-rinse stage or as a second hot wash using water at 71°C (160°F) without detergent. In the rotary conveyor type of machine, the tray racks circulate continuously through the various compartments and around the outside to facilitate direct loading and unloading of tableware from bench or trolley with a relatively large loading area. These machines have three or four compartments and require separate vapour extract hoods in addition to hot and cold water services.

10.14 *Large spray-type machines* described as the 'flight type' are free-standing and include short sections of benching. The feed arrangements consist of a continuously moving conveyor—of the escalator type—into which plates, saucers and trays can be slotted directly, and on which cutlery and other items can be loaded in trays. Whilst this machine is in use at least two operators are continuously required, one to load and the other to unload. To facilitate this operation, mobile trolleys for both dirty and washed tableware are essential and space must be provided for these to be positioned at each end adjacent to the conveyor.

The conveyor passes, at a regulated speed, through a series of compartments—pre-rinse, main wash, second wash, and rinse/sterilize—and returns back under the machine. Capacities, in terms of meals per day handled, are in excess of 1000 and the lengths of 'flight type' machines vary from 3·96 to 7·93 m (13 to 26′).

10.15 *Specialized washing machines.* 'Flight type' washing machines may be designed for specific types of crockery, eg cups, or for other good containers such as bottles.

Specialized cutlery washing machines are compact and operate intermittently. The cutlery is given a relatively short wash (28 seconds), a long rinse (72 seconds), followed by hot air drying for 120 seconds.

Pan washing machines are also available.

Construction

10.16 The wash-up area tends to be noise producing due to the unavoidable clatter of dishes coming into contact with each other and with metal racks and baskets and to the mechanical and hydraulic processes in dishwashing machines. It is an advantage if this noise can be prevented from spreading to other parts of the kitchen and it must be excluded from the servery and dining areas. In addition,

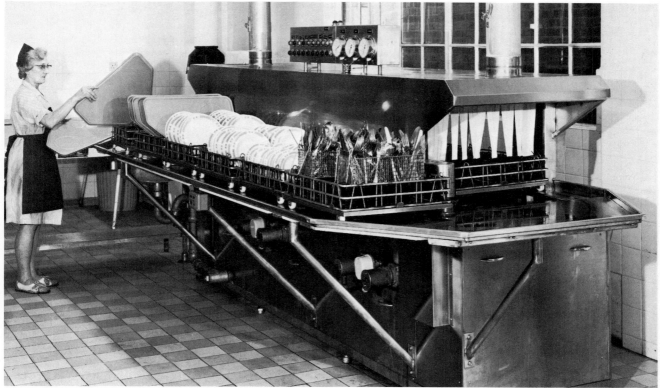

18
Staff catering, The Plessey Co. Ltd., Ilford. The Plessey Co. Ltd.
An example of a dishwashing machine showing method of
stacking cutlery, dishes and trays in mobile racks.

19
Dishwasher installation at Bentalls of Kingston. Equipment
by Hobart Ltd.
A large 'flight'-type dishwasher.

20
Dishwashing facilities. Equipment by Zoppas Ltd.
A smaller version of the 'flight'-type dishwasher with dishes
conveyed by trays through the compartments of the machine.

some discharge of steam and evaporation of water—for example, from the exposure and air drying of hot, wet dishes—produces a local high humidity which is best controlled by confining it to this area and providing a high rate of local ventilation. For these reasons, and to minimize the carry over of spillage, the wash-up section is normally separated by screens and partitions from other areas.

Screens between the wash-up and kitchen may be translucent—of wired glass or perspex—to aid light distribution and supervision. If adjacent to the dining room, the dividing wall should provide a high degree of sound insulation. For most situations a sound reduction in the order of 25 decibels should be adequate but where the dining room is

to be used for after-dinner speeches and similar purposes a noise insulation standard of 45 decibels is desirable.

10.17 The floors and walls up to at least 1·8 m (6′) are exposed to spillage, splashing and frequent cleaning and must be of hard, durable, impervious materials. Floor finishes of quarry tiles with glazed tiles for walls are, generally, most suitable and the floor surface must be laid to falls for proper drainage to a gulley.

Because of the high humidity, the ceiling and upper area of walls should not be porous but have a vapour sealed surface—such as an oil-bound or polyurethane paint. To minimize condensation, the construction must have a low thermal transmittance (U) value ensuring that the surfaces remain relatively warm.

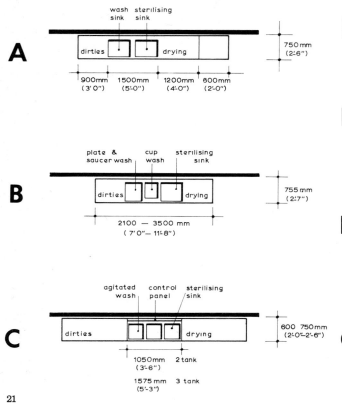

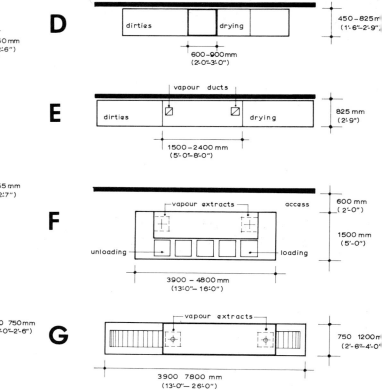

Layouts for wash-up areas and principal dimensions of equipment.
A—Manual washing-up with wash and sterilising sinks.
B—Brush type dishwashing machine.
C—Agitated water type dishwashing machine.
D—Small spray type dishwashing machine.

E—Medium size automatic conveyor type dishwashing machine.
F—Rotary conveyor type dishwashing machine.
G—Large 'flight type' dishwashing machine with continuous escalator type conveyor.

Water supply and drainage

10.18 For washing purposes, the piped supply of domestic hot water is generally maintained at 60°C (140°F). To ensure effective sterilization and rapid air drying after washing, the rinse water is supplied at a temperature of at least 77°C (170°F) and most dishwashing machines operate at temperatures of 82–88°C (180–190°F). This higher temperature may be obtained by using a booster heater, with gas, electric or steam heating incorporated in the machine. Alternatively, if the dishwashing requirements are substantial, a separate supply at 88°C (190°F) may be piped directly from the boiler. Wash periods in machines vary from 30 to 120 seconds and rinse/sterilization extends from 15 to 45 seconds.

In hard water areas, accumulation of lime scale is liable to block the jets and leave deposits on the surfaces, particularly at the high rinsing temperature. This may be remedied by installing a water softener of the base exchange or zeolite type in the cold water supply to the boiler or calorifiers. Alternatively, if the size of machine does not warrant this, an appropriate combination of detergent plus softener must be used in the machine.

Detergent is added automatically at a controlled concentration from a detergent wash tank which is supplied through a make-up line from a dispenser and, in larger machines, this concentration is regulated by electronic mechanism.

Rinse aid fluids are also employed to assist wetting and drying and sterilizing agents may be added to the rinse water.

Where the mains pressure is low it may be necessary to install an independent water pump. Water used for washing is normally recycled before being eventually discharged to waste and the drainage outlets are connected direct to the waste pipe system.

Ventilation and lighting

10.19 A ventilation rate providing 6 air changes per hour is necessary in the wash-up section to remove steam and heat and this is obtained by installing an extraction system. Separate ventilator outlets are also required to large dishwashing machines.

To ensure efficient and accurate work in this area, the level of lighting should be at least 400 lux (37 lumens/sq ft) and must be evenly illuminated all around the work area and machines.

6 STAFF FACILITIES

1 NUMBERS OF EMPLOYEES AND PROVISION OF FACILITIES

1.01 The number of staff required to operate any particular catering establishment will depend on three factors:

(a) The market catered for and the standards of service and personal attention expected

(a) In 1970, the average costs of labour as a percentage of total sales was 58 per cent in industrial canteens, 31 per cent in hotels having a bias towards food sales and about 25 per cent in other restaurants. In view of the high proportions of labour costs in catering there is invariably a close correlation between the standard of personal service provided and the cost of a meal.

Economies in staff may be obtained by passing on to the customer all or any of the functions of serving and collecting food and/or collecting and returning the used tableware.

(b) The numbers accommodated and the occupancy rate over a meal period

(b) The larger the scale of operation, the more efficient use may be made both of equipment and staff. Similarly, if a restaurant or dining room has a high rate of occupancy —that is to say, if the seats are occupied several times during the meal period—staff can be employed continuously throughout that period. Peaking of work in catering can also be offset by shift systems of employment.

(c) The efficient employment of staff and facilitation of their work

(c) Efficient operation both in food preparation and service will also be affected by the plan and layout of the premises and by use of labour-saving equipment and other aids to facilitate the work. In this context, work not only means the preparation and service of food but includes subsequent cleaning and replacement of items which have been used. It has been estimated that about 25 per cent of the work in a conventional kitchen is taken up in cleaning, and improvements in equipment and interior surfaces can reduce this proportion appreciably. As with food service, savings in labour may be obtained by passing back to the supplier all or part of the work in preparing food, e.g. by the use of so called 'convenience foods'.

1.02 In view of the wide variations in staff requirements from one premises to another, it is difficult to draw comparisons on a common basis. The following table represents the average number of staff expressed in ratio to the number of meals served during the peak meal period. For the purposes of assessing staff facilities it is the maximum number of persons working in the premises at any one time which is more significant than, say, the numbers employed in smaller shifts.

Staff facilities in hotels—such as the staff dining and rest rooms—tend to be used in common by all the hotel employees and it is necessary to take account of these total numbers in providing staff accommodation.

Type of premises (1)	Average ratio of employees* : meals served** (2)
Canteens	
Total canteen staff preparing 1 cooked main meal/day with part waitress service part self service	1 : 20
Cooking staff only (preparing, cooking and plating meals and cleaning kitchen)	1 : 40
Coffee Shop operations	
Cooking and washing up staff	1 : 50
Counter and waitress service	1 : 36
(3 sittings during meal period) (3)	
Restaurants	
Kitchen staff (preparing and serving food and washing up)	1 : 10 to 1 : 30
Waiter/waitress service	1 : 8 to 1 : 24
(2 sittings during meal period) (3)	
Hotels	Employees : Residents
Total employees compared with number of residents, depending on type of hotel and extent of personal service provided :	
Luxury	1 : 1
Grade A	1 : 3
Economy	1 : 10

Notes: (1) These ratios reduce as the size of the premises reduces.

(2) Equating * 2 part-time employees = 1 full time.

** 1 main meal = $2\frac{1}{2}$ snack items.

(3) A proportionately higher ratio of staff will be required where there are fewer sittings during the meal period.

Legal provisions

1.03 The physical conditions in which persons are required to work and the standards of facilities which must be provided for employees are governed by legal requirements. In the case of most hotels and restaurants, statutory control is enacted under the Offices, Shops and Railway Premises Act, 1963, whilst premises involved in the manufacture of food products are covered by the Factories Acts. In addition, less specific requirements concerning health and welfare, such as general dilapidation and nuisances, are contained in the Public Health Acts, 1936–61. The provisions of the Occupiers Liability Act, 1957 protect both the customer and employee alike in requiring that the premises shall be kept safe and suitably maintained. Such matters as the safety and stability of the building, safe and adequate means of access and egress and the provision of proper sanitary accommodation are all governed by public health legislation and control is further strengthened by the Licencing Acts when premises are used for the sale of intoxicating liquor.

With regard to the handling of food, the Food Hygiene (General) Regulations, 1970, ensure that suitable and adequate provision is made for cleanliness and hygiene.

Responsibility

1.04 With the exception of structural requirements for the building itself, it is usually the occupier of the premises who is held to be responsible for compliance with the above-mentioned legal requirements.

Staff dining rooms

1.05 Emoluments to staff usually include their own meals and, where meals are taken on the premises, suitable and sufficient facilities for this purpose must be provided (Offices, Shops and Railway Premises Act, 1963; Section 15). In most premises this can be met by the use of the main dining room at times when it is closed to the public, but in the case of hotels and large restaurants, particularly where the accommodation is of an expensive standard, it is usually desirable to provide a separate dining room exclusively for staff. In addition, to ensure close control over food costs, employee meals may be prepared separately from those for the public restaurant and are often based on a different menu to provide a more popular range of traditional rather than exotic food.

The Industrial Society Survey, 1969, revealed that the meals preferred in industrial canteens were, in order: roast beef, steak and kidney pie or pudding, and fish and chips, followed by apple (or fruit) pie, steamed pudding and milk pudding.

Space requirements for staff dining rooms are similar to those for canteens generally and average 0·9 to 1·0 m²/person (10 to 11 sq ft per person). The constructional and design features of canteens also apply.

Cloakroom accommodation

1.06 Arrangements must be made for hanging outdoor clothing and the clothing such as overalls and 'whites' required for work. Where practicable, this should include some means of drying clothes. Precautions against theft, and contamination or soiling must also be considered and these requirements are best met by providing a locked room or separate enclosed lockers with a key for each employee. Drying is obtained by the provision of guarded hot water pipes or tubular heaters under the clothes stands or lockers and the interiors must be ventilated by air circulating through grilles or slats.

Washing facilities and sanitary conveniences

1.07 Legislation concerning the provision of washing facilities is contained in both the Food Hygiene (General) Regulations, 1970, and the Offices Shops and Railway Premises Act, 1963.

The former requirement is to ensure that hand washing facilities are conveniently available to all persons engaged in handling food and, for this purpose, at least one hand wash basin should be located in or adjacent to the kitchen and accessible from the servery. A supply of soap or detergent, nail brush and towel or hand drier must be provided. Washing facilities for employees, generally, are specified under the Washing Facilities Regulations (SI 1964, No. 965) and include provisions based on the numbers of employees of each sex. Similarly, the Sanitary Conveniences Regulations, 1964 (SI 1964, No. 966), lay down detailed requirements for sanitary accommodation.

1.08 Standards

(a) Separate washing and sanitary accommodation must be provided for each sex where this is reasonably practicable and where there are more than 5 persons employed.

(b)

Number employed at any one time Separate for males and females	Wash basins	Water closets*
1 to 15	1	1
16 to 30	2	2
31 to 50	3	3
51 to 75	4	4
76 to 100	5	5

With an additional 1 wash basin and 1 water closet for every 25 employees in excess of 100.

* A reduced standard is allowed for males where urinals are also available.

In certain cases, the washing and sanitary facilities provided for customers may be used to meet the legal requirements for employees with the proviso that an extra wash basin and water closet for each sex, must be included if more than 10 persons are employed.

The Regulations also contain other provisions concerning privacy and the ventilation, lighting and cleanliness of these facilities.

Miscellaneous requirements

1.09 Legal provisions also relate to the provision of first aid materials (SI 1964, 970), including waterproof dressings for persons handling food; of drinking water; of seats for those employees who have reasonable opportunities for sitting without detriment to their work; of proper and

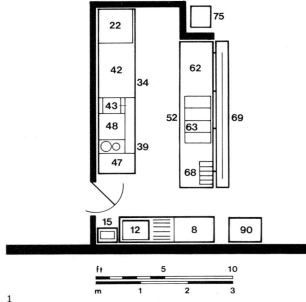

1
The Post House, Leeds/Bradford. Trust Houses Forte Ltd. The layout of the staff kitchen in the Leeds/Bradford Post House which is separate from the main kitchen facilities and is based on the supply of food ready prepared for use thus requiring the minimum of equipment.

secure guards to dangerous parts of machinery.

2 CUSTOMER TOILET AND CLOAKROOM FACILITIES

2.01 Section 89 of the Public Health Act, 1936, as amended, empowers the Local Authority to require the owner or occupier of any refreshment house—that is, any building in which food or drink is sold to and consumed by the public—to provide such number of sanitary conveniences as are considered necessary for persons using the premises. The adequacy and suitability of the sanitary accommodation is also a factor to be taken into account before a licence may be granted to sell alcoholic drink on the premises.

Standards

2.02 Guidance on standards of sanitation is contained in British Standard Code of Practice CP3, Chapter 3, 1950, which recommends the following provisions:

Restaurants and public rooms of hotels		
Fitments	For male public	For female public
Water closets	1 per 100 up to 400 For over 400— 1 per 250 or part	2 per 100 up to 200 For over 200— 1 per 100 or part
Urinals	1 per 25	
Wash basins	1 for 1 to 15 persons 2 for 16 to 35 persons 3 for 36 to 65 persons 4 for 66 to 100 persons Above 100— add at 3 per cent	As for males

2.03 The positioning and design of public conveniences must satisfy both legal and functional requirements. Ideally the cloakroom and toilet facilities should be located adjacent to each other and obviously, but discreetly, alongside the main route followed by customers entering and leaving the dining areas. From any public area in the vicinity of sanitary accommodation it must not be possible to view the interior of any closet compartment or urinal even when all the doors are left open. To provide such screening, the sanitary conveniences may be positioned at an obtuse angle to the line of entrance or separated from the main entrance by an antespace—which may be used as a cloakroom or powder-room and contain wash basins.

The use of an anteroom or intervening space is legally compulsory where sanitary conveniences, including urinals, are entered from a room in which there is food or in which persons are working. Such a space must be separately ventilated from the sanitary conveniences to minimize the risk of odours escaping.

Dimensions for sanitary appliances are indicated in 2.06 with typical space requirements.

Construction and services

2.04 The floors exposed to splashing and requiring frequent washing should be impermeable and stain resistant. Polyvinylchloride and composition tiles are commonly used but must be laid on a waterproof base and adhesive. Mastic asphalt, terrazzo or granolithic floorings may be used to provide a jointless finish or a floor may be constructed of ceramic tiles or mosaics to give a hard wearing surface.

Walls must also be impermeable up to about 1400 mm (4′ 6″) and glazed tiles or sheets of laminated plastic are often used to form suitable surfaces. The partitions between closet compartments and screens may be of block construction similarly finished or of preformed plywood and block-board panels faced with laminated plastic. The latter, being relatively thin, allow considerable saving in space and can be supported on lightweight frames 150 mm (6″) clear of the ground for ease of cleaning and about 1900 mm (6′ 3″) high to allow better light distribution over the ceiling. The doors to the closet compartments are also best constructed with smooth-faced plastic surfaces. Ceiling construction should provide some degree of noise absorbency and light fittings and other services should be recessed to provide a level surface. Suitable shelves and clothes hooks should be provided in the compartments.

To minimize noise, space and risk of damage, flushing cisterns should, where possible, be concealed in a service duct and noise is also reduced by fitting buffers and properly adjusted closure springs on the doors. The main entrance doors, in particular, should be sound deadened and close fitting.

An average lighting of 100 lux (9·3 lumens/sq ft.) is necessary in the public toilets, although this may be graded in the entrance area to avoid an excessive contrast with an exterior of much lower illumination. The positioning of lights around the mirrors to give a higher local illumination is critical and light sources should be screened from view. Colour selection is also important and mirrors may be tinted pink to reduce harsh reflection.

To comply with legal standards, a minimum of three air changes per hour must be installed with provision for emergency plant to maintain this ventilation at all times. In practice, mechanical ventilation is usually designed to give six air changes per hour and must be completely separate from the ventilation to other parts (except sanitary conveniences) of the building. Alternatively, where an external wall is available, natural ventilator openings, equal in size at least 1/20th of the area of the floor, may be used where security considerations allow.

Wash basins arranged in a row should, preferably, be set into a continuous surface cantilevered from the wall.

2.05 Cloakroom: space allowances

Attendant operated									
		Space allowances—widths							
		Counter		Along front of rows		Between rows of hooks		Average area per user	
		ins	mm	ins	mm	ins	mm	ft²	m²
1. With direct access to counter		24	600	27	700	36	900 (1)		9	0·08 (2)
2. Enclosed—served by a corridor 1200 mm (48″) wide on public side		24	600	27	700	36	900	11	0·10 (3)

Unattended								
	Along front of rows		Along rear of rows		Between rows of hooks		Average area per user	
	ins	mm	ins	mm	ins	mm	ft²	m²
Direct access—no counter	42	1050	42	1050	36	900	11	0·10

Note: With hinged and mobile racks the dimensions may be reduced as follows:
   (1) 850 mm   (2) 0·07 m²   (3) 0·09 m²

2.06 Space allowances for washing facilities and sanitary accommodation

Appliance	Unit size				Space required including access*	
	Width		Depth			
	ins	mm	ins	mm	ft^2	m^2
Water closet compartment	33	840	59	1500	32	3·0
Urinals	24	610	12	300	14	1·3
Wash basin	25	630	18	460	16	1·5
Towel holder	14	350	10	250	12	1·1

* *Note:* The areas will vary slightly with different layouts. Typical areas stated.

Spray taps providing mixed water at a suitable temperature are most economical since most washing is in the nature of hand rinsing. Soap or liquid soap dispensers are required and towels, in suitable holders, should be available nearby. If disposable towels are used, careful consideration must be given to the facilities for their disposal.

7 FOOD SERVICE AND DISTRIBUTION

1 CONSIDERATIONS

1.01 The arrangements used for food service may form an integral feature of the restaurant design, occupy a part of the kitchen or comprise a separate area. In each case the most appropriate method of serving meals will be determined—as is the style of the restaurant—by two main considerations:

(a) *The customer*—the types of meals likely to be required; the numbers of persons involved; the periods over which meals will be taken; the speed of service desired and the standard of personal attention expected.

In a word, this may be described as the 'market' and information concerning these potential customers and their preferences is obtained by carrying out market surveys.

(b) *The premises*—the location of the premises in relation to this 'market'; the limitations imposed by space and physical features of the building and the relative costs of the various alternatives.

'Feasibility studies' involve making comparisons between different schemes and the financial returns which might be expected from each investment.

1.02 It is essential that a specific market is clearly identified before the premises are designed since success in catering, as in any other sphere of commerce, depends on being able to satisfy effectively a demand for a particular product or facility—whether this be an expensive restaurant or a fish and chip saloon.

The same criteria may be applied equally to employee catering since the measurement of success is, to a certain extent, reflected in the percentage of employees taking the meals provided. The percentage take up is a good index of satisfaction with the catering facilities but may give an exaggerated impression of their suitability because of the distance to the employees' homes, lack of competition and high subsidies of the true cost. Similarly, in most forms of residential catering the market is, in effect, semi-captive and other methods of measurement must be used to determine whether the catering is suitable for the purpose.

Location

1.03 The location of the premises is of paramount importance since prominence and convenience are two of the main considerations in restaurant selection particularly where transient customers are involved. A restaurant which is satisfactory in all other respects may fail simply because the public at large is not aware either of its existence or its availability. This applies equally to the hotel restaurant which has no direct entrance from the street as it does to a commercial venture sited off a main travel route or in the wrong setting for the market it is intended to serve.

Service

1.04 Ease and speed of service assume increasing importance when the time available for a meal is limited or when catering is provided for large numbers—either simultaneously or by way of repeated sittings. Under these conditions, food service must be designed to avoid confusion and congestion and a number of new techniques, such as the 'free-flow' systems, have been introduced to simplify the selection and collection of meals. In the case of transport catering, hospital catering and similar situations involving restrictions on both time and movement, emphasis has been given to developing more rapid methods of distribution.

1.05 The degree of personal attention provided in a restaurant may range from full waiter or waitress service to individual self service with or without the self-clearance of tables and, at the other extreme, to automatic vending machines. The arrangement which is most appropriate for any particular establishment will depend on a number of considerations, for example:

(a) The nature of the meals available and the prices charged, which may be presumed to reflect the extent of service involved.

(b) The type of customer and the standard of service which would normally be expected in the situation or circumstances concerned.

(c) The image of hospitality or service which the restaurant may wish to project.

(d) The limitations on space or physical features which may restrict self service.

(e) The need to cater for large numbers, for fast service or for meals outside the normal times which, because of staffing and other practical difficulties, are best operated with self service.

Where the market is sufficiently large it may be advantageous to provide different restaurant facilities within the same establishment in order to cater for a variety of needs. Thus, in an industrial situation, a canteen may be available for fast self-service meals at economical prices, an executive dining room with waitress service and vending machines for use outside the main meal periods. Similarly, an hotel may operate a coffee shop or buttery in addition to its main restaurant in order to extend the range of customers.

Clearance of tables

1.06 With all forms of self service a degree of organization and direction is necessary and this is even more emphasized when self-clearance of tables is involved. Generally, self-clearance of used tableware is not readily accepted by the customer and is difficult to operate satisfactorily in competitive catering because of irregular use and varied co-operation. Areas in which customer participation can be relied upon to clear the tables include school meals and certain forms of residential and employee catering but, in all cases the arrangements must be simple and convenient if they are to be effective.

In most situations where self service of meals is operated it is necessary to provide staff and facilities for table clearance whether by trolley or direct to a collection point. Adequate spacing and clear access between tables must be provided for this purpose.

Factors affecting meal service

1.07 The relationships between the various aspects of meal service can be expressed by simple formulae which may also be represented on graphs and nomograms. Basic information for self-service meals may be summarized as follows:

Number of meals to be served — M

Length of dining period * (minutes) — p

Time for each meal, from occupation to vacation of seat * (minutes) — t

Rate of service (diners per minute) — r

Number of seats available — S

Number of times * each seat is occupied during the meal period, i.e. number of sittings — N

(* In each case, the mean times are taken as being representative.)

Number of seats = rate of service × time for a meal

$$S = r \times t$$

Number of meals = number of seats × number of sittings

$$M = S \times N$$

Length of dining period = time of meal × (number of sittings + 1)

$$p = t(N + 1) \text{ minutes}$$

As example of calculations:

(a) With a self-service rate of 9 per minute and an average meal time of 25 minutes, 225 seats will be occupied during this period. To serve 500 meals there will be 2·2 sittings and the total meal period will extend over 85·5 minutes.

(b) If the speed of service is improved to 12 per minute a maximum of 300 seats will be occupied and 500 meals can be served in 1·7 sittings extending over a total of 67·5 minutes.

(c) If a reduction in the time of the meal can be obtained—for example by providing a separate coffee lounge—to say 20 minutes, with a service rate of 12 per minute, 240 seats will be required and 500 meals can be served in 2.1 sittings over a total dining period of 62 minutes.

Modified formulae may be applied to table service.

2 FOOD SERVICE ARRANGEMENTS

Methods of serving food may be considered under four main headings:

(a) Waiter or waitress service to tables.

(b) Self service.

(c) Counter service.

(d) Assembled meal service.

2.01 Design requirements for waiter or waitress service and self service by the customer are, essentially, similar since the needs for organized flow routes and fast service are the same in both cases. The main distinctions arise from the need to provide the customer with more direction and assistance in selecting items of food and the opportunity which then arises, to use the service counter for salesmanship to generate impulse buying by attractively setting out the items on display. In the case of waiter or waitress service, part of the work involved in serving food or beverages from the counter can be transferred to them and the service counter and fittings can thus be simplified and modified, eg by providing a still room, to facilitate this dual role.

2.02 Counter service differs in that the diner although stationary is seated at, or adjacent to, the service counter and is thereby able to select items from food on display or in course of preparation. This type of operation tends to specialize in quick informal service with a limited menu of popular dishes prepared on back-bar equipment within view of the customer. To extend the dining area, tables may also be provided served by waitresses or used by customers served from the counter. There is a wide variation in counter systems ranging from snack and sandwich bars to speciality grills providing high-quality meals to call order.

2.03 In the case of assembled meals, emphasis is given to the attractive presentation of the food on the plate or tray supplied. To this end, cold food items may be pre-wrapped in transparent film to maintain their appearance and trays are usually designed to ensure correct separation and the minimum of disturbance of the food during handling. A number of systems are in use to keep hot food heated whilst in transit from the kitchens including mobile hot cupboards and bains-marie for bulk quantities and heated pellets for individual made-up dishes.

3 SELF SERVICE

3.01 Self-service arrangements can be identified with four basic principles, each of which is capable of many variations to suit particular requirements.

(a) *The cafeteria system*—consisting of a number of units arranged in series to form a continuous counter along which the customer travels with a tray to select various items of the meal which are paid for at the end of the counter line.

(b) *The free-flow system*—based on several separate counters which are approached in parallel, the customer using any one of the counters which is free to obtain the particular meal required. Payment is made on leaving the area at any one of several cash desks.

(c) *Mechanical systems*—may be part of the counter service or form an independent unit. Mechanical systems include rotary turntables which slowly circulate to convey a selection of meal items to the serving area.

(d) *Automatic systems*—comprise vending machines which are operated by coin or key to provide hot or cold meals or various kinds of beverages. Vending machines may also be used to augment a counter service or be arranged as a self-sufficient unit.

4 THE CAFETERIA SYSTEM

4.01 The simplest cafeteria arrangement is a single straight counter with various sections for cold service, hot dishes, sweets and beverages. For large numbers the

1

Stotts of Oldham.
A specially designed bulkhead serving counter.

counter lines may be doubled or trebled; on plan, counters may be straight, curved, extend round internal corners or around the outside of an island service area. Specialist sections at one end of the line may be used for grills, salads or snack items and by-pass arrangements provided. A variety of alternative arrangements are employed for serving beverages and for payment.

Position

4.02 The cafeteria layout needs careful planning to ensure efficient use bearing in mind that the self service will often be operated by customers of different ages, sizes and aptitudes, many of whom may be unfamiliar with the arrangements. To enable food to be easily transferred to the service counter this should be close—preferably adjacent—to the production area with heated and refrigerated pass-through cabinets forming a link between the two areas. Satellite counter systems supplied with prepared food, by elevator or trolleys, from a central commissary are more adaptable in location and can be designed in island arrangements.

The counter must be conveniently placed in relation to the traffic routes followed by the customers entering the restaurant, but should be sufficiently set back from the entrance to avoid congestion and confusion when groups of customers wait in this area. It is also necessary to arrange the layout in a way which will minimize the risk of collision—particularly when trays are being carried—

and avoid disturbing persons who are dining. This is achieved by planning flow routes for customers entering to approach directly to the serving area without crossing or meeting those who are leaving.

Space can be saved if movements to and from the serving counter are confined to distinct passages and, depending on the shape and size of the space available, it may be advantageous to site the serving counter in a separate room with individual 'in' and 'out' openings. This room may form the entrance hall to the restaurant proper or be fully, or partly, partitioned off from the dining area. Other advantages which derive from screening the counter include improved appearance and privacy in the dining area, less noise transmission and easier control. Such screens may be decorative as well as functional or may merely suggest a division by providing a break in the continuity of the space—such as with portable plant troughs or ornamental iron work.

In dining rooms which are for multipurpose use, for example in schools and institutional canteens, it is usually necessary to provide shutters or doors to close off the serving counter when it is not required. Under these conditions, a separate counter for beverages and, perhaps, snack items is desirable to allow flexibility in the use of the room.

Speed of service

4.03 The rate at which customers can pass along a serving

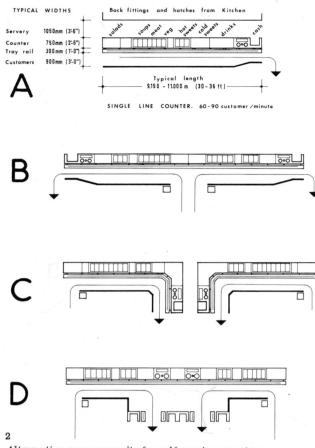

2
Alternative arrangements for self-service counters.
A—Single line counter   *E—Parallel flow*
B—Divergent flow   *F—Bypassing*
C—Convergent flow   *G—Free flow with counters*
D—Multiple outlets   *in line*
                              H—Free flow with counters
                                 in perimeter

counter is affected by many things—the meals served, the design and layout of the counter and slowness and indecision on the part of the customer. A steady flow can be facilitated by minimizing the congestion in those areas which are potential bottlenecks.

(a) *Menu selection*
The menu and price list of individual items must be clearly visible well in advance to minimize hesitancy in selection.

(b) *Serving*
Delays are most likely to occur where customers are unable to serve themselves. These areas are usually in the hot service and beverage counters and at the cash desk.
Solutions include:
(i) Preplating of meals where practicable.
(ii) Adequate service—using interchangeable counters to extend or reduce different sections as required to meet varying demands.
(iii) Fast replenishment of food.
(iv) Location of call-order, or hot meals section at one end with by-pass facilities for customers requiring other food items.
(v) Separation of beverage area which may be an individual counter or vending machines.
(vi) An average of 9 customers per minute can be served by one cashier. To increase this flow the cash desk must be duplicated.
(vii) Arrangement of food in correct sequence of selection, eg soup-entrée-gravy-vegetables.

(viii) A limited menu usually facilitates faster service but is more liable to serious hold up unless adequate provision has been made to cope with the peak demand. The greater the range of choice the longer the counter required for display and service.

4.04 For most cafeteria counters offering a choice of meals a typical customer flow rate is between 6–9/minute for single line and one cash desk and 10–14/minute with some by-pass facilities and double cash desks.
Increased flow rates may be achieved by duplicating the counter lines. Under peak conditions a linear space of about 600 mm (2′ 0″) is taken up by each person in line.

Counter design
4.05 A straight counter is usually adopted for simplicity in layout and operation and to allow economy with the use of standard counter sections and interchangeable units. The counters may have to be arranged to fit the space available but counters extending around external corners are liable to cause tray spillage and the negotiation of internal corners tends to slow down movement. Where changes in direction are necessary these are best accommodated in a slow curve if this is possible.
The length of a counter depends on the types of meals and range of choice offered and may vary from 6·10 to 15·25 m (20′ to 50′). For, say, school meals and certain types of residential catering operating a simple menu with limited choice, the counter would need to be no longer than 6·10 m (20′ 0″). A typical counter length of 9·15–11·0 m (30–36′)

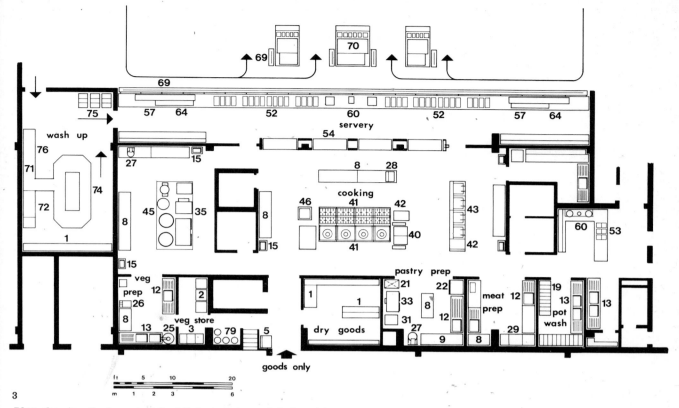

3

Plan showing the layout of the kitchen equipment designed to serve approximately 900 personnel.

4

Employees' canteen, General Foods Ltd., Banbury. Equipment by G. F. E. Bartlett and Son Ltd.
The main serving counter, which is heated by steam, is 24·4 m (80 ft) long. Circulation is from both ends towards the centre with alternative cash desks positioned at right angles some distance from the counter to provide a part free flow system. Pass through hatches are built into the partition wall behind the counter.

would be suitable for a canteen meal offering a range of 2/3 choices and serving about 80–90 customers in 10 minutes. The same length of counter in a public restaurant, providing a wider range of choice, would probably serve 60 to 70 persons in the same time. The trend in counter design is towards the use of shorter counters supplemented by mobile units and vending machines or multiple counter arrangements.

4.06 The overall depth of the counter should allow:
(a) 750 mm (2′ 6″) minimum, 1150 mm (3′ 9″) average behind the counter as a gangway for serving staff;
(b) 750 mm (2′ 6″) for an average depth of counter;
(c) 300 mm (1′ 0″) for a tray slide using 350 mm (1′ 2″) trays;
(d) 900 mm (3′ 0″) as an approximate width for customers using the counter.

The width allowed for customers will, in fact, vary depending on the need for by-passing—where a minimum width of 1200 mm (4′ 0″) or, preferably, 1350 mm (4′ 6″) is more appropriate—or for funnelling as in the approach to the cash desk. If back-bar cooking units are installed a further space of about 750 mm (2′ 6″) should be allowed behind the counter.

Counters should have a uniform height—usually a standard height of 900 mm (3′ 0″) is adopted—but display cabinets and shelving may be arranged in tiers to increase the display area within convenient reach. It is desirable, particularly where confectionery items are exposed, to provide a rail as a sneeze guard and this form of protection can be incorporated into the design.

All counter units must be kept 150 mm (6″) clear of the floor to facilitate cleaning underneath and may be on height-adjustable feet or castors. Units such as tray stands, plate lowerators, ice cream conservators and others which require frequent replacement, must be mobile.

4.07 The design and installation of tray slides warrants

119

particular attention to minimize the risk of accidents and spillage. Solid shelves for this purpose are more difficult to clean and offer greater variation in frictional resistance than circular rail types, although the latter are more liable to produce tilting and spillage. The joints must be formed in a way which does not cause obstruction and this applies equally to the rim of the counter. For a typical tray size of 350 mm (14″), the slide should be 300 mm (12″) wide. A greater width tends to limit reach over the counter whilst narrow slides increase the risk of trays being tipped or sliding off the rails. To facilitate reaching over the tray whilst guiding the tray along the slide, the slide is fixed lower than the counter top and must be sufficiently rigid and strong to withstand a person leaning for support on the edge.

Heating and refrigeration

4.08 Counter units may be gas or electric heated or cooled with self-contained refrigeration equipment and this applies both to the cupboard area and to the counter top. The latter may be in the form of a bain-marie with individual heated shallow containers for different items of food or as an open or enclosed well for cold meats, salads and chilled sweets.

For warming hot dishes on display, quartz lamps may also be fitted or suspended above the counter emitting radiant heat in addition to providing a good appearance.

Hot cupboards are maintained at a temperature between 76–88°C (170–190°F) to avoid excessive drying and spoilage of the food awaiting serving. Bains-marie of the fitted container type should ensure that food in the containers is maintained at a temperature of at least 73°C and, in the case of dry heat equipment, there must be no local overheating to cause burning or scorching of the food.

5
Stotts of Oldham.
Beverage unit showing enclosure for the boiler and cup stands.

6
G. F. E. Bartlett and Son, Ltd.
A hot cupboard fitted with bain-marie top designed for use as a serving counter unit.

7
Staff catering facilities, British Steel Corporation. Equipment by Stotts of Oldham.
One of the two electric service counters which contain refrigerated and infra-red display sections in addition to a bain-marie. In the foreground is an iced water dispenser.

120

8

The back-bar units in the services include gas heated grillers, an electric griddle plate and 3-ring boiler unit, hot cupboards, deep fat fryers and a refrigerated sandwich section. Under-counter space allows positions for mobile plate lowerators and chip trolleys.

9

Stotts of Oldham.
Hot cupboard counter unit with overshelves and infra-red lamps.

Although insulation requirements for hot cupboards are not so stringent as those for ovens and other high-temperature cooking equipment, it is important that the heat loss is not excessive because of the uncomfortable conditions this may produce for counter staff and the effect of the heat transfer to other 'unheated' sections. BS 4167: Part 11:1970 and BS 2512: Part 10:1963 for electrically heated and gas burning appliances respectively, specify the methods of test and standards for surface temperature rise.

To comply with the Food Hygiene (General) Regulations, 1970, cold made-up dishes containing meat, fish, gravy, imitation cream, or dairy or egg products must be kept at a temperature below 10°C (50°F) until served and this cool temperature can only be effectively maintained in practice by refrigeration. Legal requirements, under the Ice Cream (Heat Treatment) Regulations, 1959, also stipulate the temperature at which ice cream must be kept, namely, below −1·7°C (29°F), and it is unlawful to refreeze ice cream which has thawed out unless it is first heat treated.

4.09 Food conveyed from the preparation kitchen may be passed through cabinets built into, and accessible from, the back of the service area. These 'pass-through' units are heated or refrigerated as required and serve for temporary storage of the food until it is required. Alternatively, mobile trolleys or cabinets may be used to bring the replacement food to the counter and are arranged at right angles to form a work centre at the side of a person serving food. The trolleys are replaced when new food dishes are required.

Lighting

4.10 Lighting in the area of food service needs to be at a high level of intensity, particularly around the cash desk area. Suitable illumination levels are:

Situation	Minimum level of illumination	
	Lux	Lumens/sq ft
Servery area generally	400	37
Service counter*	600	56
Price lists, menu details*	600	56
Cash desk*	600	56

* Locally

In addition, careful colour selection of light fittings is essential. With fluorescent lighting, the British Standard 'colour' most suitable for display purposes is 'De luxe natural' (55), which produces a soft light emphasizing the red colours of meat, etc.

Light fittings positioned low over the counter area must provide sufficient screening so that the light source is not directly visible and liable to cause glare. This can be achieved by using deep individual shades for light bulbs, or by mounting—say fluorescent tubes—behind a fascia. In the former type of fitting, quartz lamps provide the dual function of illumination and warming.

Ventilation of the servery

4.11 Some form of local ventilation is usually required in the servery to prevent the accumulation and condensation of steam and fumes from food which is being served and also to reduce the build up of heat from the exposed surfaces of the bains-marie counters, hot cupboards and other equipment and from the large numbers of people who may congregate in this area.

In many cases, where the servery is open to the kitchen, the extraction system in the latter will provide an adequate air flow over the counters but some form of balancing is desirable by providing plenum air inlets at strategic points.

When the servery is separated from the kitchen, local extraction must be provided in or over the counter and also over any back-bar or other types of cooking equipment. Cooking smells and fumes from the latter must be confined and removed from the source using extraction hoods to prevent staining on the adjacent walls and ceiling. To balance the air being extracted and avoid excessive smoke and odours being drawn into the servery, plenum air inlets are often also provided around the ceiling or canopy perimeter. As with all ventilation systems, careful regulation and balancing of the air distribution is necessary.

Sequence and display of food

4.12 In deciding the best positions for various kinds of food along the counter, consideration should be given to the possibility of delays whilst waiting for food to be prepared and/or served, and to the use of the counter as a display to generate impulse buying of attractively pre-

sented prepared food dishes.

At the end of the counter—or well before the counter line if by-passing arrangements are encouraged—a purposely designed stand must be provided for clean trays. It may be advantageous to use a mobile trolley stand for this purpose if this position is remote from the wash-up area.

The normal sequence of food service is:

(a) Cold service—salads, cold meats, etc.

(b) Bread, rolls, butter, cheese, biscuits, sandwiches.

(c) Hot food service—in order of soup, main dish, gravy, vegetables.

(d) Hot puddings.

(e) Cold sweets, pastries, ices.

(f) Tea and coffee, milk and other beverages.

(g) Cashier.

By positioning the cold service at the front of the line, impulse buying and by-passing is encouraged if there is any hold-up along the hot section. There is also a similar advantage in providing prepacked items such as sandwiches, cakes and chilled sweets, in the section adjacent.

Hot food should, where possible, be kept farthest along the line to minimize cooling off before the food reaches the table. This also applies to hot beverages where they are served in the counter system, but the tendency is to take the tea, coffee and cold drinks service out of the line and provide a supplementary counter or vending machines for this purpose. To extend the range of choice of meal this may be combined with a repeat section of cold sweets, pastries and snack items under the control of a separate cashier.

If a high turnover of use is desired in the restaurant dining area, the tea or coffee service may be provided in a separate lounge to encourage customers to move out to the lounge as soon as the meal is finished.

A variation of this counter sequence may be used where it is desirable to separate customers requiring hot food, such as grills, prepared to call order from those wanting pre-plated quick-service meals. In this case, the front end section of the counter may be devoted to call order service with a by-pass corridor for other customers. Yet a third method is to take orders in advance and deliver the dish to the customer at an appropriate later stage.

Cutlery and condiments, etc

4.13 To reduce congestion in the vicinity of the service counter, cutlery should be provided in conspicuous display stands situated to one side of the flow route followed by customers leaving the cash desk. The stand must include a well supported rest area for trays and suitably shaped compartments for cutlery pieces which will allow their easy removal by the handles. This area can create as much obstruction to the flow as the service counter itself and is, possibly, more liable to produce accidents whilst trays are being balanced. Careful positioning and adequacy of size or the number of alternative points are, therefore, important considerations.

Where the menu is fixed or the choice limited, cutlery may be collected before the meal. In this case the tendency is to take up more pieces than are required and it is better to pre-wrap the cutlery in a napkin and place them in a shallow container next to the tray stand.

Water glasses should be available on the tables or on a trolley stand next to a water supply point. The latter must have a sink and drainage outlet and is usually supplied through refrigerated water cooling apparatus.

Salt, pepper, mustard and sauce containers are usually provided on the tables and sugar may also be available in a dispensing container or pre-wrapped in portions.

From the counter to the dining area

4.14 When customers leave the counter area, carrying trays, their concentration is usually divided, mainly on balancing the tray and its contents without spilling and partly on looking for a suitable table or other destination. Under these conditions the customer is vulnerable to accidents, collisions and errors of judgement in distance and position, and the exit route must not be obstructed—particularly by low objects. There must be no steps nor changes in level, the slipperiness of the floor must not increase and there must be sufficient width to allow passing but not to encourage crossing over.

In establishments catering mainly for the shopper, or having a high proportion of older customers, there are many advantages in providing staff to carry the customers' trays from the cash point to the tables.

Equipment requirements guide: self-service cafeteria

Equipment for servery		Meals served per day—based on main meal period								
		50	100	200	400	600	800		1000	
							1	2	1	2
							(1—single line 2—double line)			
Trays										
tray storage length	ft	1' 6"	1' 6"	3' 0"	3' 0"	4' 6"	4' 6"	2 × 3'	4' 6"	2 × 3'
	m	0·45	0·45	0·60	1·35	0·60	1·35	2 × 0·6	1·35	2 × 0·6
Bread, rolls, butter, etc (2) Unheated counter with self-service display above: length	ft	1' 6"	2' 0"	2' 6"	4' 0"	5' 6"	6' 0"	2 × 4'	7' 6"	2 × 5'
	m	0·45	0·45	0·75	1·20	1·65	1·80	2 × 1·2	2·30	2 × 1·5
Cold meats, salads, etc (2) Refrigerated counter with dole plate and glass display above, refrigerator under of capacity:	ft	2' 0"	2' 6"	3' 0"	4' 0"	6' 0"	7' 6"	2 × 4'	8' 6"	2 × 5'
	m	0·45	0·75	0·90	1·20	1·80	2·30	2 × 1·2	2·60	2 × 1·5
	ft³	2	2	3	4	3	4	2 × 3	5	2 × 4
	m³	0·06	0·06	0·08	0·08	0·11	0·11	2 × 0·08	0·14	2 × 0·11
Hot foods Hot cupboard with sectioned bain-marie and heated service shelf: length	ft	3' 0"	5' 0"	8' 0"	12' 0"	16' 0"	20' 0"	2 × 12'	24' 0"	2 × 14'
	m	0·9	1·5	2·4	3·6	4·9	6·1	2 × 3·6	7·3	2 × 4·3
Beverages—hot drinks (1) Counter length	ft	3' 0"	3' 6"	4' 0"	4' 6"	5' 0"	6' 0"	2 × 4'	7' 0"	2 × 5'
	m	0·9	1·1	1·2	1·4	1·5	1·8	2 × 1·2	2·1	2 × 1·5
Comprising water boiler capacity	pints/hr	100	200	300	400	600	800	2 × 400	1000	2 × 500
	litres/hr	55	115	170	225	340	455	2 × 225	570	2 × 285
Tea/coffee urns No × capacity	gals	1 × 3	2 × 3	2 × 5	2 × 10	2 × 15	2 × 20	4 × 10	2 × 25	4 × 15
	litres	1 × 15	2 × 15	2 × 25	2 × 45	2 × 70	2 × 90	4 × 45	2 × 115	4 × 70
Storage racks under counter for cups/saucers:	capacity	50	100	150	200	250	350	2 × 200	450	2 × 250
Reserve cup and saucer storage behind counter:	capacity	—	—	50	200	350	450	2 × 200	550	2 × 250
Cold Drinks, etc (1) Counter length	ft	2' 0"	3' 0"	4' 0"	6' 0"	7' 0"	8' 0"	2 × 6'	9' 0"	2 × 7'
	m	0·6	0·9	1·2	1·8	2·1	2·4	2 × 1·8	2·7	2 × 2·1
Comprising refrigerator capacity	ft³			2	3	3	4	2 × 3'	4	2 × 3'
	m³			0·06	0·08	0·08	0·11	2 × 0·08	0·11	2 × 0·08
Cold shelf length	ft	1' 6"	2' 0"	2' 0"	3' 0"	4' 0"	4' 0"	2 × 3'	5' 0"	2 × 4'
	m	0·45	0·6	0·6	0·9	1·2	1·2	2 × 0·9	1·5	2 × 1·2
Ice cream storage (2)	gals			1	2	3	4	2 × 2	5	2 × 3
	litres			4·5	9·0	13·5	18·0	2 × 9·0	22·5	2 × 13·5
Squash dispenser		1	1	1	1	1	1	2	1	2
Iced water point				1	1	1	1	2	1	2

Equipment for servery		Meals served per day—based on main meal period								
Cutlery counter (1)										
length	ft	1' 0"	1' 0"	1' 6"	2' 0"	2' 0"	3' 0"	2 × 2'	3' 0"	2 × 2'
	m	0·30	0·30	0·45	0·60	0·60	0·90	2 × 0·6	0·90	2 × 0·6
Cutlery boxes fitted in top-capacity pieces		250	300	400	600	900	1000	2 × 500	1700	2 × 650
Reserve cutlery under			200	600	1400	2200	3000	2 × 1400	3800	2 × 1850
Cashier counter-cut away for cash desk										
length	ft	4' 0"	4' 0"	4' 0"	4' 0"	4' 0"	4' 0"	2 × 4'	4' 0"	2 × 4'
	m	1·2	1·2	1·2	1·2	1·2	1·2	2 × 1·2	1·2	2 × 1·2
Standard cash desks		1	1	1	1	1	1	2	1	2
Automatic change machine						1	1		1	1

Notes: (1) May be located away from service counter.

(2) Depends on type of meals and customer preferences.

(3) Based on equipment by Stotts of Oldham.

5 FREE-FLOW SYSTEMS

5.01 The main disadvantage of the cafeteria counter arrangement is the way in which customers have to pass in line along the whole length of the counter in order to select the particular meal required. Any delay in the flow is liable to hold up the remainder of the line and a certain amount of queueing is almost inevitable during peak periods. The efficiency of a continuous counter can be improved by providing by-pass facilities and this principle is extended in the 'free-flow' or 'multi-point' system.

The latter may be described as the supermarket approach to meal service and may take several forms depending on the type of establishment and the space available.

Principle

5.02 Customers entering the food hall may select their meals from a number of service counters each offering a particular choice of course. Depending on the type of meal and size of establishment there may be three for the main course, two for sweets and one for sundries such as ice cream, confectionery, etc. A separate chilled counter is provided for salads and cold meats otherwise the counters are adaptable to allow flexibility in operation, for example, if there is a heavy demand for a particular dish, this may be duplicated in a second service counter. Each counter

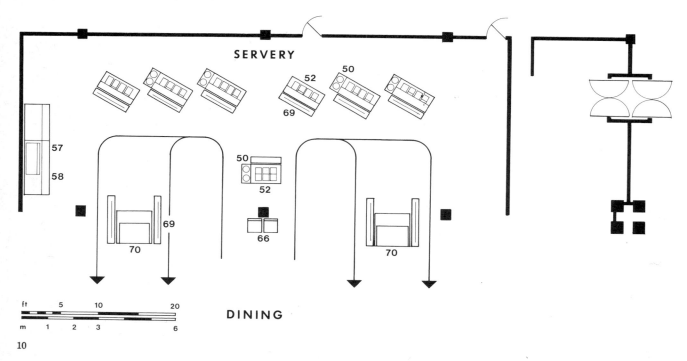

10

Free flow servery, Players Ltd. Lenton. Equipment by Stotts of Oldham.
The echelon units forming a staggered counter arrangement based on the 'free flow' system. Also shown are mobile stands for cutlery self service and for trays.[11]

11

12

13

14

Staff catering facilities, The Plessey Co. Ltd., Ilford. The Plessey Co. Ltd., Equipment by Oliver Toms Ltd.
A view of the echelon bain-marie hot cupboard units with infra-red lamps providing individual service counters for the 'free flow' system. Cashier points interspaced with cutlery stands are shown to the left.

Staff catering, The Plessey Co Ltd., Ilford. Equipment by Oliver Toms Ltd.
The Cold Buffet[13] and Grill Bar[14] sections of the serving hall. To allow for some delay in preparing meals to order, the latter section is located to one side of the main circulation area.

serving the main course would include an entrée, two vegetables and gravy or sauce as required.

By distributing the service over a number of counters, a large number of customers can be served in a short time and this arrangement is particularly suitable for large-scale employee catering where the number of meals per day is in excess of about 600.

Payment for the meal is made on leaving the food hall before entering the dining area and the same free-flow principle is applied by providing a number of cash desks in line thereby enabling the customer to select one which is free.

Planning

5.03 The individual counters may be arranged in a line along one side of the room but must be seen to be separated into distinctive meal sections to ensure effective use of the system. An alternative arrangement which promotes better distribution is to offset the sections so as to produce a staggered layout. Salads and cold dishes, approp-

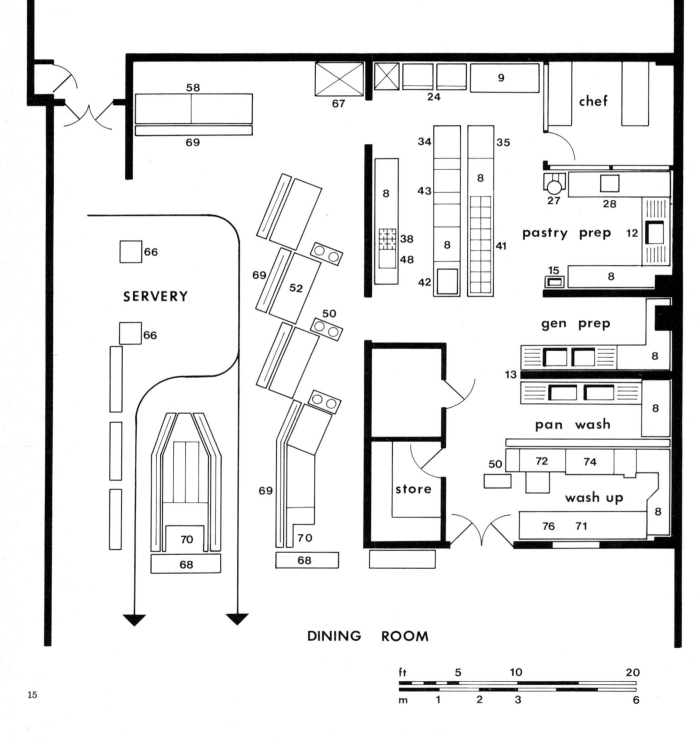

DINING ROOM

Staff catering, Girlings Ltd., Pontypool. Equipment by Stotts of Oldham.
Plan of the kitchen and servery.

16

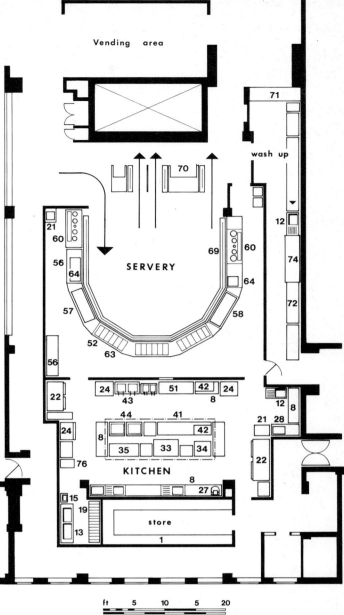

Vending area

71

wash up

SERVERY

70

21
60
56
64
57
52
63
56
22
24
43
44
24
76
35
15
19
13

69
60
64
58
51
42
24
8
41
42
33
34
KITCHEN
8
27
store
1

12
74
72
12
8
21 28
22

18

ft 5 10 5 20
m 1 2 3 4 5 6

17

Staff catering, Girlings Ltd., Pontypool. Equipment by Stotts of Oldham.
An example of a servery arrangement based on the 'free flow' system with offset counter units.[16] *A view of the kitchen, which is separated from the servery, shows the compact arrangement of the equipment.*[17]

riate for quick service, are usually kept to a separate section at one side of the main flow to encourage by-passing. Similarly, the beverage counter must be sited adjacent to the exit to minimize the length of carry. A call order bar specializing in grills and other individually prepared dishes may be provided but located at the other remote side of the main area to minimize congestion.

The counters thus arranged may form a U shape to allow maximum use of the perimeter for service, and many other combinations of counter systems are possible including part cafeteria style counters to allow a wider choice of salads, cold dishes and pastries.

In view of the risk of cross traffic and possibility of collisions between customers moving across the food hall, some form of control by guided routing is desirable using deliberately positioned islands for this purpose. It is also necessary to ensure adequate spacing and numbers of serving counters to avoid congestion and the total area occupied in serving, say 800–1000 meals at one time, is in the order of 186 m² (2000 sq ft).

Staff catering facilities, John Lewis Ltd., Oxford St. Equipment by Oliver Toms Ltd.
The staff catering facilities are situated on the 7th floor and have been designed to serve a variety of 1600 meals over a period of 2¼ hours.

Counter details

5.04 Counters used for 'free-flow' systems are similar to the hot and cold sections comprising a cafeteria line, and include a counter rail as a stand for trays during service. Adequate space must be provided behind the counters for serving staff and for replacement of food items by trolleys or otherwise. In this respect the location of various counters is important and, where required, each should be backed up by an appropriate supply arrangement for food:

Service	Supply arrangements
Salad counters Cold Meats Chilled sweets	Refrigerated pass-through cabinets providing temporary storage between preparation and service areas.
Ice cream	Refrigerated ice cream conservators—preferably mobile.
Hot foods	Heated pass-through cabinets and hot cupboards between production and service areas.

Service	Supply arrangements
Large plates	Mobile lowerators or dish dispensers which are self levelling and heated or unheated.
Grills Short order items	Back-bar cooking equipment fitted behind counter together with worktop and preparation facilities. Refrigerated storage for raw food items, preferably mobile, if remote from main production area.
Beverages	Under-counter boilers fitted with café sets or other tea and coffee making equipment. Refrigerated fountains for cold drinks.

Identification

5.05 Successful operation of the free-flow system is dependent on the customer being familiar with the arrangement. With this objective, menus must be clearly displayed and counters easily identified, so that the customer can easily locate the courses served. Flow routes must be carefully planned to guide the customer and avoid cross traffic. The stands for trays and cutlery, etc are conveniently positioned near the entrance and exit, respectively, to the service area and the operational and environmental considerations which apply to cafeteria service are also relevant to this area.

Variations

5.06 On a smaller scale, the free-flow principle of self selection may be introduced as a modified version of the snack and sandwich bar. In this case a choice of sandwiches, pastries and ices, which may be pre-packed for self service or served by counter staff, are available at a number of display counters around the perimeter or on one or more sides of a service area.

Beverages are also provided but in a position near the cashier to minimize the length of carry to the dining area. In addition, a section may be devoted to short order items prepared as required on equipment behind the counter.

The service hall may form the entrance area to a dining room or be a partitioned off section. In each case the design of both the service and dining facilities is based on a need for quick, convenient, light meals and is capable of a very high and continuous occupancy ratio. It may also be possible to use the service area alone for take-away meals and facilities for this purpose should be provided.

6 WAITER AND WAITRESS SERVICE

The service counter arrangements for waiters and waitresses are similar to those for cafeteria but modified to allow for the following:

Screening

6.01 In conventional waiter or waitress service the counter is invariably divided from the restaurant. Separate 'in' and 'out' swing doors are usually necessary for proper circulation and these must be:
(a) Self closing with the minimum of noise;
(b) provided with kicking and finger plates to reduce damage;
(c) fitted with transparent viewing panels if there is any risk of collision;
(d) preferably screened from the restaurant to reduce noise, draughts and glare disturbing diners at nearby tables.

To prevent congestion in the service corridor a clear width of 1350 mm (4' 6") should be provided which will allow one person to pass whilst another is being served.

Counters

6.02 Since the counters have no merchandising value they are kept as simple and functional as possible and are made up from hot and cold cupboards with bain-marie or plain tops. Depending on the type of restaurant, the hot cupboard capacity may have to allow space for large serving platters and dishes, and mobile plate lowerators are usually provided to aid the transport and storage of plates. For banqueting use, the temporary storage of plated meals and serving dishes will normally have to be increased because of the quick service demanded. This requirement may be met by using mobile cupboards—both heated and refrigerated—which can be brought into the serving line as needed.

Self help

6.03 Economy and speed may be promoted by the waiter or waitress serving themselves with certain items, but this advantage must be balanced against the need for food and cost control. A still room is often provided for self-service of tea, coffee and similar beverages and, in hotels particularly, this area is frequently used for light breakfast and supper service when the main counter is closed and should include grilling, toasting and frying equipment where necessary to form a supplementary kitchen.

From an operation viewpoint, firm discipline in the movement and functions of waiting staff is essential and this must be facilitated by appropriate planning. It is, for example, usually considered necessary to provide some form of barrier—by counters or otherwise—between the waiting area and the kitchen proper.

Dirty dishes

6.04 Arrangements must be made for used tableware to be deposited on a suitable receiving counter sited conveniently near the entrance to the serving counter. Details of space and functional requirements for the wash-up area are given in Chapter 5 (9).

The procedure for collecting and depositing used tableware also needs precise organization.

Cutlery and table items

6.05 Cutlery and tableware may be collected from the serving area from stands provided near to the counter line. Alternatively, to save journeys and time in attending to the customers' needs, the waiter or waitress may operate from a station in the restaurant with a sideboard for cutlery, table items and replacement linen to serve a particular number of covers.

7 COUNTER SERVICE

7.01 By taking meals at the counter, the customer can select the meal required without having to carry it away to a table. Such an arrangement lends itself to visual cooking where dishes are prepared to call order, and grilled or fried as required on back-bar equipment in the view of the customer. It is also used extensively for snack meals selected from display cabinets located around the counter area or described on the menu boards exhibited. Generally, for practical reasons, the range of choice of call order dishes is limited to 2 or 3 of the most popular items which can be easily, and quickly, prepared on restricted equipment, but this menu may be supplemented by meals cooked in an adjacent finishing kitchen. The latter is also necessary for the preparation work involved in pre-portioning, pre-cooking and plating or packaging of the food, but may only be a relatively small area if mainly 'convenience' food is used.

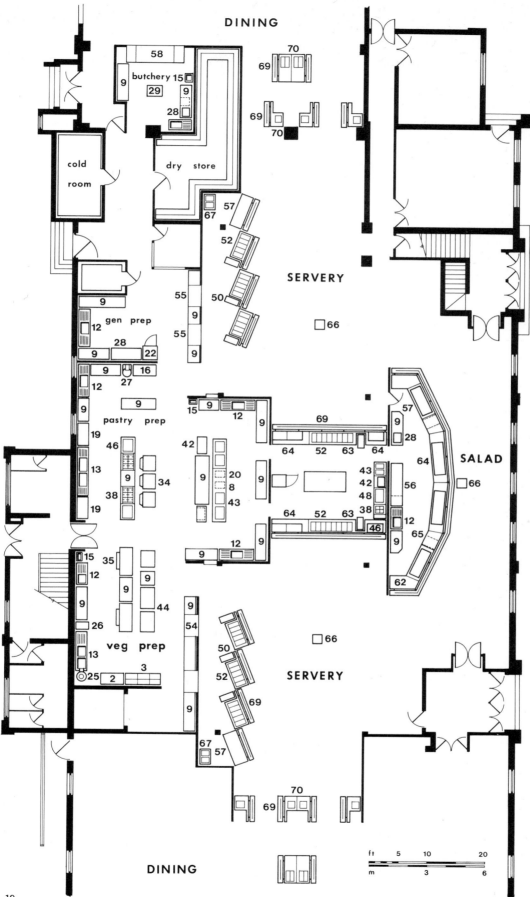

DINING

58

9 | butchery 15
29 | 9
28

70
69
69
70

cold room

dry store

57
67
52
50
55
9
55
9

SERVERY

66

9 | gen prep
12
28
9 | 22
9 | 16
27
12

9

pastry prep

19
46
13
9 | 34
38
19

42
9 | 20
8
43

15 | 9
12
9

9

64 | 52 | 63 | 64

69

9
28

57

9
64

SALAD

56
66

43
42
48
38

46

12

65

9

9

62

15 | 35
12
9 | 9
26
13
44
9
54

64 | 52 | 63

9

12 | 9

veg prep

25
2 | 3

9

50
52
69

SERVERY

66

67
57

70
69

19

DINING

ft   5   10   20
m   3   6

Staff catering facilities, The Plessey Co. Ltd., Liverpool.
Equipment by Oliver Toms Ltd.
The arrangement of the kitchen and servery is designed to
provide up to 4000 meals within a period of 2½ hours.

129

7.02 To enable maximum use of the area, the counter needs to be the greatest length possible which is commensurate with reasonable access to both sides, and this is achieved by arranging it in a series of 'tunnels' with the service corridor extending between counters on each side and one end. The tunnel layout is advantageous in that it allows easy and unobstructed access to each counter place for the counter staff who are able to serve rather more customers than would be possible with a normal waiting system. A further merit from a commercial point of view is the high occupancy ratio of the counter seats arising partly from the nature of the meals, partly from the fact that customers are more conspicuous at the counter than at a table, and tend to leave immediately they have finished their meals.

To cater for the customer who prefers individual choice of company or solitude, it is desirable that part of the area should have conventional tables and chairs, and this is often advantageous in using the spaces in which counter construction might be difficult or uneconomic. For this purpose seats may be individual chairs or of the bench type, arranged as banquettes forming booths around the perimeter walls or in island groupings.

Service to the tables may be by waitress or self service from the counter depending mainly on the nature of the meals and prices charged. For call order meals, waitress service is preferable in view of the delay involved.

Details of counter design and seating are given in the book *Restaurant Planning and Design*.

8 ASSEMBLED MEALS AND CENTRALIZED PRODUCTION

8.01 The problems associated with the service of meals which are pre-assembled before being delivered to the customer are mainly matters of distribution and temperature control or, more precisely:
(a) Efficient plating or packaging and transportation to the customer in the shortest possible time to ensure that the food remains in a freshly prepared condition; and
(b) regulation of the temperature, moisture and other conditions which may affect the quality of the food as a meal.
Preportioning and distribution of meals to each individual customer is necessary in many situations where the person concerned is unable to dine in a collective area. The various reasons may include:

Circumstances	Example
(a) immobility due to ill health or infirmity, etc.	hospitals, institutions and welfare catering
(b) isolation by time	shift workers and night staff
(c) isolation by distance	room service in hotels; employee catering for individuals or groups working in isolated areas
(d) restrictions on movement	aircraft passengers

8.02 In addition, the advantages of speed and control conferred by preportioning meals in advance of their requirement have wide applications in other spheres of catering. Self service in restaurants and canteens, in particular, is greatly facilitated by the use of pre-packaged meals and, even where meals are served individually on traditional lines, the use of preportioned supplements—butter, sauces, condiments, cheeses, conserves, etc—is an aid to convenience and food cost control.

Meal assembly lines
8.03 Production arrangements which terminate in the portioning and plating or packaging of large numbers of individual meals more closely resemble those of a factory assembly line than a traditional kitchen. Usually some form of conveyor belt or moving platform is required and, in this case, the various constituents of the meal or dish concerned are added from a series of service counters positioned at right angles and at intervals along the conveyor line in an appropriate sequence. These service points must be continuously supplied with freshly prepared food throughout the period of operation and this is best achieved by using mobile replacement units or food trolleys to convey food direct from the cooking and production areas. Mobility of service units also facilitates their rearrangement and allows greater flexibility in the type of meal assembled.

8.04 The use of an assembly line for meal production depends on several factors—the type of establishment, number of meals involved, and speed of service required—and is normally warranted for:
(a) Centralized systems of hospital meal service;
(b) large-scale production of packaged meals such as for flight catering; and
(c) production kitchens employing cook-freeze systems of distribution.

Trays and containers
8.05 To facilitate handling, carrying and subsequent use by the diner, meals are usually assembled on trays which may be of a standard plain design for use with conventional plated meals or be moulded to provide appropriate spaces for the various items which comprise the meal.
Plated meals may be kept hot by using:
(a) Individual insulated containers which may enclose a heated insert to maintain the temperature during distribution; or
(b) heated mobile hot cupboards or trolleys for transportation.
The former method is used for individual trayed meals whilst the latter is appropriate when meals are taken in bulk to subsidiary pantries before final distribution. Both systems are employed in hospital catering and in hotel room service.

8.06 Moulded trays and food boxes are mainly used when food has to be transported over long distances and are designed to provide protection in addition to serving as containers. The use of a moulded tray obviates the need for plates and saucers and is particularly suitable for use in, say, flight catering, where space, time and handling facilities are restricted. Boxed meals are becoming increasingly popular for occasional use in situations or circumstances in which catering would, otherwise, be impracticable.

Temperature control
8.07 Unless food is intended for immediate consumption, some form of preservation is necessary. From a practical point of view, hot food can only be maintained at a suitably high temperature for a relatively short time without deterioration of flavour, crispness and those other properties which characterize freshly prepared meals. Hence, the range of distribution of hot meals direct from a central kitchen is generally limited by time and any system operating on this basis must be highly organized in terms of transportation and handling facilities.
8.08 If direct distribution of meals in a hot condition is not

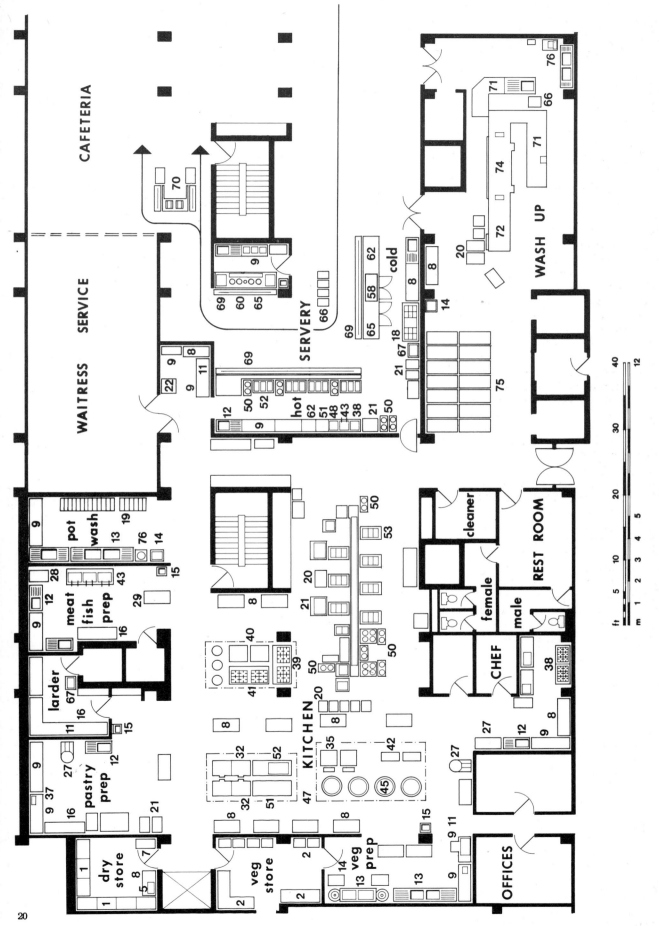

20

Equipment by Glynwed Ltd.
Plan showing the layout of a typical 'Ganymede' system used
in hospital catering.

possible, the food after being fully or mainly cooked, must be cooled quickly to below 10°C (50°F) and be stored and conveyed at this low temperature until it is subsequently re-heated for use. Re-heating can be carried out most economically in small finishing kitchens serving each area of distribution and many types of fast end-cooking or re-generating equipment, eg forced air convection ovens, microwave ovens, infra-red ovens, high-pressure steam ovens, are available for this purpose. Accelerated cooking equipment is described in Chapter 4.

The same requirements for low temperature storage apply to food dishes which are intended to be consumed cold and which contain perishable cream, eggs, meat or fish products.

In order to ensure that suitable temperatures are maintained, the food must normally be kept in a refrigerated store with the temperature regulated just above freezing point to maintain chilling conditions. Subsequently, the food may be kept for short periods, for instance, during transportation, in an insulated container but should not be allowed to rise above 10°C (50°F) until it is ready for reheating or consumption.

Commissary systems

8.09 The storage life of chilled foods is limited and, depending on its perishable characteristics, such food must normally be used within 48 hours of preparation. Hence these arrangements are most appropriate for a commissary system with food prepared in a central kitchen one or two days in advance of requirements and immediately distributed to a number of small finishing kitchens for end cooking and service.

Centralized production

8.10 Limitations on time and quantity generally mean that the advantages of centralized production in terms of scale and organization are also restricted. In order to realize these advantages—

· economies in the purchase of food in bulk and in season;
· long production runs allowing better organization and higher efficiency;
· better use of equipment;
· more regular employment of staff;
· accurate quality and portion control of food;
· less wastage—

the production process should, ideally, be operated independently of food distribution and service and this can only be achieved by introducing some form of extended preservation for the food.

Preservation of meals

8.11 General methods of preserving individual food commodities are described in Chapter 2 on food storage, and various types of pasteurized, sterilized, dehydrated and chemically preserved foods are widely used—particularly for convenience—in domestic and commercial kitchens. The preservation of prepared meals in catering is most commonly achieved by deep freezing to temperatures of between −10°C and −20°C (14°F and −5°F), depending on the storage life required, and this process is made possible by the use of rapid freezing techniques.

Requirements for quick freezing

8.12 The slow freezing of water in food is liable to produce a number of undesirable changes which may impair its

21

Grosvenor House Production kitchens. Equipment by Foster Refrigeration UK Ltd.
The unit to the right is a blast-freezer designed to effect rapid cooling of food to subzero temperatures by blasts of cold air

directed at high velocity over the food surfaces. Floor grooving allows the use of mobile racks to facilitate loading and removal of frozen food to storage. A two-temperature 'walk-in' cold room is shown on the left.

flavour, texture and nutritional value. Such effects result from the increasing concentration of salts and enzymes as ice begins to form first in the weakest solutions, from changes in the fats and proteins and from the disruptive effect of large crystals collecting in the cellular structure. By reducing the temperature rapidly—particularly through the critical interval between −1°C and −5°C (30° and 23°F) when most of the water freezes—these changes can be minimized.

This is achieved by:

(a) limiting the thickness of the food and thereby reducing the time taken for heat to be conducted away from the centre; and

(b) by using high performance refrigerating equipment which ensures adequate contact between the surface of the food and a low temperature cooling medium: air, nitrogen, metal plates, etc.

For refrigerating equipment such as the blast freezer, the standard of performance normally specified is that it should be capable of reducing the temperature at the centre of food 25 mm (1″) thick from 70°C (160°F) to −20°C (−5°F) within 90 minutes.

Food freezing processes

8.13 The main methods of freezing in use at the present time are:

Process	Typical applications
(i) *Plate freezing* between refrigerated plates pressed together against the sides of each food portion to ensure intimate contact.	Food made into slabs—fish, cartoned fruits and other foods.
(ii) *Immersion freezing* in a non-tainting liquid refrigerant, eg 'Freon 12' which boils at atmospheric pressure at −30°C (−23°F).	Initial freezing of chickens and turkeys.
(iii) *Cryogenic freezing* using a spray of liquid nitrogen at −196°C (−321°F) across food travelling through a tunnel on a variable speed conveyor.	Shrimps, scampi, mussels, cockles. Some bakery and confectionery products. Large-scale food production.
(iv) *Fluidized freezing* employing a cushion of refrigerated air blown upwards through perforations designed to keep the food in suspension and impart a rolling movement.	Small products such as peas, fruit and vegetables.
(v) *Blast freezing* with a refrigerated air flow directed at high velocity over the food surface. An air temperature of not less than −32°C (−25°F) with a velocity over the food of at least 50 m/s (1000 ft/min) is required.	Medium-scale catering operations.

Blast freezing

8.14 The most common equipment used for intermittent production in catering operations is the blast freezer, although the liquid nitrogen freezing tunnel is usually appropriate for continuous freezing processes when the weight of food frozen is in excess of 1800 kg/day (4000 lb/day). Blast freezers may be designed as cabinets or as tunnels having 1, 2, 3 or 4 sections for use with trolleys. The capacities are generally expressed in loadings or weights of food per batch, each batch taking a maximum of 90 minutes to reach −20°C (−5°F). For an average working day, it is reasonable to allow for six batch freezings but this output can be increased with shift working.

Example	Typical capacity range per freezing	
	kg	lbs
Cabinets	11·3–22·7	25–50
Twin trolley freezers	54·4–68·0	120–150
Triple trolley and heavy duty freezers	90·7–181·4	200–400

For calculation purposes the following average values are assumed in order to determine the required refrigeration capacity:

*	Imperial	Metric
Weight of food/meal	1 lb	0·454 kg
Maximum temperature assumed	80°F	27°C
Temperature when frozen	−5°F	−20°C
Specific heat of food before freezing	0·9 Btu/lb °F	3·768 kJ/kg °C
Latent heat of fusion	105 Btu/lb	50·4 kJ/kg °C

(* Depending on type of premises and the extent of food which is:
1. Prepared and frozen in the blast freezer.
2. Bought in ready frozen.
3. Prepared fresh each day.)

Process

8.15 Production processes terminating in refrigeration and cold storage are based on the preparation and cooking of food in batches, each batch run being sufficient to enable economies of scale and organization. The production line follows flow patterns of food in the same way as normal kitchen practice with the addition of the following stages:

⇨

portioning

⇨

packaging

⇨

freezing   and

⇨

storing.

As an additional step, precooling may be introduced prior to freezing. The advantages of cooling food after cooking and before refrigeration arise from better utilization of the freezing plant and from a reduction in the moisture loss of food during freezing. On the other hand, the introduction of cooling involves the possibility of delay and loss of quality and, where through processes of refrigeration are employed, precooling may be unnecessary and undesirable.

Cold stores

8.16 Cold storage of food is expensive and maximum utilization of the refrigerated space must be obtained by:

(a) Accurate calculation of the required capacity in terms of both volume and refrigeration loading;

(b) Proper design of the shelving to allow efficient use and access for stock control and rotation. Mobile racking may be used for the purpose;

(c) Maintenance of correct conditions of storage by minimizing temperature and humidity fluctuations. Where there is a need for frequent access, the refrigerated store should be entered through an air lock or air curtain.

The capacity of a cold store will depend on the method of

packaging and boxing, the size of portions and the individual loading characteristics of the refrigerator—which may be described as the volume factor. Typical volume factors are:

Trayed portions: 80 kg/m³ (5·0 lb/cu ft).

Blocked portions: 145 kg/m³ (9·0 lb/cu ft).

8.17 In calculating storage requirements, allowance must be made for:

(a) Anticipated meal demand, range of choice to be offered and cyclic variations proposed in the menu—from which the types and quantities of food appropriate for freezing and storage can be determined.

(b) Proposed foods to be 'bought in' ready frozen for which additional refrigerated storage will be needed.

(c) Duration of storage—which will depend on the particular operating conditions. The following periods are commonly adopted:

21 days—foods infrequently used

14 days—foods moderately used

 7 days—foods regularly used.

The operating temperature for a deep freeze store should be in the range −22 to −18°C (−7 to 0°F) or lower depending on the type of food and storage life required.

At this low temperature microbiological spoilage and enzyme activity is virtually suspended.

Suitability of food for freezing

8.18 Not all food can be frozen successfully and in some cases the recipe or normal methods of cooking, cooling and/or reheating may need to be modified to obtain better results. To show comparisons, food products may be grouped into four categories according to the way they respond to cook-freeze processing:

Characteristics of food	Examples
1. Products which may be frozen, stored and thawed without marked change.	Bread rolls, cakes, biscuits, pies, clear soups.
2. Products normally changed by freezing, storing or reheating but made suitable by:	
(a) Modification of recipe, eg substitution of wheat flour by starch of high amylopectin content to avoid curdling and breakdown.	Sauces, thickened soups, meat, etc in sauce.
(b) Reduction of initial cooking time to allow for further softening in storage and reheating.	Pastry tops, fried or poached fish, sauté and roast potatoes, carrots and green vegetables.
(c) Use of thinner consistency to allow for evaporation on reheating.	Milk puddings, sauces.
3. Products which deteriorate rapidly at ordinary storage temperatures and must be prepared and used quickly or held at unusually low temperatures (−10°C or lower).	Shellfish, fatty fish.
4. Products which are greatly changed by freezing and reheating and are unsuitable for this purpose.	Cooked egg white, vegetable salads.

8.19 The thickness of the food is also critical and is limited by two considerations:

(a) The penetration rate of freezing is about 15 mm/hour. To achieve deep freezing within the standard time it may be necessary to limit the food thickness to about 23 mm (1″).

(b) In fast end cooking, the food must not be so thick that the outside is overcooked before the centre is ready.

In practice, the maximum thickness of food is limited to about 38 mm (1½″).

Packaging

8.20 Prior to freezing, food must be portioned and enclosed in containers, enclosure being necessary to reduce dehydration and darkening—described as 'freezer burn'—caused by loss of moisture from the food to the refrigerated air. Containers may be of 2 kinds:

(i) *Reusable containers*

Metal or polypropylene trays divided into portion sizes. The sizes most commonly used in the UK are:

Dimensions (interior)		Portions	Weight each portion	
mm	ins	No	gm	oz
240 × 240 × 40	9½ × 9½ × 1	7	113	4
230 × 180 × 40	9 × 7 × 1	5	113	4

The normal procedure is to use the container only as a mould and, when the food has been frozen, it is knocked out and repacked in a suitable disposable packaging material.

(ii) *Disposable containers*

Disposable containers used in the refrigeration process include aluminium trays which, subsequently, serve for storing, transporting, reheating and serving the food. The foil containers are of a similar size to the moulds although 40 mm (1½″) deep. A 10-portion tray of 320 × 200 mm (12½ × 7¾″) is also frequently used.

Other packaging materials used in refrigeration, storage and transport of food include:

Material	Examples of uses
Waxed drums and cartons	Vegetables, soft fruits, soups and sauces
Polythene bags and films	Vegetables, fruit, meats and cooked foods with low fat content
Aluminium shaped and foil containers	All pre-cooked dishes and unbaked pies
Polyethylene film	Irregular shapes, joints, chicken and baked products
Polyester parcels and bags	Irregular shapes, joints, chicken

8.21 The properties necessary for packaging materials are:

· Virtually impermeable to grease, gas, moisture.

· Non-toxic, non-tainting, compatability with food.

· Capable of being evacuated and heat sealed under vacuum and of withstanding expansion of food.

· Stable under low freezing temperatures, high production temperatures, long storage periods.

Distribution of frozen food

8.22 To obtain the advantages of scale it is necessary to concentrate food preparation, cooking and freezing into large central production kitchens from which the frozen food is, subsequently, distributed to the areas in which it is to be used. During distribution frozen food must be maintained at the low temperature necessary to avoid any risk of deterioration and this presents some difficulty when the food needs to be transported over a long distance. Therefore, quite apart from other operating conditions, questions of size, siting, transportation and handling facilities must be considered together, ie.

(a) The size of the central production unit in relation to the numbers of outlets served.

(b) Its position and the distances involved in distribution.

(c) The frequency of distribution and storage capacity required for frozen food.

(d) The methods of transportation used, the costs of suitable vehicles and their operation.

(e) Facilities needed for loading, unloading and handling the frozen food.

(f) Related economic and practical considerations.

Transportation

8.23 Alternative methods used for transporting frozen food are, broadly, in two groups:

(i) Reliance on insulated containers and vans.

(ii) Use of refrigerated vehicles.

Method	Features
Insulated containers and vans (a) with insulated enclosure of expanded polystyrene or (b) cooled by solid carbon dioxide ('dry ice') or eutectic* liner.	Low initial and operating costs. Limited to short distances and time. Seriously affected by: (i) any delay—traffic, breakdown, etc. (ii) ambient conditions—heat, sunshine. (iii) method of packing. (iv) frequency of opening.
Refrigerated eutectic holdover vans* Insulated enclosure with large eutectic plates in ceiling cooled by refrigerator. The refrigerator is normally operated overnight by connecting lead to electricity supply.	Usually requires electricity supply connections for cooling. Relies on thermal reservoir effect of eutectic plates. Liable to be affected by: (i) delays in transit. (ii) frequency of use. (iii) distance from base—recooling may be necessary for extended journeys.
Refrigerated cold air blast vans Insulated vans incorporating refrigerated air circulation powered by auxiliary motor.	Expensive in initial cost and generally limited to large size. Practically independent of time and outside conditions continuous freezing whilst auxiliary motor operating.
Liquid nitrogen vans Insulated vans having tank of liquid nitrogen from which evaporating gas is sprayed on to food. Includes automatic cut out when door is opened.	Low capital outlay but high operating costs. Limited use depending on capacity of tanks. After opening doors, 1–2 minutes must be allowed before entering—to allow gas to clear.

* Eutectic—filled with brine for cooling.

Development of centralized food production

8.24 The separation of food production from the various places in which meals are served provides a number of advantages which, in many cases, will outweigh the additional capital costs incurred in the refrigeration, storage and distribution of the food. Some of these benefits have already been considered in relation to production control and efficiency but, examined in total, the advantages of centralized production using the cook-freeze system may be summarized under the following headings:

(a) Food quality and control.

(b) Organization and economy in food production.

(c) Convenience and economy in food usage.

Food quality derives from selective buying of raw food materials, close supervision over the production and storage of the food and the use of the most efficient equipment for the purpose—all of which are facilitated by the use of large central kitchens. By reducing cooking times and holding at high serving temperatures the appearance, palatability and nutritional value—particularly in vitamin C—of the food are improved.

The organizational and economic advantages of large-scale production stem from the opportunities for bulk purchase of raw food in season and from the higher productivity generated when food of the same type is prepared and cooked in large batches. In addition, the use of deep freeze storage allows production to be organized on a time scale independent of distribution and usage ensuring more regular employment of labour and equipment.

8.24 The use of frozen and other food which has been prepared in advance of delivery has a considerable effect on the design of the finishing or service kitchens. Compared with conventional kitchens, the overall area and equipment required for preparation and cooking can be reduced, fewer staff are required and meals can be made ready for service in a shorter time. Storage space for raw food may also be reduced although this is offset by the need to provide additional refrigerators for the stocks of deep-frozen food. The storage capacity necessary for this purpose will depend on the turnover of food used in the restaurant, and the intervals between deliveries.

Figures showing comparisons between examples of conventional and finishing kitchens are outlined below for illustration.

Equipment and space	For 250 main meals per day		For 500 main meals per day	
	Conventional kitchen	Finishing kitchen	Conventional kitchen	Finishing kitchen
Convection ovens	2	1	3	2
Deep fryers	2-standard	2-standard	2-large	2-large
Boiling tables	2	1	2	1
Boiling pans	2 × 20 gal	1 × 10 gal	3 × 20 gal	1 × 20 gal
	2 × 90 litre	1 × 45 litre	3 × 90 litre	1 × 90 litre
Steamers	1 × 11 cu ft	—	1 × 22 cu ft	—
	1 × 0·3 m³	—	1 × 0·6 m³	—
Grillers	1-large	—	1-large	—
Potato peeler	1 × 14 lb	—	1 × 28 lb	—
	1 × 6 kg	—	1 × 13 kg	—
Slicer	1		1	

Equipment and space	For 250 main meals per day		For 500 main meals per day	
	Conventional kitchen	Finishing kitchen	Conventional kitchen	Finishing kitchen
Mixer	1 × 20 qt	1 × 20 qt	1 × 30 qt	1 × 30 qt
	1 × 20 litre	1 × 20 litre	1 × 30 litre	1 × 30 litre
Preparation sinks	4	1	4	1
Pot-wash sinks	1	1	1	1
Hand-wash basin	1	1	1	1
Sterilizer wash-up area	1 × 8′ 0″	1 × 8′ 0″	1 × 11′ 6″	1 × 11′ 6″
	1 × 2·5 m	1 × 2·5 m	1 × 3·5 m	1 × 3·5 m
Preparation tables—worktops	3	—	3	—
Hot cupboards and plating area	no change		no change	
Total cost of equipment (1972)	£4400	£2400	£6200	£3800
Areas required (sq ft)	1500	800	2500	1500
(m²)	140	75	230	140

Use of convenience foods

8.25 The attitude towards convenience foods—in frozen, dried or other forms—varies widely not only from the reaction of the consumer but also from the viewpoint of those involved in food preparation and service. It would appear, however, that the customer is more influenced by the way food is presented as a meal than the method of its preparation and this total 'meal experience' may be equally affected by the standard of service, the décor and atmosphere of the restaurant and the cleanliness, hygiene and other physical features of the catering.

8.26 Trends in recent catering developments show that there are three more or less distinct variations in the type of food used:

(a) Small expensive restaurants specializing in traditionally prepared meals with emphasis on food quality. Within this category are a growing number of speciality restaurants serving so called 'natural foods'.

(b) Restaurants and catering facilities based entirely on pre-prepared frozen and similar convenience foods because of restrictions on space, labour, capital cost or time available for food preparation. These also include large-scale catering organizations operated on a central production basis.

(c) Catering premises using part convenience foods—in steadily increasing quantities—but also taking advantage of local fresh vegetables and other freshly delivered foods when available. This arrangement is preferred in most cases, whether for employee or public catering. Where fresh vegetables are used, they are normally obtained ready washed and peeled, etc to minimize the extent of preparation necessary on the premises.

In determining catering policy it is important to bear in mind the fact that, whilst kitchens planned on traditional lines can be adapted for exclusive use of frozen food, the reverse conversion of finishing kitchens is often not possible without enlarging the preparation area.

9 AUTOMATIC VENDING

9.01 As a means of serving beverages, snacks, and even full meals, automatic vending has a number of advantages over other methods:

(i) Food and beverages can be made available at a large number of places and without any limitations on the time of service.

(ii) Individual service is relatively quick—an average of 12 seconds for a beverage and 5 seconds for a snack meal.

(iii) Meals can be selected, heated by microwave and supplied hot within a short time.

(iv) The minimum of labour is required for attendance.

(v) Machines can be refrigerated to ensure the food or cold drink remains in prime condition over a reasonable storage life.

(vi) The permanent display and availability of snacks and beverages generates trade through 'impulse' buying.

9.02 Vending machines cannot, however, be regarded as a substitute for conventional methods of food service on a large scale partly because of the large numbers of machines which would be required and the space they would occupy, and partly because of the higher costs involved with such an installation. The numbers of vending machines needed to provide service within a short period of, say, 10 minutes, comparable with self service from a counter, are quoted below:

	Numbers of meals to be served within 10 minutes			
	50	100	200	400
Machine service	Numbers of machines required			
Hot drinks	1	3	4	6
Cold drinks	1	1	2	2
Hot main meals	3	5	10	20
Refrigerated meals	3	4	6	8
Unheated sweets	1	2	4	8
Snacks, sandwiches	1	2	3	6

Source: Stotts of Oldham.

Over a longer interval of time, the numbers of machines indicated would be capable of serving a much larger number of meals or, alternatively, for the same number of meals but spread over a longer period, fewer vending machines would be required.

Practical applications

9.03 The three main areas in which automatic vending has become widely used are in:

(a) Providing a meals service at times when the main catering services are closed—for example for travellers, shift workers and night staff.

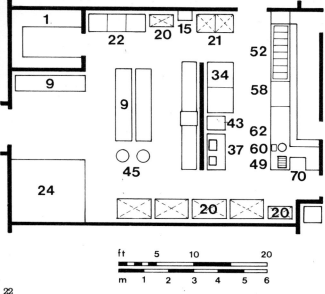

1 22 20 15 21

9

9

24

34

52 58 43 62 37 60 49 70 45

20 20 20

ft 5 10 20
m 1 2 3 4 5 6

22

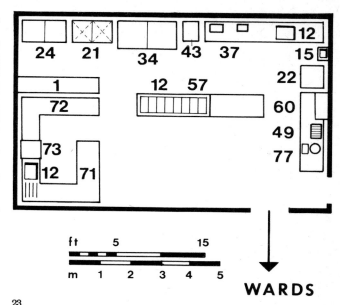

24 21 34 43 37 12

1 12 57 15

72 22

73 60

12 71 49

77

ft 5 15
m 1 2 3 4 5

WARDS

23

Finishing kitchens for frozen meals systems. King's Fund Catering Advisory Service.

The proposals of the Catering Advisory Service illustrate finishing units(22. 23. 24) *suitable for use with frozen meals in both large and small hospitals.*

Example 22 is a combined finishing kitchen for a small hospital. low temperature storage is provided for a week's supply and recovery of meals is by 2 forced-air convection ovens. There is a small area for preparation of fresh foods—salads, etc. It is intended that a plated meals/tray service is used for the wards and service to staff is by cafeteria/self service supported by 2 vending machines for beverages.

Example 23 shows a peripheral finishing kitchen in which frozen food storage is reduced to 1 day. Two forced-air convection ovens and a deep fat fryer comprise the main equipment. This unit is appropriate for service to wards which are all on one level and it is suggested that a dining room is attached to the kitchen for ambulant patients. With this system the wash-up is also centralized.

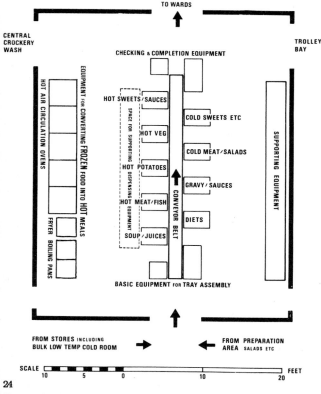

TO WARDS

CENTRAL CROCKERY WASH

TROLLEY BAY

CHECKING & COMPLETION EQUIPMENT

HOT AIR CIRCULATION OVENS

EQUIPMENT FOR CONVERTING FROZEN FOOD INTO HOT MEALS

FRYER BOILING PANS

SPACE FOR SUPPORTING DISPENSING EQUIPMENT

HOT SWEETS/SAUCES

HOT VEG

HOT POTATOES

HOT MEAT/FISH

SOUP/JUICES

COLD SWEETS ETC

COLD MEAT/SALADS

GRAVY/SAUCES

DIETS

CONVEYOR BELT

SUPPORTING EQUIPMENT

BASIC EQUIPMENT FOR TRAY ASSEMBLY

FROM STORES INCLUDING BULK LOW TEMP COLD ROOM

FROM PREPARATION AREA SALADS ETC

SCALE 10 5 0 10 20 FEET

24

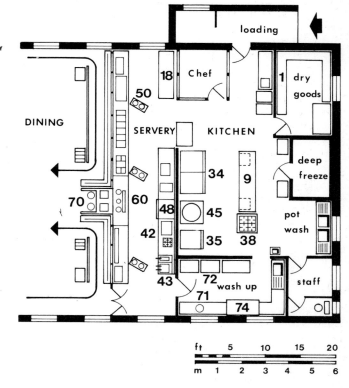

loading

18 Chef 1 dry goods

50

DINING

SERVERY KITCHEN

deep freeze

70 60 34 9

48 45 pot wash

42 35 38

43 72 wash up 71 74 staff

ft 5 10 15 20
m 1 2 3 4 5 6

25

Example 24 is a more sophisticated central tray operation suitable for up to 500 patients. The arrangement shown is based on the 'Gannymede' system but it could be operated with other systems. Boiling pans and supplementary equipment are included to allow for the use of soups and custards, etc. from other convenience packs.

Conversion kitchen. Equipment by Stotts of Oldham.
A typical layout for a conversion kitchen for end-cooking and regeneration of frozen food.

26

Staff catering, Unigate Ltd. Installation by Roboserve Ltd.
A small automatic vending installation serving a canteen
restaurant with part manual service available. The vending
unit includes a microwave oven for heating meals selected from
the display.

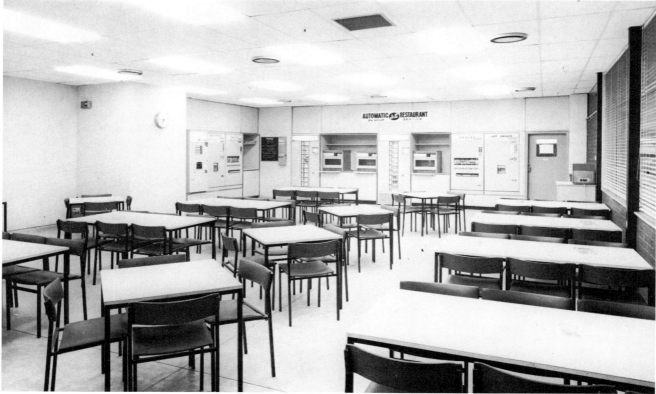

27

Automatic restaurant. Equipment by G. K. N. Sankey Ltd.
An example of an automatic vending installation providing a
24-hour catering service for employees. The design illustrates
the way in which vending machines can form an integral part
of the restaurant design.

(b) Supplementing the main catering area to provide a more efficient and wider ranging service. Examples include the use of beverage machines with main counter service to reduce congestion; automatic vending in subsidiary areas as an alternative or extension to the catering facilities; the use of beverage machines near places of work and traffic routes in lieu of trolley service.

(c) The provision of completely automatic cafeteria or vending bars where the size and situation warrants this as an alternative to personal service. Vending bars may be used as a form of service counter filled directly from a small store room positioned behind the banks of machines. The store room must contain deep freeze and refrigerated storage for reserves of food and may include limited kitchen facilities for preparing sandwiches and snack meals.

Operation

9.04 Vending machines may be operated by the company using them or, on their behalf, by a contractor specializing in catering services. The capacity necessary for a machine or machines will be determined by the user demand and by the intervals between filling, but may also be limited by the number of containers, eg cups, stored.

Machine mechanisms may be gravity or electrically operated by coin, token or key, or by manual control. In a large installation it may be an advantage to provide separate coin-changing machines.

Mounting

9.05 Alternative designs may allow for fixing to a wall, mounting on the floor or assembling in a group. In deciding the best location and arrangement, consideration must be given to the means of access for refilling, cleaning and servicing. The visual appearance of vending machines of different size, shape, illumination and features is unattractive and machine groupings should, preferably, be of the same manufacture and be fitted into continuous fascia panelling to form a unified matching frontage. The external finishes may be stove or vitreous enamelled, stainless steel, anodized aluminium or laminated plastic, and must be sufficiently robust to withstand repeated usage, risk of pilfering and other damage.

Selection of machines

9.06 In selecting a vending machine it is necessary to take into account two main areas of requirements. Firstly, the machine must meet the specific needs of the vending operation in terms of the type of products dispensed; range of choice; mode of operation; facilities for refrigerating and heating, etc. In addition, all machines should comply with more general requirements, such as:
· Simplicity of operation.
· Reliability in use.
· Accuracy in dispensing.
· Ease of servicing and refilling.
· Hygienic construction and operation.
· Appearance and durability.

Services

9.07 Provision will need to be made for engineering services appropriate for the type of vending machines required. The range of services involved include:

Services	Requirements
Electricity supply	For lighting, heating—in beverage vending and for heating food by microwaves—and supply of power to refrigeration machines and electrically operated mechanisms.
Water supply	Mains connection for beverages. As an alternative, the machine may be supplied from a water storage reservoir. A hot water supply in the vicinity is desirable for cleaning.
Drainage	Where necessary machines may have a permanent connection, flexible connection or discharge to a storage receptacle. For multiple installations, a local drainage gulley is desirable for washing down the equipment.
Refrigeration	Machines used for perishable food must be refrigerated. The refrigeration is normally an integral part of the construction.
Refuse	Tables may be cleared by staff or self-cleared by diners. Disposable cups and plates, etc are normally used and later deposited: (a) in bins or sacks—which must be frequently emptied, and cleaned before re-use. (b) through boxes—which may have self-closing flaps—to hidden containers.

Surroundings

9.08 The area in which vending machines are located should be treated in the same way as a normal servery counter. Flooring must withstand continuous traffic and spillage of grease and water without becoming dangerously slippery or difficult to clean and maintain in a good condition. Vinyl asbestos and composition tiles are commonly used for this purpose. Similarly the adjacent walls must be impervious and easily cleaned, and are often surfaced with mosaic or other forms of glazed tiles to form a decorative and functional background.

Good lighting in this vicinity is essential and, in addition to a general level of lighting equal to 600 lux. (50 lumens/ft^2) over the area, lighting is often provided within the compartments of a machine to show the contents. Concealed lighting may also be mounted above, and in front of, machines arranged in a range to provide additional local illumination.

10 BAR SERVICE

Planning

10.01 In many areas of catering provision will need to be made for the sale of alcoholic drink, either as a part of the meal or as an ancillary function. Where this is limited to service during meals the drink may be supplied from a small dispense bar, conveniently located in or adjacent to the dining room. Such a unit is normally planned simply as a storage and serving area with local facilities for cooling wines and washing glasses.

In contrast, a bar counter intended as an independent facility for direct sale of drink to customers is often designed with considerable elaboration as a distinctive feature to attract attention. Frequently, the bar design endeavours to create 'atmosphere' in the room which, to be fully effective, should also be reflected in the choice of furniture and the general décor of the surroundings.

Ornamentation, however, must normally be limited to the façades since the primary purpose of a bar is to act as a service area for drinks and the layout, fittings and construction must be considered on a strictly functional basis. The activity concentrated behind the counter is often intensive, a wide variety of drinks being served, using different techniques and glasses, and with many ancillary functions such as bottle opening, cash handling and glass washing being carried out all within a confined space of movement. Hence, an important aspect of bar design and planning involves studies of bar operation and practice.

In layout, a bar usually consists of two counters separated by a serving space about 1050 to 1150 mm (3′ 6″ to 3′ 9″) wide.

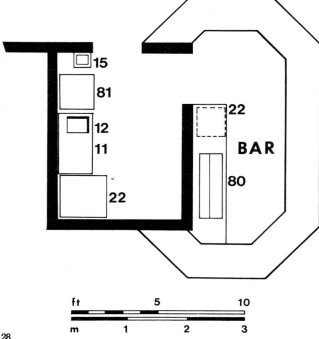

15

81

12

11

22

22

BAR

80

ft　　　5　　　10
m　　1　　2　　3

28

Post House, Washington. Trust House Forte Ltd.
Plan of the waiters' dispense bar.

The back counter acts as a storage and display area whilst drinks are served over the front counter, which may also be used by customers drinking at the bar. Normally the two counters are straight and parallel but curved and island layouts may be used to provide a more prominent or extensive frontage.

Bar details

10.02 The upper part of the back counter is used for display of spirits and other drinks and also forms a decorative background. A worktop—for dispensing—is provided at counter level, and storage shelves below for bottled lagers and beers. The top shelf of this unit should be refrigerated to allow chilling of bottled drinks prior to service. Space on the back counter should be provided for the cash register which must be in a position visible to the customer, convenient for use, but not obstructive to other servers.
Front counters are usually a convenient height for leaning on—1000 to 1150 mm (3′ 3″ to 3′ 9″)—and a foot rail and counter stools may or may not be provided depending mainly on the style of the restaurant.
The width of the counter is determined by length of reach and is normally a total of 600 to 700 mm (2′ 0″ to 2′ 3″) in two sections, the counter top being 450 to 550 mm (1′ 6″ to 1′ 9″) wide and the under counter work area or sink extending out a further 150 mm (6″) to allow easier access.
10.03 In a bar which is subsidiary to a restaurant, virtually all sales of drink will be in bottled or canned form, and pumping equipment is rarely installed. It is, however, desirable to have facilities for wine cooling and also an ice-making machine should be fitted either under the counter or in the vicinity convenient for use in both bar and restaurant service.
A sink with draining board must be provided in the bar for washing glasses unless alternative provision is made for the glasses to be taken to a central wash-up area. In a large bar a glass-washing machine may be installed and built into the counter unit with the necessary plumbing and electrical connections. Provision should also be made for empty bottles, broken glasses and other refuse by provid-

ing suitable bins in the bar unit.
To allow access to the bar servery the counter may be fitted with a lift up flap and hinged door panel. Secondary access for supplies of drink and for the removal of empty bottles usually requires a separate entrance to the side or rear of the servery and provision should be made for isolating and securing the drinks store when it is not under supervised use.
Similarly, when the bar is not functioning, provision should be made for either the whole bar or the back counter—in which the drinks are kept—to be shuttered off for security and several designs of rolling or sliding shutters or grilles are available for this purpose.

Construction and services

10.04 The bar counter, fittings and shelves should be of hard, smooth, impervious materials which are easily cleaned and plastic laminates, glass, chrome plated and stainless steel are commonly used. To provide an illusion of depth, sparkle and multiple display the back counter is often fitted with mirrors.
Servery floors must also withstand frequent spillage, washing and traffic, but to allow for standing at the bar and comfort a very hard surface is not desirable. Suitable materials are asphalt thermoplastic, resin-rubber and composition tiles and sheeting, coved at the junctions with the counters. Depending on the extent of use and traffic, similar materials may be used in the area immediately in front of the bar, but for light usage the carpeting of the lounge may be continued up to the bar with provision for replacement of this section when necessary.
Walls in the vicinity of the bar, and the counter front itself, should be covered with durable materials which will resist burning and marking and permit wiping over. The wall surfaces can often be protected by a dado rail or panel at the height most susceptible to damage, and less damage is likely when tables and chairs are in fixed positions.
10.05 The engineering services required to create a satisfactory environment include controlled ventilation, heating and lighting. To allow for smoking a ventilation rate of 4–6 air changes each hour should be available. Extraction should not be concentrated within the bar area—since this will cause the smoke to collect—but rather distributed in front of the bar canopy. An exception applies when the bar is used for catering, and in this case extraction must be provided to cooking equipment.
In the bar area a high illumination is essential—300 to 400 lux (28–37 lumens/sq ft)—and care must be taken to screen the bright light sources from view to avoid glare.
The ambient temperature should be maintained at about 18°C (65°F). Initially this will depend on heating—by warm air or otherwise—but when the room becomes heavily occupied, temperature regulation becomes more a function of ventilation and air conditioning to remove heat.

11 DINING AREAS

11.01 The layout of a dining area will be largely dictated by operational considerations such as the method used for meal service and clearance of tables. Adequate aisle space must also be allowed for customers entering and leaving the room, for movement to and from the service counters and for access to the tables. In addition, the sizes and disposition of tables may be influenced by other factors such as the group sizes of customers and the need to take advantage of a view or to divide up a large open room.
As a summary, the following requirements should be taken into consideration:

Feature	Requirements
Service	
Self service	Corridor space must be allowed for customers approaching and leaving the service counters in addition to the area taken up by meal service.
	Relatively wide aisle spaces are needed for customers carrying trays:

Aisle width	mm	ins
Entrance, exit and access routes to service area	1800 (1500)	72 (60)
Main corridors between tables	1350 (1100)	54 (42)

(The figures quoted in brackets are the minima.)

Feature	Requirements
Trolley clearance	Tables should be arranged in parallel lines to allow the trolleys to circulate behind rows of diners with a clear width of at least 1350 mm (54'') for bypassing.
Waiter/waitress service	Table groupings can be arranged closer together. The minimum clear space between adjacent chairs or furniture for service is 900 mm (3' 0'').
Counter service	Counter service planning is described in Chapter 7.07. The width occupied by each diner is normally 600 mm (24'') with 550 mm (22'') as a minimum.
	A counter arrangement is generally not economical in the use of space unless it is combined with tables or wall units.
Furniture	A tabletop height of 700 mm (28'') together with a seat height of 430 mm (17'') is now recommended.
	For seating on opposite sides, the width across the top of a table should preferably be 750 mm (2' 6'') and at least 600 mm (2' 0'').
Conventional tables and chairs	Tables 750 mm (2' 6'') square are most commonly used, being suitable for 2–4 diners.
	Where appropriate, the local seating density can be increased by positioning the chairs in diagonal rather than square formations. Larger rectangular and circular tables, seating 6 or more, also increase the density.
	An occupied seat extends about 450 mm (18'') from the table but a total width of at least 700 mm (2' 4'') must be allowed to permit access and manoeuvring in sitting down.
Fixed tables and chairs	Fixed furniture will usually allow economies to be made in the space required. Seats are generally of the banquette type, arranged around the perimeter of the room or in booths. Typical dimensions for a booth seating 2 persons on each side of the table are

	length (table plus seats)	width (2 persons)
optimum	1900 mm (6' 3'')	1200 mm (4' 0'')
minimum	1600 mm (5' 3'')	1100 mm (3' 6'')

Feature	Requirements
Banquet layouts	Tables joined together for banquet dining allow high local densities of seating. The normal width of a banquet table is 750 mm (2' 6'') and a linear space of 600 mm (2' 0'') is usually allowed per person.
	Generous corridor spaces—at least 1500 mm (5' 0'') wide—should be allowed for fast service.
Level of sophistication	The more elaborate the meal and method of service, the greater the space allowance per seat.
	An exception may apply where, to allow for entertainment or dancing, the tables are concentrated around the perimeter.
Surroundings	
Shape of room	The arrangement of furniture and corridor spaces may be determined by the shape and dimensions of the room. Room widths giving the highest local densities, with 2 lines of table groupings separated by an access corridor, are:

	Optimum width	Minimum width
Tables and chairs	5000 mm (17' 0'')	4500 mm (15' 0'')
Booth seating (at right angles)	4000 mm (13' 0'')	3500 (11' 6'')

Feature	Requirements
External	The positions of the tables and seating may be arranged to take advantage of the view through windows or to avoid disturbance—from the entrance, kitchen, etc.

11.02 Space allowances based on average requirements

Type of premises	Area per diner		Notes
	m²	ft²	
Commercial restaurants			
Table service			
—loose furniture	1·0–1·7	11–18	
—fixed tables and chairs	0·7–1·0	8–11	(arranged in booths)
Counter service	1·4–1·9	15–20	
Cafeteria service	1·4–1·8	15–19	(includes service area)
Banquet service			
—long tables	0·9–1·3	10–14	
Canteens (industrial and office)			
Cafeteria service			
—tables of 4 to 6	1·3–1·8	14–19	(includes service areas
—table of 8 or over	1·1–1·6	12–17	and trolley lanes)
School dining rooms			
Primary schools			
—counter service	0·74	8	
—family service	0·83	9	
Secondary schools	0·9	10	
Colleges of further education	1·1	12	

Constructional features

11.03 The internal finishes, coverings, furniture and fittings in a dining room will normally be selected on the basis of function, appearance, service and cost. For most purposes, the need to satisfy functional requirements will be the primary consideration and, where intensive use is envisaged, serviceability will be an equally important factor. Greater emphasis is generally given to an appearance of comfort or luxury where the customer is likely to be more discriminating, the standard of service and attention higher and the duration of meals longer. This is reflected in the greater use of soft textured fabric materials—tablecloths, carpets, curtains, etc.—and purposely designed furniture and fittings in more expensive restaurants.

However, regardless of other considerations, it is an essential rule that the surfaces of those areas which are exposed to any risk of soiling must either be easily cleansable or easily removed and replaced.

The following summary outlines the main considerations in specifying requirements for various internal surfaces in dining rooms. The relative importance of these requirements will depend on the situation and use of the surface in question.

Consideration	Requirements
Ease of cleaning	Smooth non-absorbent surfaces which are capable of being wiped clean and which are free from inaccessible crevices or exposed joints.
Retention of appearance	Durable, permanent finishes which are unaffected by repeated soiling, washing or the use of recommended cleaning agents.
Resistance to damage	Surfaces which are resistant to scratching, abrasion, impact, staining and heat. Adequate support, strength and rigidity in the structural components and joints.
Maintenance	Facility for renovation, redecoration or recovering as a whole or in part.
Safety	Freedom from slipperiness, exposed sharp edges or projections.
Comfort	The resilience, warmth and noise absorbency of the surface as appropriate for the situation together with adequate thermal and sound insulating properties in the structural background.
Appearance	A selection and combination of colour, pattern and texture which will create interest and appreciation.
Integration	Unit sizes and proportions which are in balance and harmony with the surroundings.

The selection of appropriate materials to meet these functional requirements and the subject of 'atmosphere' creation in dining rooms are more specifically described in the book *Restaurant Planning and Design*.

Engineering services

11.04 A high standard of environmental control is expected in a modern dining room and a large proportion of the cost of constructing or renovating catering facilities is incurred in providing more sophisticated engineering equipment and services.

The level of lighting over the general area of a dining room needs to be in the order of 200 lux (18 lumens/sq ft) with higher local intensities—400 lux (37 lumens/sq ft)—over the servery and cashier's sections. Light points must be so positioned and screened that the source of light is not directly visible as a point of glare.

Whilst daylighting is psychologically beneficial and is generally preferred in most canteens, large windows facing south can give rise to excessive penetration of solar heat unless properly screened. Overheating is also liable to occur when large numbers of diners congregate in the room and some means of air-conditioning is usually necessary to obtain efficient temperature, odour and smoke control. Typical design temperatures and rates of air flow adopted in restaurants are:

Situation	Air changes/hour	Temperature	
		°C	°F
Canteens, coffee shops	8–12	18	65
Restaurants	10–15	18	65

In winter, problems of heating are often aggravated by the intermittent occupancy of a dining room which may only be used for a short period during the mid-day or in short intervals extending over the day. In addition, the high rate of air extraction required in the kitchen and servery creates a large outflow of warm air from the dining room which must be balanced by the heating system. To some extent, the control of temperature can be effected by use of good insulation and provision of means of recirculation for part of the room air when the premises are not in full use.

8 SUPPLEMENTARY INFORMATION

1 METRICATION

1.01 With the view to eventual simplification of measurements and expression of quantities, the existing British or Imperial units are in the process of being substituted by an International system of metric units—the 'Système International d'Unités', which is usually abbreviated to the symbol 'SI'. The change-over to metric is being introduced in phases starting with the primary manufacturing and construction industries and extending through to the distribution and retail organizations. Architects and engineers are already using SI units in general design work but in the catering industry, metrication is in an intermediary stage with new building work usually being measured in metric whilst most equipment, utensils and commodities are still based on their traditional British sizes.

To try to meet the difficulties being encountered in this transitional stage—which is likely to continue for many years—the quantities in this book have been quoted, where possible, in dual units. It is hoped that this provision will be of value in familiarizing the caterer with metric units and their size equivalences and, in this context, the detailed dimensions may be of practical value in the USA and elsewhere, bearing in mind the international trade in catering equipment and the trend towards metrication on a world-wide scale.

Introduction to SI

1.02 The subject of metrication has been explained in depth in many other books specifically devoted to this subject and a list of references for further reading is given in the appendix. For the purposes of explanation, this brief outline is intended only as a guide to those metric units which are most commonly used in catering.

Units

Under the SI, all quantities can be reduced to 6 primary units of measurement:

Quantity	Unit	Symbol
Length	metre	m
Mass	kilogramme	kg
Time	second	s
Electric current	ampere	A
Temperature	degree kelvin	°K
Luminous intensity	candela	cd

From various combinations of the primary units is obtained an extensive range of secondary and derived units appropriate for other quantities. A few common examples of such units are given below showing this inter-relationship.

Quantity	Unit	Symbol	Relationship
Area	square metre	m²	Length (m) × width (m)
Volume	cubic metre	m³	Area (m²) × height (m)
Velocity	metre per second	m/s	Distance (m) ÷ time (s)
Frequency	hertz	Hz	Intervals per second
Density	kilogramme per cubic metre	kg/m³	Mass (kg) ÷ volume (m³)
Force	newton	N	kgm/s²
Pressure	newton per square metre	N/m²	Force (N) ÷ area (m²)
Work, energy, quantity of heat	joule	J	Force (N) × distance (m)
Power, rate of heat flow	watt	W	Work (J) ÷ time (s)
Temperature	degree Celsius	°C	Comparative Unit (1°K = 1°C)
Thermal conductivity	watt per metre degree	W/m°C	
Specific heat capacity	joule per kilogramme degree	J/kg°C	
Electric tension potential difference	volt	V	watt (W) ÷ amp (A)
Electric resistance	ohm	Ω	volt (V) ÷ amp (A)
Luminous flux	lumen	lm	Intensity (cd) × solid angle of light (sr)
Illumination	lux	lx	lumen (lm) ÷ area (m²)

Size of units

1.03 The units quoted above may be too large or too small for convenience and the facility of a metric system allows for the basic units to be expressed in multiples or sub-multiples of 10 by adding a prefix or symbol.

Multiple	Prefix	Symbol	Variations
1,000,000	mega	M	The Megagramme (Mg) is also known as the tonne (t) or metric ton
1,000	kilo	k	
100	hecto	h	10 000 square metre is also known as the hectare (ha) : 100 ha = 1 square kilometre
10	deca	da	
1	—	—	The gramme, metre, newton, joule, watt, etc
0·1	deci	d	The cubic decimetre (dm³) is also known as the litre (1) : 1000 litres = 1 cubic metre
0·01	centi	c	1 cubic centimetre (cm³) = 1 millilitre (ml)
0·001	milli	m	
0·000001	micro	μ	

For simplification, it is recommended that multiples of 1000 should be used where practicable, eg Megagramme—kilogramme—gramme—milligramme.

Other units

1.04 Units in common usage which, whilst they do not strictly conform to the SI, will probably remain in practical use include:

(a) *For capacity*

Litre (cubic decimetre)

$$1000 \text{ litres } = 1 \text{ cubic metre}$$
$$1 \text{ millilitre } = 1 \text{ cubic centimetre}$$

(b) *For time*

Hour (3·6 kiloseconds) and day (86·4 kiloseconds)

(c) *For angular measurement*

Degree ° (π/180 radians)

Conversions

1.05 The metric values quoted in this book are not exactly equal to the British measurements and quantities previously used (as shown in brackets) but have been rounded off to the nearest appropriate number. Where a metric standard has been recommended—as in the preferred dimensions for building work—this has been adopted but, in other cases, a suitable value for the metric equivalent has had to be assumed. As an illustration, the British Standard measurement of 1 foot has been converted to a metric standard of 300 mm although the exact equivalent is 304·8 mm. Similarly, 10 gallons has been converted to 45 litres (strictly, equal to 45·46 litres) and 10 lbs into 4·5 kg (4·546 kg).

At this stage in the metrication of British measurements, few standards have been universally adopted in catering. A number of enterprising equipment manufacturers have individually introduced modular equipment based on metric dimensions and the majority are now producing equipment with internal dimensions appropriate for the Gastro-norm and British Standard system of sizes for containers and trays. The standard module size recommended for this purpose is 325 mm × 530 mm with fractional sizes of ½, ¼, ⅓ and ⅙ and with depths from 20 mm to 200 mm in 20 and 50 mm intervals.

Recommended standards for food package sizes

In changing over from traditional British sizes of food containers to SI, the following metric sizes have been recommended in the interests of standardization:

Prepacked solid food for retain trade—
range of sizes which are mandatory or preferred in existing British and recommended SI sizes

Typical retail sizes	1 oz 25 g	2 oz 50 g	¼ lb 125 g	½ lb 250 g	¾ lb 375 g*	1 lb 500 g	1½ lb 750 g	2 lb 1 kg
Typical catering sizes	3 lb 1·5 kg*	4 lb 2 kg	6/7 lb 3 kg	8 lb 4 kg	10 lb 5 kg	21 lb 10 kg		

* During transitional period only

Based on recommendation of
Food Trades Metrication Liason Committee;
Tripartite Standardization Committee and
National Association of Flour Millers.

Recommended sizes for milk, cream, butter and fats for use in hotels and catering.

Milk	1 qt 1	1 gal 4	4 gal 16⁺	20 gal 20 litres⁺	⁺ with dispenser. Pergal type of system preferred
Cream	¼ pt 0·125	½ pt 0·25	1 pt 0·5	2 qt 2 litres	individual containers of 30 ml and 60 ml in sets of 10 or 12 preferred
Butter and fats	½ lb 0·25 kg	14 lb (bulk) 6 kg	28 lb (bulk) 12 kg		Individual portions of 10 or 15 gm in sets of 100.

Based on recommendation of
Hotel and Catering Advisory Committee
to the Council of Industrial Design

For precise determination of metric equivalents, the following conversion factors cover some of the more common measurements and quantities used in catering practice.

British	to Metric	Metric	to British
Length			
1 mile	= 1·6093 km	1 kilometre	= 0·6214 mile
1 yard	= 0·9144 m	1 metre	= 1·0936 yd
1 foot	= 0·3048 m	1 metre	= 3·2808 ft
1 foot	= 304·80 mm		
1 inch	= 25·40 mm	1 millimetre	= 0·0394 in
Area			
1 square mile	= 2·590 km²	1 square kilometre	= 247·105 acre
1 square mile	= 258·999 ha	1 hectare	= 2·471 acre
1 acre	= 0·405 ha		
1 acre	= 4046·86 m²		
1 square yard	= 0·8361 m²	1 square metre	= 1·1960 yd²
1 square foot	= 0·0929 m²	1 square metre	= 10·7639 ft²
1 square inch	= 645·16 mm²	1 square millimetre	= 0·0016 in²
Volume			
1 cubic yard	= 0·7646 m³	1 cubic metre	= 1·3080 yd³
1 cubic foot	= 0·0283 m³		
1 cubic foot	= 28·3168 dm³	1 cubic decimetre	= 0·0353 ft³
1 cubic foot	= 28·3168 litre	1 litre	= 0·0353 ft³
1 cubic inch	= 16·387 mm³	1 cubic centimetre	= 0·0610 in³
1 cubic inch	= 0·0164 litre		
Capacity			
1 bushel	= 36·3687 litre	1 litre	= 0·2200 gallon
1 gallon	= 4·5461 litre	1 litre	= 0·2642 US gal
1 US gallon	= 3·7854 litre	1 litre	= 0·8800 quart
1 quart	= 1·1365 litre	1 litre	= 1·7600 pint
1 pint	= 0·5683 litre	1 litre	= 7·0400 gill
1 gill	= 0·1421 litre	1 litre	= 35·2113 fl oz

1 fluid ounce	= 0·0284 litre		
1 fluid ounce	= 28·413 ml		
1 fluid ounce	= 28413 mm³		

Mass
1 ton	= 1·016 tonne (t)	1 tonne	= 2204·62 lb
1 ton	= 1016·05 kg		
1 hundredweight	= 50·8023 kg		
1 quarter	= 12·7006 kg		
1 stone	= 6·3503 kg	1 kilogramme	= 0·1575 stone
1 pound	= 0·4536 kg	1 kilogramme	= 2·2046 lb
1 ounce	= 28·3495 g	1 kilogramme	= 35·2736 oz
1 dram	= 1·7719 g	1 gramme	= 0·0353 oz
1 pennyweight	= 1·5552 g		

Time
1 day	= 86·40 ks		
1 hour	= 3·60 ks	1 kilosecond	= 0·2761 hour
1 minute	= 60·00 s		

Velocity
1 mile per hour	= 1·6093 km/h	1 kilometre per hour	= 0·6214 mph
1 mile per hour	= 0·4470 m/s		
1 foot per second	= 0·3048 m/s	1 metre per second	= 3·2808 ft/sec
1 foot per minute	= 0·0051 m/s	1 metre per second	= 196·848 ft/min
1 foot per minute	= 5·080 mm/s		
1 inch per second	= 25·400 mm/s		
1 inch per minute	= 0·4233 mm/s		

Acceleration
1 foot/second. second	= 0·3048 m/s²	1 metre/second. second	= 3·2808 ft/sec²

Mass per Unit Length
1 pound per yard	= 0·4961 kg/m		
1 pound per yard	= 4961 g/mm		
1 pound per foot	= 1·4882 kg/m	1 kilogramme per metre	= 0·6720 lb/ft
1 pound per inch	= 17·8580 kg/m		
1 ounce per inch	= 1·1161 kg/m	1 kilogramme per metre	= 0·0560 lb/in

Mass per Unit Area
1 pound per sq foot	= 4·8824 kg/m²	1 kilogramme/ sq metre	= 0·2048 lb/ft²
1 pound per sq inch	= 703·070 kg/m²		
1 ounce per sq foot	= 305·152 g/m²	1 kilogramme/ sq metre	= 0·0014 lb/in²

Density (Mass per Unit Volume)
1 ton per cubic yard	= 1328·94 kg/m³		
1 ton per cubic yard	= 1·3289 t/m³		
1 pound per cubic foot	= 16·0185 kg/m³	1 kilogramme/ cubic metre	= 0·06214 lb/ft³
1 pound per cubic inch	= 27·6799 Mg/m³		
1 pound per cubic inch	= 0·0277 g/mm³	1 gramme/ cubic millimetre	= 36·1011 lb/in³

Concentration
1 pound per gallon	= 0·0998 kg/1	1 kilogramme/litre	= 10·0200 lb/gal
1 pound per gallon	= 99·7760 g/1	1 gramme litre	= 0·0100 lb/gal
1 ounce per gallon	= 6·2360 g/1	1 gramme litre	= 0·1603 oz/gal
1 ounce per pint	= 49·8882 g/1		

Force
1 ton force	= 9·9640 kN		
1 pound force	= 4·4482 N	1 Newton	= 0·2248 lbf
1 ounce force	= 0·2780 N		

Pressure:Stress
1 pound force per square foot	= 47·8803 N/m²		
1 pound force per square inch	= 6894·76 N/m²	1 kilonewton/ square metre	= 20·8854 lb/ft²
1 foot water	= 2989·07 N/m²		
1 inch mercury	= 3386·39 N/m²		

Volume Rate of Flow
1 cubic foot per min	= 0·4719 l/s	1 litre/second	= 0·2200 gal/s
1 gallon per hour	= 4·5461 l/h	1 litre/second	= 13·2058 gal/min
1 gallon per hour	= 0·0013 l/s		
1 gallon per minute	= 1·2670 ml/s		
1 gallon per minute	= 0·0758 l/s		
1 gallon per second	= 4·5461 l/s		

Mass Rate of Flow
1 ton per hour	= 1016·05 kg/h	1 kilogramme/hour	= 2·2046 lb/hr
1 ton per hour	= 1·0161 t/h	1 gramme/second	= 0·1322 lb/min
1 ton per hour	= 0·2822 kg/s		
1 pound per hour	= 0·4536 kg/h		
1 pound per hour	= 0·1260 g/s		
1 pound per minute	= 0·0076 kg/s		
1 pound per minute	= 7·5599 g/s		

Heating and Refrigeration
1 British Thermal Unit	= 1055 J		
1 British Thermal Unit	= 1·055 kJ	1 kilojoule	= 0·9478 Btu
1 Therm	= 105·506 MJ		
1 Btu per hour	= 0·2931 W	1 watt	= 3·4118 Btu/hr
1 Btu/sq ft hour	= 3·1546 W/m²	1 kilowatt	= 3411·8 Btu/hr
1 Btu/pound	= 2326 J/kg	1 Megajoule/hour	= 947·8 Btu/hr
1 Btu/pound °F	= 4186·8 J/kg °C		
1 Btu/cubic foot	= 37·2589 J/l		
1 Btu/cubic foot	= 37·2589 kJ/m³		
1 horse power	= 0·7457 kW	1 kilowatt	= 1·341 hp
1 ton refrigeration	= 3519 W	1 Megajoule/hour	= 0·3725 hp

Illumination
1 lumen/sq foot	= 10·7639 lux	1 lux	= 0·0929 lm/ft²
1 candela/sq foot	= 10·7639 cd/m²	1 candela/sq metre	= 0·0929 cd/ft²
1 candela/sq inch	= 1550·00 cd/m²		

2 SOURCES OF INFORMATION

1.06 For general information and statistics relating to the hotel and catering industry, the following references are particularly useful:

Hotel and Catering EDC, *Your Market 1971*, National Economic Development Office, London, 1971. (*Sources of market information and surveys.*)

Hotel and Catering EDC, *Investment in Hotels and Catering*, National Economic Development Office, London, 1971. (*A study of investment in hotels and large-scale catering.*)

Food Manufacturing EDC, *Food Statistics*, National Economic Development Office, London, 1971. (*A guide to the statistics of food production and consumption.*)

Annual Survey of canteen prices, costs and subsidies, The Industrial Society, London, 1972. (*Annual surveys of employee catering services.*)

Catering, Hotel and Institutional Managers Yearbook 1972, Kogan Page Ltd., London, 1972. (*A comprehensive guide for managers in accommodation and food services.*)

Directory of Products and Members, Catering Equipment Manufacturers Association, London, 1972. (*Lists of catering equipment and manufacturers.*)

Bryn Jones, M., *Food Services in Britain, 1970-1980*, New University Education, London, 1970.

Kotas, R., *Labour Cost in Restaurants*, Intertext, London, 1970.

Medlik, S., *Profile of the Hotel and Catering Industry*, Heinemann, London, 1972.

INDEX

Figures in italic refer to pages in which illustrations occur

146